CLEP® WESTERN CIVILIZATION II

Dr. Preston Jones

Associate Professor of History
John Brown University
Siloam Springs, Arkansas

Research & Education Association
Visit our website at: www.rea.com

Research & Education Association
61 Ethel Road West
Piscataway, New Jersey 08854
Email: info@rea.com

CLEP® Western Civilization II with Online Practice Exams

Published 2015
Copyright © 2013 by Research & Education Association, Inc.
Prior edition copyright © 2006 by Research & Education Association,
Inc. All rights reserved. No part of this book may be reproduced in
any form without permission of the publisher.

Printed in the United States of America

Library of Congress Control Number 2012950343

ISBN-13: 978-0-7386-1049-8
ISBN-10: 0-7386-1049-6

REA® is a registered trademark of
Research & Education Association, Inc.

CONTENTS

CHAPTER 3:

CHAPTER 4:

CHAPTER 5

CHAPTER 6

CHAPTER 7

CHAPTER 8

CHAPTER 9

ABOUT OUR AUTHOR

Dr. Preston Jones has been a Fulbright scholar and a fellow of the Pew Program in Religion and American History. He received his doctorate in History from the University of Ottawa (Canada) in 1999 and an M.A. in History from California State University at Sonoma in 1995. Dr. Jones has taught courses in European, American, and world history at the secondary and university levels. He also teaches Latin. He has published over 200 articles in scholarly journals, magazines, and newspapers. Currently he teaches at John Brown University in Arkansas.

ABOUT RESEARCH & EDUCATION ASSOCIATION

Founded in 1959, Research & Education Association (REA) is dedicated to publishing the finest and most effective educational materials—including study guides and test preps—for students in middle school, high school, college, graduate school, and beyond.

Today, REA's wide-ranging catalog is a leading resource for teachers, students, and professionals. Visit *www.rea.com* to see a complete listing of all our titles

ACKNOWLEDGMENTS

We would like to thank Pam Weston, Publisher, for setting the quality standards for production integrity and managing the publication to completion; John Paul Cording, Vice President, Technology, for coordinating the design and development of the REA Study Center; Larry B. Kling, Vice President, Editorial, for his supervision of revisions and overall direction; Diane Goldschmidt and Michael Reynolds, Managing Editors, for coordinating development of this edition; Transcend Creative Services for typesetting this edition; and Weymouth Design and Christine Saul, Senior Graphic Designer, for designing our cover.

A Note from the Author

The first college-level credit I earned was from CLEP exams I took while I served in the U.S. Navy. By the end of my four-year enlistment, in 1990, I had completed enough CLEP exams, and had done well enough on them, to have a very good head start on my university career. The discipline it took to study for the CLEP tests prepared me for university-level work.

If you are reading this, I assume not only that you want to pass the CLEP Western Civilization II exam but also that you want to be better educated. If you use this book well and if you commit yourself to learn what is in it, you will be in a very strong position to pass the exam—and you will be a more knowledgeable person. My advice on how to use this book in preparation for the CLEP exam is as follows:

1. Pay attention to everything that is in **bold.** The information surrounding each word or phrase in bold will tell you why that item or idea is important.

2. Know the correct answer to every question in both practice exams that follow the survey of Western Civilization since 1648.

3. In addition to knowing the right answer to every question on the practice exams, know why every correct answer is correct. This will involve studying the answers to the questions, which follow the exams. It is important to study these paragraphs, for some information is included in them that does not appear in the main narrative. It is also important to note that there is not a question about every item that is in bold. This is why it is important to emphasize all three of these steps.

In addition to providing a straightforward narrative of Western Civilization since 1648, this text introduces each chapter with quotations from the period under study, and most chapters conclude with brief discussions—under the title "For Your Information..."—of topics that are raised in the chapter (called out with the symbol°). These items will help students to understand the broader context of the events and concepts they are studying. I also hope they will spark or sustain an interest in history.

Inevitably, this text is a synthesis of syntheses. The works I have consulted while writing it are Philip Cannistraro and John J. Reich, *The Western Perspective: A History of Civilization in the West* (Belmont, CA: Thomson, 2004); Jacques

Barzun, *From Dawn to Decadence: 500 Years of Western Cultural Life* (New York: HarperCollins, 2000); Norman Davies, *Europe: A History* (New York: HarperPerennial, 1996); Lynn Hunt et al., *The Making of the West: Peoples and Cultures* (Boston: Bedford/St. Martin's, 2005); Donald Kagan et al., *The Western Heritage* (Upper Saddle River, NJ: Prentice Hall, 2001); David M. Kennedy et al., *The American Pageant* (New York: Houghton Mifflin Company, 2002); Brian Levack et al., *The West: Encounters and Transformations* (New York: Pearson, 2004); Marvin Perry, *Western Civilization: A Brief History* (New York: Houghton Mifflin, 2005); and Jackson J. Spielvogel, *Western Civilization* (Belmont, CA: Wadsworth, 1999). The quotes in the text can be found in the sixteenth edition of John Bartlett's *Familiar Quotations* (New York: Little, Brown and Company, 1992); in John L. Beatty et al., *Heritage of Western Civilization: From Revolutions to Modernity* (Upper Saddle River, NJ: Pearson/Prentice Hall, 2004); and in Katharine J. Lualdi's documents companion to Hunt's *Making of the West*. I have also benefited from teaching European and Western history at the University of Ottawa (Canada), the California State University at Sonoma, the University of Dallas, Dallas Christian College, The Cambridge School of Dallas, and John Brown University.

I am grateful to my trusted teacher's assistant, Ruby Vazquez, who saved me from numerous errors and who makes my life easier. I also wish to thank Judy Balla, administrative assistant in the School of Social and Behavioral Studies at JBU, whose constant help made it possible to write a text like this while juggling many other responsibilities.

I have dedicated this manuscript to Mr. Charles Grande, my Western Civilization teacher at Eisenhower High School in Rialto, California. The world would be better if everyone could have a teacher like him. *Admira-bantur turbae super doctrinam eius.*

Preston Jones
John Brown University

CHAPTER 1

Passing the CLEP Western Civilization II Exam

PASSING THE CLEP WESTERN CIVILIZATION II EXAM

Congratulations! You're joining the millions of people who have discovered the value and educational advantage offered by the College Board's College-Level Examination Program, or CLEP. This test prep fouses on what you need to know to succeed on the CLEP Western Civilization II exam, and will help you earn the college credit you deserve while reducing your tuition costs.

GETTING STARTED

There are many different ways to prepare for a CLEP exam. What's best for you depends on how much time you have to study and how comfortable you are with the subject matter. To score your highest, you need a system that can be customized to fit you: your schedule, your learning style, and your current level of knowledge.

This book, and the online tools that come with it, allow you to create a personalized study plan through three simple steps: assessment of your knowledge, targeted review of exam content, and reinforcement in the areas where you need the most help.

Let's get started and see how this system works.

Test Yourself and Get Feedback	Assess your strengths and weaknesses. The score report from your online diagnostic exam gives you a fast way to pinpoint what you already know and where you need to spend more time studying.
Review with the Book	Armed with your diagnostic score report, review the parts of the book where you're weak and study the answer explanations for the test questions you answered incorrectly.
Ensure You're Ready for Test Day	After you've finished reviewing with the book, take our full-length practice tests. Review your score reports and re-study any topics you missed. We give you two full-length practice tests to ensure you're confident and ready for test day.

THE REA STUDY CENTER

The best way to personalize your study plan is to get feedback on what you know and what you don't know. At the online REA Study Center, you can access two types of assessment: a diagnostic exam and full-length practice exams. Each of these tools provides true-to-format questions and delivers a detailed score report that follows the topics set by the College Board.

Diagnostic Exam

Before you begin your review with the book, take the online diagnostic exam. Use your score report to help evaluate your overall understanding of the subject, so you can focus your study on the topics where you need the most review.

Full-Length Practice Exams

Our full-length practice tests give you the most complete picture of your strengths and weaknesses. After you've finished reviewing with the book, test what you've learned by taking the first of the two online practice exams. Review your score report, then go back and study any topics you missed. Take the second practice test to ensure you have mastered the material and are ready for test day.

If you're studying and don't have Internet access, you can take the printed tests in the book. These are the same practice tests offered at the REA Study Center, but without the added benefits of timed testing conditions and diagnostic score reports. Because the actual exam is Internet-based, we recommend you take at least one practice test online to simulate test-day conditions.

AN OVERVIEW OF THE EXAM

The CLEP Western Civilization II exam consists of 120 multiple-choice questions, each with five possible answer choices, to be answered in 90 minutes.

The exam covers the material one would find in the second semester of a two-semester course in Western Civilization. The exam questions cover European history from the seventeenth century through the post–Second World War period, including political, economic, and cultural developments.

The approximate breakdown of topics is as follows:

7–9%   Absolutism and Constitutionalism, 1648–1715

4–6%   Competition for empire and economic expansion

5–7%   The scientific view of the world

7–9%   Period of Enlightenment

10–13%   Revolution and Napoleonic Europe

7–9%   The Industrial Revolution

6–8%   Political and cultural developments, 1815–1848

8–10%   Politics and diplomacy in the Age of Nationalism, 1850–1914

7–9%   Economy, culture, and imperialism, 1850–1914

10–12%   The First World War and the Russian Revolution

7–9%   Europe between the wars

8–10%   The Second World War and contemporary Europe

ALL ABOUT THE CLEP PROGRAM

What is the CLEP?

CLEP is the most widely accepted credit-by-examination program in North America. The CLEP program's 33 exams span five subject areas. The exams assess the material commonly required in an introductory-level college course. Examinees can earn from three to twelve credits at more than 2,900 colleges and universities in the U.S. and Canada. For a complete list of the CLEP subject examinations offered, visit the College Board website: *www.collegeboard. org/clep*.

Who takes CLEP exams?

CLEP exams are typically taken by people who have acquired knowledge outside the classroom and who wish to bypass certain college courses and earn college credit. The CLEP program is designed to reward examinees for learning—no matter where or how that knowledge was acquired.

Although most CLEP examinees are adults returning to college, many graduating high school seniors, enrolled college students, military personnel, veterans, and international students take CLEP exams to earn college credit or to demonstrate their ability to perform at the college level. There are no prerequisites, such as age or educational status, for taking CLEP examinations. However, because policies on granting credits vary among colleges, you should contact the particular institution from which you wish to receive CLEP credit.

How is my CLEP score determined?

Your CLEP score is based on two calculations. First, your CLEP raw score is figured; this is just the total number of test items you answer correctly. After the test is administered, your raw score is converted to a scaled score through a process called *equating*. Equating adjusts for minor variations in difficulty across test forms and among test items, and ensures that your score accurately represents your performance on the exam regardless of when or where you take it, or on how well others perform on the same test form.

Your scaled score is the number your college will use to determine if you've performed well enough to earn college credit. Scaled scores for the CLEP exams are delivered on a 20-80 scale. Institutions can set their own scores for granting college credit, but a good passing estimate (based on recommendations from the American Council on Education) is generally a scaled score of 50, which usually requires getting roughly 66% of the questions correct.

For more information on scoring, contact the institution where you wish to be awarded the credit.

Who administers the exam?

CLEP exams are developed by the College Board, administered by Educational Testing Service (ETS), and involve the assistance of educators from throughout the United States. The test development process is designed and implemented to ensure that the content and difficulty level of the test are appropriate.

When and where is the exam given?

CLEP exams are administered year-round at more than 1,200 test centers in the United States and can be arranged for candidates abroad on request. To find the test center nearest you and to register for the exam, contact the CLEP Program:

CLEP Services
P.O. Box 6600
Princeton, NJ 08541-6600
Phone: (800) 257-9558 (8 A.M. to 6 P.M. ET)
Fax: (610) 628-3726
Website: *www.collegeboard.org/clep*

The new CLEP iBT exams

To improve the testing experience for both institutions and test-takers, the College Board's CLEP Program has transitioned its 33 exams from the eCBT platform to an Internet-based testing (iBT) platform. All CLEP test-takers may now register for exams and manage their personal account information through the "My Account" feature on the CLEP website. This new feature simplifies the registration process and automatically downloads all pertinent information about the test session, making for a more streamlined check-in.

OPTIONS FOR MILITARY PERSONNEL AND VETERANS

CLEP exams are available free of charge to eligible military personnel and eligible civilian employees. All the CLEP exams are available at test centers on college campuses and military bases. Contact your Educational Services Officer or Navy College Education Specialist for more information. Visit the DANTES or College Board websites for details about CLEP opportunities for military personnel.

Eligible U.S. veterans can claim reimbursement for CLEP exams and administration fees pursuant to provisions of the Veterans Benefits Improvement Act of 2004. For details on eligibility and submitting a claim for reimbursement, visit the U.S. Department of Veterans Affairs website at *www.gibill.va.gov.*

CLEP can be used in conjunction with the Post-9/11 GI Bill, which applies to veterans returning from the Iraq and Afghanistan theaters of operation. Because the GI Bill provides tuition for up to 36 months, earning college credits with CLEP exams expedites academic progress and degree completion within the funded timeframe.

SSD ACCOMMODATIONS FOR CANDIDATES WITH DISABILITIES

Many test candidates qualify for extra time to take the CLEP exams, but you must make these arrangements in advance. For information, contact:

College Board Services for Students with Disabilities
P.O. Box 8060
Mt. Vernon, Illinois 62864-0060
Phone: (609) 771-7137 (Monday through Friday, 8 A.M. to 6 P.M. ET)
TTY: (609) 882-4118
Fax: (866) 360-0114
Email: ssd@info.collegeboard.org

6-WEEK STUDY PLAN

Although our study plan is designed to be used in the six weeks before your exam, it can be condensed to three weeks by combining each two-week period into one.

Be sure to set aside enough time—at least two hours each day—to study. The more time you spend studying, the more prepared and relaxed you will feel on the day of the exam.

Week	Activity
1	Take the Diagnostic Exam. The score report will identify topics where you need the most review.
2—4	Study the review chapters. Use your diagnostic score report to focus your study.
5	Take Practice Test 1 at the REA Study Center. Review your score report and re-study any topics you missed.
6	Take Practice Test 2 at the REA Study Center to see how much your score has improved. If you still got a few questions wrong, go back to the review and study any topics you may have missed.

TEST-TAKING TIPS

Know the format of the test. Familiarize yourself with the CLEP computer screen beforehand by logging on to the College Board website. Waiting until test day to see what it looks like in the pretest tutorial risks injecting needless anxiety into your testing experience. Also, familiarizing yourself with the directions and format of the exam will save you valuable time on the day of the actual test. .

Read all the questions—completely. Make sure you understand each question before looking for the right answer. Reread the question if it doesn't make sense.

Read all of the answers to a question. Just because you think you found the correct response right away, do not assume that it's the best answer. The last answer choice might be the correct answer.

Work quickly and steadily. You will have 90 minutes to answer 120 questions, so work quickly and steadily. Taking the timed practice tests online will help you learn how to budget your time.

Use the process of elimination. Stumped by a question? Don't make a random guess. Eliminate as many of the answer choices as possible. By eliminating just two answer choices, you give yourself a better chance of getting the item correct, since there will only be three choices left from which to make your guess. Remember, your score is based only on the number of questions you answer correctly.

Don't waste time! Don't spend too much time on any one question. Remember, your time is limited and pacing yourself is very important. Work on the easier questions first. Skip the difficult questions and go back to them if you have the time.

Look for clues to answers in other questions. If you skip a question you don't know the answer to, you might find a clue to the answer elsewhere on the test.

Be sure that your answer registers before you go to the next item. Look at the screen to see that your mouse-click causes the pointer to darken the proper oval. If your answer doesn't register, you won't get credit for that question.

THE DAY OF THE EXAM

On test day, you should wake up early (after a good night's rest, of course) and have breakfast. Dress comfortably, so you are not distracted by being too hot or too cold while taking the test. (Note that "hoodies" are not allowed.) Arrive at the test center early. This will allow you to collect your thoughts and relax before the test, and it will also spare you the anxiety that comes with being late.

Before you leave for the test center, make sure you have your admission form and another form of identification, which must contain a recent photograph, your name, and signature (i.e., driver's license, student identification card, or current alien registration card). You may wear a watch to the test center. However, you may not wear one that makes noise, because it may disturb the other test-takers. No cell phones, dictionaries, textbooks, notebooks, briefcases, or packages will be permitted, and drinking, smoking, and eating are prohibited.

Good luck on the CLEP Western Civilization II exam!

CHAPTER 2

Absolutism, Constitutionalism, The Dutch Republic, and Russia

CHAPTER 2

ABSOLUTISM, CONSTITUTIONALISM, THE DUTCH REPUBLIC, AND RUSSIA

During the time men live without a common power to keep them all in awe, they are in that condition which is called war; and such a war, as is of every man, against every man.
—Thomas Hobbes

Wherever Law ends, Tyranny begins.
—John Locke

I would have been glad to have lived under my woodside, and to have kept a flock of sheep, rather than to have undertaken this government.
—Oliver Cromwell

From 1618 to 1648 the **Thirty Years' War** raged in Europe. It is called a "war of religion"; Calvinists, Lutherans, and Catholics in and from present-day Germany, Austria, Denmark, Sweden, France, and other regions fought one another, sometimes with incredible ferocity. Entire villages—including the elderly and children who lived in them—were destroyed. The various countries' interests actually had more to do with political power and prestige than with theology. But because there was no separation of church and state in the early 1600s, theological language inevitably got wrapped up in political scheming and combat.

The war-ending **Treaty of Westphalia** (1648) set the stage for the development of modern Europe. The treaty made permanent the religious changes that had come to Europe since the **Protestant Reformation**. Local rulers were given authority to determine the faiths of the regions they ruled. The treaty also signaled the declining influence of the papacy; the Pope openly opposed it, but he was ignored. Thus, the Treaty of Westphalia paved the way for the **secularization** of European politics. The treaty also recognized the political independence of the **Swiss Confederacy** (modern Switzerland) and the United Provinces of Holland, from which the admirable **Dutch Republic** would spring. Further, because the devastating war had not been fought on French soil (most of it was fought in central Europe), France was in a position to become the European continent's dominant power.

The German state that emerged strongest from the Thirty Years' War was Brandenburg-**Prussia**, which would become the core of present-day Germany. Prussia's **Great Elector, Frederick William** (r. 1640–1688), along with his son **Frederick I** (r. 1688–1713), and grandson, **Frederick William I** (r. 1713–1740), laid the foundation on which the powerful German nation would be built. They did so partly by gaining the favor of Prussia's nobles, the **Junkers**, who were given **exemptions from taxes** and whose rights over serf labor were established in law. The Fredericks also created an organized bureaucracy, governed by the **Central Directory**, which was staffed not only by nobles but also by professionals who came from common stock. Finally, Prussia's rulers focused on building a **powerful army**, which grew from about thirty thousand men in 1690 to about eighty thousand in 1740. For many years to come, the words *Prussia* and *army* were tightly linked.

What would become the **Austro-Hungarian Empire** also began to take shape in the decades following the Treaty of Westphalia. Unlike Prussia, however, it contained many radically different ethnic and religious groups. Many **Muslims**, for example, came under the rule of Austria's **Hapsburg monarchy** as a result of Hungary's liberation from the Ottoman Turkish Empire to the east. Not even Austria's military, which one would expect to be quite disciplined, functioned smoothly, because of **linguistic, cultural, and political differences** among subjects from different parts of the empire. Until its demise following the First World War, the Austrian Empire would rarely be stable.

ABSOLUTISM: PHILOSOPHICAL BACKGROUND

In the period following the Thirty Years' War, two very different political trends developed. One of these trends, **absolutism**, emphasized the complete authority of a nation's ruler. The English philosopher **Thomas Hobbes** (1588–1679) argued this point of view in his highly influential and still much-read work *Leviathan* (1651). Left to their own devices, Hobbes famously wrote, people will create miserable lives for themselves and others because they are naturally selfish, greedy, and shortsighted; their lives will be "solitary, poor, nasty, brutish, and short." To solve this problem, Hobbes continued, people give their power to an absolute authority, the "Leviathan," who keeps order and makes peaceful living possible. Though Hobbes quoted the Bible frequently—his title comes from the biblical book of Job—he had no use in his politics for theology. Thus, his philosophy is symbolic of the increasing **secularization** of Europe, which had begun around the early 1500s.

Another philosopher who advocated absolutism, **Louis XIV**'s tutor **Bishop Bossuet** (1627–1704), did so from a strictly religious point of view. In *Politics Drawn from the Very Words of Scripture*, Bossuet argued that since a king derived his power only from God, the king was accountable to God alone. In Bossuet's view no one could criticize the king, and revolution was beyond consideration. Kings were chosen by God; they ruled by "**divine right**." Bossuet is an example of the continuation of conservative religious belief in seventeenth-century Europe, and he built on the well-organized political foundation set by **Cardinal Richelieu** (1585–1642), France's powerful secretary of state and chief minister to Louis XIII (1601–1643).

In 1648 what Hobbes and Bossuet agreed on—that the monarch's power was absolute—was widely accepted in Europe. But another very different view was being offered by another English philosopher, **John Locke** (1632–1704). Of fundamental importance—in England and later in the English colonies that would become the United States—was Locke's idea that a ruler could rule only so long as he or she kept the people's trust. The ruler did this by respecting the inherent rights human beings possess to **life, liberty, and property**. And if a ruler trampled on those rights, Locke argued, the people had a responsibility to replace that ruler.

Locke's ideas would become popular among French thinkers, or *philosophes* (see the section on the Enlightenment in Chapter 4). In France, Bossuet's concept of the divine right of kings to rule would hold sway. Revolution would not come to that country until 1789.

Monarchs in England would try to keep power for themselves, but they would not be able to do so. In the seventeenth century England experienced political turmoil and, finally, civil war.

FRANCE AND THE REIGN OF LOUIS XIV

Before **Louis XIV** (1637–1715), no European monarch had the level of power he would eventually acquire. Having witnessed street revolts against his father as a child, Louis XIV came to the throne in 1661 determined to hold total power. While he was never able to gain *complete* control over all of France, he did accumulate vast power. He was not too far from the mark when he supposedly said, "**I am the state**" (in French, "L'état c'est moi"). He censored books and tortured political opponents.

One way the clever Louis gained power was by concocting elaborate rituals at his stunning palace in **Versailles** near Paris. Nobles, whose loyalty was gained partly with tax breaks, were invited to bask in the glow of the **Sun King**; it was considered an honor to hand the king his slippers in the morning or to hold his night candle as he prepared for bed. In time about ten thousand officials, nobles, and soldiers lived at Versailles. Meanwhile, Louis took actual decision-making power away from the nobles. He never convened the **Estates General**, the weak medieval French representative institution that had not convened since 1614 and that would not meet until 1789.

Louis XIV gained further prestige by promoting science (see the section on the Scientific Revolution in Chapter 4). And he kept the French public occupied with constant wars—against England, the Dutch, Spain, and the **Holy Roman Empire**, which roughly corresponds to present-day central Europe. These wars, which will be discussed in the next chapter, added significantly to France's power and territory. But they were also very costly. Combined with the lavishness of Versailles, with its fourteen hundred fountains, France's wars led to many decades of troubled financial health for the nation. Louis also weakened France in 1685 by revoking the **Edict of Nantes** (1598), which had allowed for some religious tolerance, and chasing many of France's highly skilled Protestants, the **Huguenots**,° out of the country.

ENGLAND: THE ROAD TO CONSTITUTIONAL GOVERNMENT

Many of France's Huguenots fled to England, where they knew they would enjoy greater liberty. In contrast to the French monarchs, the kings of England had seen their power significantly reduced by 1685, and in 1688

England would experience a bloodless **Glorious Revolution**. A hundred years later, England's colonists in America would complain about oppression under the British monarchy but they could only do so because they already enjoyed considerable freedom to criticize the government.

The road to the monarch's limited power in England began partly with a personality conflict between **James I** (r. 1603–1625) and England's **Parliament**. Where Louis XIV won nobles over by lavishing gifts and honors on them, King James flatly asserted that he ruled by divine right and that Parliament's purpose was merely to advise him. Parliament saw this as an effort by the king to remove its traditional power to make law and levy taxes, albeit not without the king's approval. Because James I never acted on his claims, serious trouble was averted until the reign of his son, **Charles I** (r. 1625–1649). In response to Charles's effort to raise money for war against Spain without Parliament's consent, the Parliament passed the **Petition of Right** in 1628. This important document claimed that English subjects possessed basic rights that no king could trample on. Charles assented to this petition but also refused to reconvene Parliament until 1640, by which time the Protestants in Parliament believed that Charles wanted to return England to Roman Catholicism. Charles's introduction of new Catholic-seeming rituals in Scotland led to war between England and its northern neighbor. It was to raise funds to prosecute this war that Charles called Parliament into session. The stage was set for conflict.

ENGLAND'S CIVIL WAR

In 1640 Parliament impeached many of Charles I's ministers, dismantled the judicial system Charles had built, and declared Charles's non-parliamentary taxes null. Charles's effort to have five members of Parliament arrested for treason sparked the **English Civil War**. The forces of Parliament, called "**Roundheads**" because Puritan hats did not have hat bands, created the efficient, well-trained **New Model Army**, led by **Oliver Cromwell** (1599–1658). Soon after its 1648 victory over the king's forces, called the "**Cavaliers**," Parliament began to fracture. **Puritans,** who saw Cromwell as their leader, purged **Presbyterians** from Parliament. In 1649 this **Rump Parliament** destroyed the House of Lords (Parliament's upper house) and the monarchy itself. In that year **Charles I was executed**, and England became a **republic** governed by what remained of Parliament.

Rule by the victorious Parliament would not last, however. Some radical republicans, called "**Levellers**," wanted every Englishman to have the vote. Others believed that only men who owned property should have the vote. At the same time, the army, still led by the very pious Cromwell, did not believe that the Rump Parliament was creating a godly society. This led to another purge of Parliament. But even the members in this so-called **Bare Bones Parliament** were divided. In 1653, Cromwell was proclaimed **Protector of England, Scotland, and Ireland**. He shared power with what remained of Parliament, and England enjoyed relative stability until his death in 1658. By 1660 there was general agreement that England should restore the monarchy.

CHARLES II, JAMES II, AND THE GLORIOUS REVOLUTION

Both **Charles II** (r. 1660-1685) and **James II** (r. 1685–1688) shared Louis XIV's belief in the divine right of kings. But given England's recent history, they were realistic enough to know that they would never be able to rule absolutely. One crisis involved an effort by certain members of Parliament, called **Whigs**, to prevent Charles II's Catholic brother, James, from taking the throne. (Charles's supporters were called Tories, a label which later became synonymous with Britain's political conservatives.) Another, more serious crisis involved exemptions from laws that James II gave to Catholics who, as a result, could serve in the army, the courts, and local governments. The fear of England becoming Catholic again united Parliament's Whigs and Tories. In 1688 an invitation was sent from the Parliament to **William III of Orange** (in the Dutch Republic) to take the English throne from his uncle. William's wife, Mary, was James's oldest daughter, which meant that she too had a claim to England's throne. Best of all, William and Mary were Protestants.

William invaded England with twelve thousand men. The army of James II defected, and he fled to France. This Glorious Revolution was bloodless. In 1689 William and Mary were crowned as England's co-monarchs. They assented to a **bill of rights** drawn up by Parliament. Among other things, the English Bill of Rights denied the power of a monarch to pass laws without Parliament's consent, protected people from "excessive bail" and "cruel and unusual punishments," and gave England's residents the right to address their grievances to the government. This document would have a great influence on the writers of the U.S. Constitution and Bill of Rights.

THE DUTCH REPUBLIC

Although France would never approach republican government in the seventeenth century, and England would flirt with it only briefly, the **United Provinces of the Netherlands** better known as the **Dutch Republic,°** maintained a republican form of government through the seventeenth century. The Dutch Republic was actually made up of sovereign states that formed a loose confederacy. The strongest province was **Holland**, but it could not control its counterparts. What Hollanders could do, however, was promote international trade from their port city of **Amsterdam**. Through the seventeenth century, Holland was a major economic and maritime power: Dutch merchants traded in Asia, Africa, the Caribbean, and North America. Dutch settlers moved into South Africa, where the Dutch language Afrikaans is still spoken. The **Dutch East India Company** was established to conduct trade in Asia and served as a model to the English and French. With so much wealth passing through Dutch ports, it is no surprise that Amsterdam became an international banking center and that Dutch philosophers such as **Hugo Grotius** (1583–1645) would advocate **free trade** among nations. At the same time the seventeenth century witnessed significant **religious toleration** in the Netherlands (which became a refuge for Europe's persecuted people) and the **Dutch Golden Age** in painting. Artists like **Rembrandt** (1606–1669) painted intensely realistic and elegant scenes of businessmen at work, landscapes, and portraits.

By the early eighteenth century the Dutch Republic would no longer be a major world power. England and France would displace it.

PETER THE GREAT AND THE WEST

Until the late seventeenth century Russia drew very little from Western culture. Over the centuries, having borders in Asia and Europe, Russia has often had a conflicted national personality. **Tsar Peter the Great** (also called **Peter I**) turned Russia toward the West. He could see that the western European powers were building powerful militaries and economies, and he wanted Russia to catch up with them. He required men in Russia's upper classes and government officials to **shave their beards**, and the **French** language and **Western clothing** became the fashion among Russia's important people. Privileged Russian youth were sent to western Europe for their educations, while Western art was imported into Russia.

Peter also copied Western methods of **military and economic organization** and thus made Russia's army and economy much stronger. In his **Northern War** (1700–1721), Peter fought against the Swedish military using techniques he had learned from the Swedes! Peter brought Russia's **Orthodox Church under state control**, improved the administration of Russian government, and built Russia's new capital, **St. Petersburg** in western Russia. This city was Peter's "**window to Europe**."

FOR YOUR INFORMATION

The Huguenots

These French Protestants were pushed out of Catholic France. Historians now see that their leaving was an economic blow to France, for the Huguenots (like the Puritans in New England) were very industrious. By 1618 between 50,000 and 100,000 Huguenots had fled to England, where they created wealth by making watches, among other things. In 1685 Frederick William of Brandenburg-Prussia invited hardworking Huguenots to settle in his territory, and some 20,000 did. Other Huguenots went to Britain's colonies in America, where they contributed to a culture that prized liberty. Eleven U.S. presidents have some Huguenot ancestry: George Washington, John Quincy Adams, John Tyler, James Garfield, Theodore Roosevelt, William Howard Taft, Herbert Hoover, Franklin Delano Roosevelt, Harry S. Truman, George H. W. Bush, and George W. Bush.

The Dutch Republic

Most Americans do not know that New York City was founded by the Dutch. The words *Manhattan, Harlem,* and *Brooklyn* come from the Dutch language, as do many words Americans frequently use. Do you like or hate your *boss*? Either way, the word comes from Dutch. Do you believe in Santa Claus? Even if not, it's good to know that the jolly man's name is Dutch *(Sinterklass)*. Maybe you thought the words *bundle (bundel), coleslaw (koolsla), cookie (koekje), cruise (kruisen), knapsack (knapzak), skate (schaats),* and *waffle (wafel)* were English. But really they are Dutch. Not even *Yankee* is English. It comes from the Dutch name *Jan Kees*. Another legacy of the Dutch is their enduring influence in former colonies. In the South American country of Suriname, for example, Dutch remains the language of government and education.

CHAPTER 3

Empires and Conflict

CHAPTER 3

EMPIRES AND CONFLICT

Has God forgotten all I have done for him?
—Louis XIV, after receiving news of a French military defeat

You know that [France and England] have been at war over a few acres of snow near Canada, and that they are spending on this fine struggle more than Canada itself is worth.
—Voltaire

INTRODUCTION

At the end of the fifteenth century European sailors financed by Portugal, Spain, the Netherlands, England, and France began traveling around the world, accumulating knowledge and wealth and establishing colonies. The Western Hemisphere's dominant languages indicate how successful their efforts were: English (the United States and most of Canada); Spanish (Mexico, Central America, and most of South America); Portuguese (Brazil); French (Québec and Louisiana); and Dutch (Suriname). By the mid-seventeenth century Spain was in decline as a global power, though it would not lose the bulk of its American possessions until the 1820s, and it would hold Cuba until 1898. In the seventeenth century the Dutch, a new European power, would plant New Netherlands in North America. Its chief settlement there, New Amsterdam, would become New York when the English defeated the Dutch in war.

Whereas Europe's wars of the sixteenth and early seventeenth centuries had been driven largely by religious passions, the wars of the late seventeenth and eighteenth centuries had more to do with the accumulation of wealth and territory. The primary question was, Which European power would dominate? In the end, there were two answers to that question: France would dominate Western Europe, and England would dominate the seas. Although France's domination on land could not finally overcome coalitions arrayed against it, however, England would become the world's great sea power and remain so into the twentieth century.

THE FIRST GLOBAL WARS

Louis XIV's chief minister, **Jean-Baptiste Colbert**, centralized the French economy by employing an economic outlook called **mercantilism**. At the heart of mercantilism was the belief that there was a limited amount of wealth in the world. Thus the main goal of a mercantilist government was to maximize the amount of gold the nation had in its treasury. That meant bringing in gold by selling exports to other countries while being as self-sufficient as possible (i.e., not buying goods from competing countries). It meant avoiding what would come to be called "free trade." It also meant acquiring overseas colonies populated by captive customers. By the end of the seventeenth century France held trading outposts in India, West Africa, and the Caribbean. Its largest colony was New France, the center of which is present-day Québec.

Mid-eighteenth-century Britain governed a large and growing empire. It held many island colonies in the West Indies as well as the thirteen colonies along the eastern seaboard of what would become the United States. Britain had outposts established in Africa and, like France, was very interested in expanding its influence in India. In addition to Europe, those three regions—the **West Indies**, **America**, and **India**—were where Britain and France did most of their fighting for global power, prestige, and wealth. Both countries coveted North America's furs, fishing grounds, rich soil, and access to the sea. The West Indies offered tobacco, cotton, coffee and, most important, sugar. These items brought their producers great wealth.

Among other attractions (such as silk, spices, and tea), India appeared to France and Britain to be a springboard to China, which they believed to have great possibilities for trade. The **British East India Company** and the French **Compagnie des Indes** began the work of colonizing India.

The economic idea of comparative advantage—that nations should focus their economic energy on what they can do well and leave what they cannot do well to others—would have made sense to very few, if any, European leaders in the eighteenth century. Britain and France sought self-sufficiency; they put up **tariffs** and passed **navigation laws** in an effort to prevent people in the colonies from trading with outsiders. Economic competition, combined with competition for colonies and the general belief that warfare was a basic way for a nation to pursue its goals, inevitably led to conflict. **Privateers°**—that is, government-sanctioned pirates—also played a role in spurring war. Spain knew, for example, that **Sir Francis Drake's** plundering of Spanish ships was approved by the English monarch.

The **War of Jenkins's Ear** began in 1739 because Prime Minister Robert Walpole was unable to resist the pressure of the British Parliament to strike at Spain, which treated British sailors in the West Indies with contempt. (In 1731 an English captain, Robert Jenkins, had had his ear cut off by a Spaniard during a fight aboard an English ship.)

In 1740 that war merged with another, the **War of Austrian Succession** (1740–1748), sparked in Europe by France's support of Prussia's aggression against Austria. Because Austria had been a traditional enemy of France, the latter country was glad to see Austria weakened. At the same time Britain wanted to see the Netherlands remain in the friendly hands of Austria, not under the control of the French. Thus Britain and France went to war. By 1744 the conflict had expanded into the New World, where France decided to support Spain in its war against Britain. The **Treaty of Aix-la-Chapelle**, which ended the War of Austrian Succession, was more a truce than a peace treaty. In 1754 conflict between the French and the British in the New World led to another global conflict, the **Seven Years' War** (1756–1763).

The Seven Years' War was preceded by what has come to be called the **diplomatic revolution of 1756**. In that year the recent adversaries Britain and Prussia became allies as a result of the **Convention of Westminster**. Both countries saw France as a threat. One consequence was an improbable alliance between Austria and France, who had so recently been at one another's throats. As always, however, Britain and France remained adamant foes.

In North America the **French and Indian War**, which coincided with the Seven Years' War, began when an American colonial officer, **George Washington**, opened fire on French forces in the Ohio Valley. The spark to war in Europe was Prussia's invasion of Saxony, another German state that Prussia's **Frederick II** (or **Frederick the Great**) distrusted. This led to Austria, France, Sweden, Russia, and other German states joining Saxony in its war against Prussia. The death of Russia's empress in 1762, and her replacement by the pro-Prussian **Tsar Peter III**, along with significant financial aid from Britain, allowed Frederick II to prevail in Europe.

The financial assistance to Prussia was organized by Britain's secretary of state, **William Pitt the Elder** (1708–1778), who wanted to see France expend great wealth in the war. But Pitt's main focus was not Europe. His primary goal was to gain all of North America east of the Mississippi for Britain. That meant roundly defeating the French, who then held territory encompassing present-day eastern Canada, Louisiana, and much of the American Midwest. Pitt sent some forty thousand troops to America and secured the cooperation of Britain's American colonists. France, in increasingly difficult financial straits, was unable to make as significant a contribution toward defending its American colonies. The most significant French defeat took place on the **Plains of Abraham°** outside Québec City in 1759. Meanwhile, sugar taken from captured French ships in the West Indies helped to finance the war. And a major British victory over the French in India, at **Plassey** in 1757, paved the way for the conquest of much of India by the **British East India Company**.

The war-ending **Treaty of Paris** (1763) gave Canada, the Ohio River Valley, and territory east of the Mississippi (excluding Florida, which was claimed by Spain) to Britain. Britain also made important gains in the West Indies and India. In Europe, Prussia had gained significant power and territory at the expense of Austria and the **Holy Roman Empire**.

France and Spain maintained large, wealthy empires, and France remained one of Europe's great powers. As colonial forces, however, they were both in decline. The fact that neither nation was willing to accept this fate led both to join the American colonists in their war of independence against the British.

THE AMERICAN REVOLUTION

The American revolt against the government of **King George III** (1738–1820) is important for several reasons. First, it led to the creation of the United States of America, which since the end of the Cold War has been the world's unrivaled military and economic power (see Chapter 13). Second, the American Revolution contributed significantly to the growth of English-speaking Canada. Many Loyalists, or **Tories**, who opposed the revolution went north to Canada. Third, the most important documents to come out of the revolution drew heavily on some of the Enlightenment ideas that will be discussed in the next chapter. Finally, the American Revolution helped set the stage for the very different but equally important French Revolution (see Chapter 6).

The American Revolution took place within the context of eighteenth-century Europe's competing global empires and wars. After the end of the Seven Years' War, which in America was called the **French and Indian War**, the British had military and colonial commitments around the world and wanted to end fighting in North America. Consequently, in the **Proclamation of 1763** Britain prohibited American settlers from moving west of the Appalachian Mountains. This, Britain's government believed, would prevent more warfare between the settlers and American Indians. After the war Britain also decided to enforce the various navigation laws that had been passed in Parliament since the late 1600s. The Americans were notorious smugglers; they traded illegally with the French, Dutch, and Spaniards, among others. These actions of Britain, both of which were done with the interests of the British Empire in mind, sparked protest.

Perhaps the best-known act of American defiance, the **Boston Tea Party**, was also connected to the Empire. In the early 1770s the **British East India Company** was in financial difficulties. In an effort to bail out the company, the British government gave it a monopoly on sales of tea in the American colonies. As a result, tea merchants and smugglers in America were threatened—and the famous party took place in 1773.

Not long after the colonists—actually, a radicalized minority of colonists—went to war with the English, Britain's longtime foe, France, decided to assist the Americans, more out of a desire to see the British Empire harmed than of love for the thirteen colonies. **France played a decisive role in the American Revolution**, providing thousands of **troops**, great amounts of **gunpowder**, and, perhaps most important, a **navy**. Much of France's material assistance was funneled to the Americans by **Pierre Augustin Caron de Beaumarchais** (1732–1799), under the cover of a nonexistent corporation, Rodrique, Hortalez, and Company. Soon after France joined the war on the side of the Americans, the Spaniards, Dutch, and other foes of Britain from the Seven Years' War assisted the Americans.

By 1783 Britain had decided that it had more important things to do than force the Americans to stay in the Empire. Its hold on India was growing, the West Indies continued to produce fabulous wealth for slave-holding sugar producers, and it faced very serious challenges in its North African post at Tangier. Within the context of the Empire, America did not seem so important. Even with the loss of the American colonies Britain's empire in 1783 was the greatest and most powerful in the world.

FOR YOUR INFORMATION

Privateers

One distinction between early modern pirates and privateers such as Sir Francis Drake was that privateers had at least implicit approval from their governments, whereas pirates were considered outlaws. Through the early modern period, pirates—sometimes called buccaneers—operated around the world. Piracy remains a problem in the Straits of Malacca. When U.S. aircraft carriers pass slowly through the Straits, marines man .50 caliber machine guns to ensure that no unwelcomed person tries to come aboard. The phrase "to the shores of Tripoli" in the Marine Corps anthem refers to U.S. operations in the early 1800s, when President Thomas Jefferson fought an undeclared war against pirates from present-day Libya. The pirates made their living taking Americans and their ships for ransom.

Plains of Abraham

The defeat of the French on the Plains of Abraham in 1759 is an important event for the French-speaking people of the Canadian province of Quebec. That event marks the end of the French empire in America and the beginning of French-Canadian life under the British flag. The British, who soon had plenty of trouble on their hands with the American colonists south of Canada, decided not to antagonize the Quebecers and, therefore, did not make the Church of England Quebec's official religion. Catholicism in Quebec remained very conservative until the 1960s, when many French-Canadian young people joined the youth movement at work throughout Western civilization. From that time, nationalism has been a strong force in Quebec. Montreal, Quebec's metropolis, is the second-largest French-speaking city in the world. Of course, Paris is the largest.

CHAPTER 4

The Scientific Revolution and Enlightenment

THE SCIENTIFIC REVOLUTION AND ENLIGHTENMENT

Philosophy is written in this grand book—I mean the universe—which stands continually open to our gaze, but it cannot be understood unless one first learns to comprehend the language and interpret the characters in which it is written.
—Galileo Galilei

It is not enough to have a good mind. The main thing is to use it well.
—Rene Descartes

The heart has its reasons which reason knows nothing of.
—Blaise Pascal

Liberty of thought is the life of the soul.
—Voltaire

INTRODUCTION

In the late Middle Ages the Islamic world was ahead of Western civilization in scientific and mathematical knowledge. Some of the Arabic words that have come into English—*algebra, alchemy, almanac*—reflect the Muslims' advanced learning. But by the time Muslims made their second failed attempt to capture Vienna (1683), the West had far surpassed the Islamic world in scientific achievement. One reason is that the printing press had been banned completely in the Muslim world in the sixteenth century.

Through the Middle Ages, Europeans believed that the earth was the center of the universe and that the sun revolved around it. They believed this mainly because it was, to greatly simplify things, the view of the Greek philosophers Aristotle and **Ptolemy**. But certain passages in the Bible—such as when the Israelite warrior Joshua prays for the sun to stand still long enough for him to complete a battle—seemed to suggest the same thing. Some thought the earth's position at the center of the universe also suggested that the inhabitants of earth were at the center of God's concern. To challenge this view was to challenge fundamental beliefs people had about themselves and their place in the universe. Many other branches of learning, such as medicine and anatomy, developed dramatically during the Scientific Revolution. **Paracelsus** (1493–1541) observed that illness often stems from a chemical imbalance in the body; **Andreas Vesalius** (1514–1564), dissected human cadavers, a practice considered sinful by many in the Middle Ages; and **William Harvey** (1578–1657) studied the heart and blood circulation. But the best-known names of the period are linked to the study of the heavens.

A HALL OF FAME: COPERNICUS, GALILEO, KEPLER, AND NEWTON

The first work to cast doubt on the Ptolemaic view of the universe was *On the Revolutions of the Heavenly Spheres* published in 1543, the year its Polish author, **Nicolaus Copernicus**, died (b. 1473). Copernicus had written his book years before but did not publish it for fear that it would spark controversy, as indeed it did. In 1616 *On the Revolutions* was placed on the **Index of Prohibited Books**. The essential point of Copernicus's book was that the sun, not the earth, is the center of the universe. (To put it another way, Copernicus believed that **geocentrism**—earth-centeredness—was incorrect and replaced it with **heliocentrism**—sun-centeredness.) Copernicus came to this view less as a result of mathematical study than as a result of the messiness and illogic of Ptolemy's astronomical system as illustrated in confusing diagrams. Such messiness conflicted with the Greek philosopher Plato's view of a perfectly symmetrical universe.

More important than Copernicus was **Galileo Galilei** (1564–1642), the first person to use a **telescope** to study the universe. (The telescope was developed in the Netherlands.) Galileo observed craters, mountains, and valleys on the moon and spots on the sun. These facts challenged the prevailing view that the heavenly bodies were perfect. Galileo also discovered Jupiter's four moons; this challenged the view that all heavenly bodies orbited nothing but the earth.

Galileo's most important work, *The Starry Messenger*, was published in 1610. Galileo believed that the universe is a "grand book...written in the language of mathematics." From the book of the universe one could learn about the greatness of God's creation by applying reason based on observation and experimentation. Galileo had no intention of challenging Christianity, although he did challenge church authorities and scholars who accepted ancient views uncritically in his book *Dialogue Concerning the Two Chief World Systems—Ptolemaic and Copernican* (1632). If God gave people minds to think and to analyze, Galileo asked, why would He not want them to use their minds to expand their understanding of the world He made?

Whereas Copernicus stirred little real controversy during his life, Galileo faced great opposition from church authorities, who already felt embattled by the growth of the Protestant Reformation. In 1633, Galileo was summoned to Rome, tried by the **Inquisition**, and ordered to renounce his views. Believing that truth would eventually prevail, Galileo did renounce his views and spent the rest of his life under house arrest. He was forbidden to write about the universe. Copernicus's views—or Copernicanism—remained banned by the Roman Catholic Church until the 1820s. In the 1990s Pope John Paul II would formally acknowledge what everyone knew: Galileo had been right.

Johannes Kepler (1571–1630) was a German Lutheran, mathematician, and astronomer who shared Galileo's belief that God gave people the capacity to discover the truth about how the natural world operates. Kepler had been the assistant of another astronomer, the Dane **Tycho Brahe** (1546–1601), who for some twenty years had carefully recorded the positions of planets and stars. Whereas Brahe rejected the idea of a heliocentric universe, Kepler fervently accepted it, and in his book *The New Astronomy* (1609) he correctly argued that the **planets' orbit around the sun was elliptical**, not circular as other astronomers believed. Kepler was not able to say why that was, however.

The scientist who *was* able to explain the elliptical orbit of the planets, and much more, was the monumental British genius **Isaac Newton** (1642–1727). In *Mathematical Principles of Natural Philosophy*, often referred to simply as the *Principia*, Newton argued that gravity—the mutual attraction of physical objects in the universe—explained the orderly movement of the planets. Through gravity the earth acts on the sun and the sun acts on the earth. This mutual, consistent attraction causes the earth to move in a consistent, predictable order. After Newton provided mathematical proof for a heliocentric universe—drawing on the calculus he developed—opposition to the theory faded.

FAITH AND SCIENCE: BACON, DESCARTES, PASCAL, AND LEIBNIZ

Following a car accident, if someone were to ask why it happened, one response could be "God willed it." For many people that would, in some ways, be a satisfying answer. But it would not be a satisfactory answer for police officers, judges, and insurance companies. They would want the facts to be collected and analyzed; and they would want a reasonable answer to the question of why the accident happened to be derived from observable, verifiable facts. This approach to life, this emphasis on the **scientific method** (sometimes called the empirical method), did not have its complete beginning in the seventeenth century. The ancient writers Herodotus, Thucydides, and Saint Luke claimed to have set out to discover the truth about historical events and to report those events accurately. But the demand that one's understanding of life should conform to what can be observed and verified has not been shared by most people who have lived in Western civilization since ancient times. It is, essentially, a modern idea.

One of the most important early advocates of the scientific method was the Englishman **Sir Francis Bacon** (1561–1626). Though he was a philosopher (aside from being a lawyer and royal official), Bacon had little patience with philosophers and theologians who based their ideas about the world on abstract ideas. Instead, Bacon advocated **inductive reasoning**, or the **inductive method**. Following this method, one gathers particular information, pulls that information together and arrives at a general theory that can be tested using repeatable experimentation.

Bacon's best-known books are ***Novum Organum*** (1620) and ***New Atlantis*** (1627). Aware of the great changes taking place in the Western world, Bacon compared himself to Christopher Columbus, and he was one of the first major figures to argue that knowledge should be put to practical use for the betterment of society. His belief that scientific advancement and human advancement go hand in hand is still prevalent. The inductive method is the primary one relied on by biologists, chemists, medical researchers, and other scientists.

The **deductive method** is relied on by mathematicians, physicists, and, in different ways, philosophers and theologians. The person most credited with formulating the deductive method is **René Descartes** (1596–1650), author of the influential work Discourse on Method (1637). Unlike the inductive method, the deductive method begins with general principles and derives particular information from them. For example, Descartes noted that he had the capacity to think. That was a definite principle. From it he derived the particular fact that he existed. Thus, he wrote, "*Cogito ergo sum*," or, "**I think therefore I am**." (Students without an interest in ontology—the study of being—may think this idea of Descartes' silly, but it is not. The question "What can people be certain of?" is a fundamental philosophical question. For Descartes, the one fundamental belief he could be certain of was that he existed. From that, other principles followed. Descartes also argued that the human ability to contemplate the idea of perfection is proof of God's existence. People have never seen perfection, Descartes suggested, yet they can conceive of it. So the idea must come from some outside source which is perfect—namely, God. Descartes died in 1650 in Stockholm, where he had been the teacher of Queen **Christina of Sweden** (1626–1689).

Blaise Pascal (1623–1662) was a French mathematician who invented a calculating machine (1640), devised an influential theory of chance and probability, and learned much from intellectuals such as Bacon and Descartes. Like many thinkers at that time, he did not believe that religious faith and science needed to conflict. "If we violate the principles of reason," he wrote, "our religion will be absurd, and it will be laughed at." In a collection of notes, called the *Pensées* (or, *Thoughts*), Pascal argued that reason alone was insufficient to understand all of human experience. Pascal observed that life contains much mystery—things impenetrable to reason alone. And **Pascal's Wager** was simple and appealed to common sense. It is reasonable to risk believing in God, he said. For if God does not exist, then one will lose nothing in the next life. But if God does exist, then the believer has gained everything.

Another important mathematician of this period was **Gottfried Leibniz** (1646–1716). Like Pascal, he was an important mathematician who appears to have developed calculus independently of Newton. He also invented a calculating machine thirty years after Pascal. Also like Pascal, he made rational arguments in defense of the concept of God. In the *Théodicée* Leibniz attempts to explain evil and the problems of the world, maintaining that this is the best of all possible worlds—that is, neither a world with no suffering nor one with no good to counteract suffering would be as good overall as this world, which includes good and suffering.

THE ENLIGHTENMENT

By the early eighteenth century more intellectuals were becoming increasingly skeptical about religious faith. For one thing, church authorities had pitted themselves against theories (such as heliocentrism) that had been proven true. And, unlike Pascal, some scholars came to believe that all human phenomena could be understood through the study of the natural world. There were very few atheists in the eighteenth century; but many of *les lumières*, or enlightened ones, also called philosophes, were **deists**. That is, they believed in a God who is like a watchmaker who creates a clock, winds it up, and lets it run: God had created the world and now stood back from it, uninvolved and not very interested in it, performing no miracles, becoming involved in no person's life. But like a good watchmaker, this God had set laws in motion that caused the world to function as it does. Deists believed that the enlightened person's duty is to discover what these laws are and to teach others about them. Some Enlightenment figures believed that humans could create perfect societies once they uncovered the truth about how the world and the people in it operate.

Another thing the key Enlightenment figures had in common is that they were Frenchmen who, disenchanted with their country's lack of freedom, admired England's political system, in which the monarch shared power with Parliament. In some respects they had been preceded by **François Fénelon** (1651–1715), a writer and Catholic bishop who revered Louis XVI but also criticized his excessive power, calling for a limited monarchy and the equality of all people in the eyes of the law. Fénelon died in exile.

In his *Persian Letters* (1721), the *philosophe* **Charles Montesquieu** indirectly criticized France's monarchy and the Roman Catholic Church, and in *The Spirit of the Laws* (1748) he tried to explain the "natural laws" governing politics. In the latter book Montesquieu argued for the importance of **checks and balances** and **separation of powers** in government. This would have a very great impact on key American *philosophes* such as **James Madison** (1751–1836), who was most responsible for the American Constitution, and **Thomas Jefferson** (1743–1826), author of the Declaration of Independence. Drawing on

Montesquieu, the American writers built a system of checks and balances into the Constitution: the houses of Congress, the president and the courts have different responsibilities, and, ideally, none can ride roughshod over the others.

Where Montesquieu's enduring influence has been practical, the influence of **François Voltaire** (1694–1778) has been more psychological. Writers who scorn all authority, students who mock church authorities, journalists who denounce corrupt governments—all of them, and others, have a role model in Voltaire.

In his *Philosophic Letters on the English* (1733), Voltaire made plain his admiration for the English political system—its relative religious liberty and freedom of the press, among other things. His most famous novel, *Candide* (1759), urges readers to improve society by putting Enlightenment ideas to work. In his *Treatise on Toleration* (1763) Voltaire argued on behalf of religious freedom, making the very modern claim that "all men are brothers under God." Among his more famous quotes is *"Ecrasez l'infâme!"* or, "Crush the infamous thing!" For him, the "infamous thing" was unquestioning religious faith, traditional religion and superstition. A devastating **earthquake in Lisbon**, Portugal, in 1755 spurred Voltaire and other *philosophes* to further question the idea of a loving God. About 100,000 people were killed as a result of the earthquake, many of them while worshiping at Sunday church services.

Like Voltaire, **Denis Diderot** (1713–1784) attacked the church. But he is most remembered for editing the West's first multivolume collection of learning, *Encyclopedia, or Classified Dictionary of the Sciences, Arts, and Trades*, the first volume of which was completed in 1751, the last in 1772. The twenty-eight volume work, contributed to by many *philosophes*, became the enlightened person's bible. As one would expect, it attacked uncritical religious belief and superstition and advocated religious tolerance, political liberalization, and societal improvement based on reason and scientific discovery.

A friend of Diderot's, **Jean-Jacques Rousseau** (1712–1778), was also among the Enlightenment's most influential thinkers. Like some people then and now, Rousseau romanticized exotic and seemingly simple people, making famous the concept of the **noble savage**. Rousseau's *Social Contract* (1762) has been very influential, even if the meaning of one of its central concepts—that of the **general will**—is difficult to define in practical terms. Government is a necessary evil, Rousseau thought. The best thing a society can do is govern by its general will—the sum of its highest aspirations, that which seeks the good of all. And people within a society who disagree with the general will should be forced to submit to it for their own good. "This means nothing less," Rousseau wrote, "than that [the dissenter] will be forced to be free." This was very different from the protection of political minorities built into the U.S. Constitution by America's Enlightenment figures, and Rousseau's theory has found admirers among advocates both of unfettered democracy and totalitarianism.

In *Essay on Crimes and Punishments* (1764) **Cesare Beccaria** (1738–1794) advocated the humane treatment of criminals, emphasizing reform over punishment and arguing against the death penalty and the use of torture.

The book *The Wealth of Nations*, by the Scottish economist **Adam Smith** (1723–1790), promoted a *laissez-faire* approach to economics—that is, he maintained that governments should let the economy run on its own without legislative interference. Smith thought that what he called an "invisible hand" would shape the economy for the good of all who pursued their own self-interest. If, for example, a person wanted to become wealthy by selling vegetables, he or she would have to do so at prices buyers would tolerate. If the seller did so, he or she would benefit by attracting buyers, while buyers would benefit because buying vegetables from another person instead of having to grow them would give them time to pursue their own interests. This is the essence of **capitalism**, an economic school of thought that has been put into effect, to one extent or another, throughout the Western world.

Like Adam Smith, the philosopher **David Hume** is linked to the **Scottish Enlightenment** (1740–1800); Scotland's capital, **Edinburgh**, was sometimes called the "**Athens of the North**." In works such as *Dialogues Concerning Natural Religion* (published posthumously) and *Enquiry Concerning Human Understanding* (1748), Hume argued against the credibility of miracles, maintained that all religious claims are open to question, and that all beliefs people have are derived from the perceptions of their senses.

Hume's book should not be confused with the similarly titled *Essay Concerning Human Understanding* (1690) by the Englishman **John Locke** (1632–1704), whose political work was discussed in Chapter 2. In his book on the origins of human knowledge, Locke theorizes that, at birth, the human mind is a *tabula rasa*, or blank slate, that is filled in by experience. In this sense all people are born equal, and differences in status are determined by experience.

Another key British intellectual figure of the eighteenth century was **Edward Gibbon** (1737–1794), who in 1776 published his monumental and still much-read history, ***The Decline and Fall of the Roman Empire***. The multivolume work explained the historical processes that led to the downfall of Rome in **strictly secular terms**. For many, the will of God, or providence, was no longer considered a viable explanation for historical events.

Utilitarianism, which calls for the "greatest good for the greatest number," was a different philosophical innovation of the late eighteenth and early nineteenth centuries. It is most associated with the Englishman **Jeremy Bentham** (1748–1832).

Meanwhile, some women, prominent among them **Mary Wollstonecraft** (1759–1797), argued that women should have greater freedom to pursue their own intellectual and political interests. "Till women are more rationally educated," she wrote in ***The Vindication of the Rights of Women*** (1792), "the progress in human virtue and improvement" will be slowed.

Among the Enlightenment's most optimistic writers was **Marie Jean de Condorcet** (1743–1794). In ***Sketch for a Historical Picture of the Progress of the Human Mind*** (1794), Condorcet claims that there is "no limit to the perfecting of the powers of man." Through reason, study, and tolerance, Condorcet suggests in his book, humans could achieve perfection. But as American Enlightenment figure **Benjamin Franklin°** (1706–1790) learned and recorded humorously in his autobiography, perfection is beyond the human's grasp.

Like all the Enlightenment figures mentioned, **René de Chateaubriand** studied numerous topics and wrote about nearly as many. In his ***Genius of Christianity*** (1802), he discusses the effects of religious feeling on history, government, the arts, nature, and the conscience.

"ENLIGHTENED DESPOTS": CATHERINE THE GREAT, FREDERICK II, AND JOSEPH II

The quotation marks around the phrase *enlightened despots* in this section's title indicate that the rulers discussed here accepted Enlightenment thought and pursued political reform, but only within limits. This was probably inevitable. The histories of Austria, Prussia, and Russia were so different from the history of Britain that parliamentary democracy in them was not possible.

Montesquieu's theory about checks and balances in government could not apply in lands ruled by absolute monarchs. But real reforms were instituted.

Joseph II (r. 1765–1790), the emperor of Austria, was among Europe's enlightened despots. He aimed to govern according to principles of sound political and moral philosophy. The Catholic emperor's **Edict of Toleration** (1781) provided freedom of worship to Christians of various persuasions (such as Lutherans and Calvinists). After 1781 **Jews** in the Austrian empire were free to five outside ghettos, no longer had to wear yellow stars to identify them, and were allowed to attend a university. Joseph asserted that he, not the pope, controlled church lands in Austria, and he sold about one-third of the empire's monasteries and convents, using the money to support hospitals. Catholic orders that promoted education were left alone. This latter fact points to Joseph's commitment to education and his belief that education helped to make rich and poor more equal. Consequently, by the end of the 1700s, more children attended school in Austria than in any other European country or empire. Joseph also emancipated serfs, meaning that peasants were no longer legally required to work the land of property owners.

Like Joseph, Prussia's **Frederick the Great** (r. 1740–1786) admired Enlightenment thought and figures. He invited Voltaire to live for three years near Berlin. Under Frederick's rule, land was improved and made useful for farming. He allowed Catholics and Jews to settle in his mostly Protestant (Lutheran) country. He granted his subjects limited freedom of speech, and he sought to make Prussia's legal system more efficient. He also established a more professional **bureaucracy**, a collection of government offices and functions that would carry on after his death.

Russia's **Catherine the Great** (r. 1762–1796) wrote letters to, and received letters from, key Enlightenment figures such as Voltaire and Diderot. Catherine advocated several reforms. She questioned the death penalty, the value of torture in the criminal punishment system, and the institution of serfdom.

While each of these rulers pursued significant reforms, change was limited during their reigns. This was especially true in Russia, where little reform occurred. A rebellion against Russia's wealthy landowners led by **Emelyn Pugachev** led to greater repression of peasants, and by the end of Catherine's regime Russian governance had become much more unwieldy than before. Catherine had divided Russia into fifty provinces, which essentially led to fifty governments with their own interests to protect. Joseph II, meanwhile, let high taxes on imports (called **tariffs**) stand, though *philosophes* argued against them. Also, the abolition of serfdom in Austria was repealed after Joseph's death. And while Frederick the Great's reforms were important, Prussia was actually more aristocratic after his death. Prussia's nobles, like nobles throughout Europe, continued to enjoy great power, privileges, and influence.

FOR YOUR INFORMATION

Benjamin Franklin

Benjamin Franklin is one of the great Enlightenment figures. He published influential newspapers, was an early advocate of American colonial unity, and he gave away money to help the poor. In 1776, as the American Revolution began, he went to France to encourage that country to help the rebellious colonies. He remained in France until 1785, becoming for many the face of America. Dressing casually in raccoon-skin hats and other American clothing, he exemplified America's commitment to ordinary people. Franklin was a deist, and he encouraged readers to "imitate Jesus and Socrates." Franklin's experiments proved that lightning was a form of electricity, and among his many inventions are the Franklin stove and bifocals. He also began public libraries, founded the University of Pennsylvania and the American Philosophical Society, and organized firefighters.

CHAPTER 5

The Industrial Revolution

CHAPTER 5

THE INDUSTRIAL REVOLUTION

Soon shall thy arm, unconqer'd steam! afar
Drag the slow barge, or drive the rapid car
—Erasmus Darwin

All work, even cotton spinning, is noble; work is alone noble.
—Thomas Carlyle

AGRICULTURE

In addition to the great intellectual change discussed in the last chapter and the great political change to be discussed in the next chapter, eighteenth-century Europe experienced what historians call an "**agricultural revolution.**" This, like the **Industrial Revolution** that is related to it, began in England. Britain had many advantages that made significant industrial change possible. One was its large supplies of **coal** and **iron** and its longstanding tradition of **mining.** Another was its transportation system made up of roads, rivers, and canals. Some Britons had grown wealthy by investing in trade—for example, by owning slave ships that transported their cargo to the sugar islands of the West Indies. Moveover, Britain's increasingly individualistic culture often encouraged the ambitious to pursue their goals. By the mid-eighteenth century private business in Britain was all but left alone by government.

In essence, the agricultural revolution involved feeding Europe's growing population with crops raised by improved methods. **Jethro Tull** (1674–1741) argued incorrectly that manure was not useful as fertilizer, but he did employ metal plows to plant seed rather than cast seed onto the ground, as was common. This led to greater crop yields. Another Englishman, **Charles "Turnip" Townsend** (1674–1738), found that if different crops were planted in fields in

45

different years, the soil would not become depleted of minerals, because different crops take different minerals from the soil.

The desire among landowners to make their farms more manageable led to the continuation of the **enclosure** movement. This meant that land formerly shared in common was combined with other properties, fenced off, and used for sheep raising. This caused great hardship for independent small-field farmers, but it also made farming in Britain more productive. By 1800 less than half of Britain's population made its living from agriculture. A century earlier a large majority had done so.

INDUSTRY

The increased wealth gained by landowners as a result of greater crop production gave many of them an opportunity to invest in other innovations taking place elsewhere in an emerging economy. In the eighteenth century factories dedicated to producing cotton cloth emerged. They were made possible by the invention of the **spinning jenny**, which enabled one person to produce much more cloth in less time than it took when cotton was spun into fabric by hand. The **textile industry** provided jobs in cities to some people who had formerly worked the land. The city of Manchester grew substantially, and Liverpool, from where textiles were shipped and imports taken in, also grew.

Related to the growth of the textile industry was the arrival in Europe of steam-powered machines. England's **James Watt** (1736–1819) is credited with inventing the first steam-powered machine. The **steam engine** powered cotton mills and, before long, iron production. In time the steam engine, along with iron and steel, led to Britain's first **railroad**, which connected Liverpool and Manchester and many other cities by the mid-1800s. Within seventy years, railroads crossed the United States and Canada and provided transportation in Europe, Asia, Africa, and even Siberia. Railroads were a product of industrialization; reliant as they were on nonhuman power, steel, and oil, they also spurred further industrialization.

A key industrial item was cotton, which was in demand for many things, including clothing, underwear, and blankets. The American South, where **"king cotton"** ruled, provided more raw cotton to industrial Europe than did any other region. When British and French put on their new cotton clothing, they probably did not realize that they were also encouraging American slavery. And because early machines were now powered by steam rather than by people, women and children could operate them. Before long, children worked in factories throughout Western civilization.

INDUSTRIALIZATION'S HUMAN IMPACT

The factories that emerged during the **Industrial Revolution** changed the way many people lived and worked. Thousands left the country to work in factories in cities. The population of Birmingham in England was 73,000 in 1851; fifty years later it had risen to 250,000. Unlike today, there were **no laws concerning sanitation and pollution**. Streets and alleys often became open sewers, and factories pumped soot into the air. Consequently, disease spread through many cities. In the early nineteenth century, more than one-quarter of Britain's children died before the age of 5. Work in Britain's mines, or pits, was also difficult and dangerous. The expression "the pits"—as in, "that party was the pits"—comes to us from this period.

Starting and finishing a day's work at precise times tied people to **clocks**; and since workers' productivity in the factories was less directly linked to the workers' well-being (the way their labor had been when they worked as farmers), many employers kept meticulous control over their employees. Workers who were not as productive as they could be were fined, fired, or even physically punished. Moreover, eighteenth-century factories were often filthy and unhealthy. At the time, there were no laws to protect workers from overwork and employer abuse. Also, many people who moved to cities from villages lost the sense of community they had enjoyed before. They sometimes now lived in a factory's barracks or in crowded urban rooms. It is a curious fact that the closer people live to one another (such as in cities), the less they seem to know and care about one another.

REFORM

In very real ways, many people could say that they benefited from industrialization. **Incomes rose** and employment became less dependent on weather. What we call the **middle class** came into existence in the nineteenth century. But few could deny that there was also much misery associated with early industrialization.

Efforts to reform the industrial economy, like industrialization itself, began in England. Although democracy, as Americans in the early twenty-first century think of it, was nowhere to be found in Britain in the late eighteenth and early nineteenth centuries, there was more freedom and more frequent inter-relations between the middle, upper-middle, and wealthy classes there than elsewhere in Europe (though not in the United States, where aristocrats were obligated to talk in public like ordinary citizens).

The early nineteenth century was a period of reform in Britain. In 1829 Catholics received the right to sit in Parliament, and four years later slavery was abolished in the British Empire. The **Public Health Act of 1848** encouraged local cities and towns to pass sanitary measures.

Crucial to bringing about reform was the **expansion of suffrage**—that is, the vote. In the early 1800s entire cities that had grown as a result of industrialization had no representation in Parliament, while sparsely populated rural areas—sometimes called **"rotten boroughs"**—had representatives in the House of Commons. When the House of Commons passed the **Reform Bill of 1832**, the more aristocratic House of Lords refused to pass it. This led to riots, strikes, and mass meetings among workers. **King William IV** (r. 1830–1837) thought the country might be facing revolution, as France had recently (see the next chapter), and he pressured the Lords to pass the bill. The law did pass, and Britain's middle-class men were given the vote. As a result, men who represented middle-class interests were elected to Parliament, and that led to the beginnings of significant reform. The **Sadler Committee** heard reports from children about the abysmal conditions they worked in. The consequent **Factory Act of 1833** prohibited children under the age of 13 from working more than 9 hours a day and young people between the ages of 13 and 18 from working more than 69 hours a week. Another Factory Act, passed fourteen years later, prohibited women and boys under 18 from working more than 10 hours a day. In 1874 Parliament passed a law making it illegal to require men to work more than 10 hour days.

Parliament had been spurred into action partly by the **Chartist** movement. In 1838 petitions that included the language of a **People's Charter** were signed by millions of Britons. These petitions called for the vote for all adult men and for the payment of members of Parliament (to make corruption less attractive). This was the first large-scale movement of lower-class workers in history.

Labor unions also began to take shape. The British social reformer Robert Owen formed the **Grand National Consolidated Trades Union** in 1834. Its main purpose was to agitate for an 8-hour workday. The members of another union, the **Amalgamated Society of Engineers**, paid a small weekly sum and, in turn, the union provided workers with unemployment benefits.

A less successful reaction to industrialization came in the form of the **Luddites**, workers who saw their livelihoods threatened by new machines. In the early nineteenth century these workers living in northern England attacked factories and machines, destroying many of them. Since that time, people who do not like new technologies have been called "luddites."

In time, industrialization spread to other parts of Europe and eventually to much of the world. It took hold in Europe more slowly than in Britain partly because there were few good roads and because tolls along rivers made trade more expensive and thus less inviting. Also, more than in any other country except in what would become the United States, Britain's culture encouraged entrepreneurship and, increasingly individualism. Probably most important, though, were the destructive wars that had taken place in Europe between 1790 and 1815 (see the next chapter).

By the 1840s technical schools were established in France and Germany, and governments began to encourage inventiveness by providing awards and by paying to build canals and roads (making the movement of goods easier and cheaper). Railroads crisscrossed western Europe by the 1860s. Also by that time the Germans, French, and others had copied another British institution, the **joint-stock investment bank**. Leading stock corporations were the **Darmstadt Bank** in Germany and **Crédit Mobilier**° in France. European financial institutions helped to finance the building of railroads in the United States.

FOR YOUR INFORMATION

Crédit Mobilier

In 1872 officers of the Union Pacific Railroad (UPR) in the United States formed the Crédit Mobilier in America Corporation to build railroads at the expense of the government and citizens. The UPR men then placed themselves on the Crédit Mobilier payroll, giving themselves nice salaries. To prevent public figures from making this a public scandal, Crédit Mobilier gave stock to key congressmen, and even the U.S. vice president accepted payments. Events like that demonstrated that government would have to get involved in the affairs of business if the interests of taxpayers and of ethical government were to be honored. A strict *laissez-faire* approach to the economy would not work. Consequently, as the years passed the economies of Western nations emphasized both economic freedom and government regulation.

CHAPTER 6

The French Revolution and Napoleonic Europe

THE FRENCH REVOLUTION AND NAPOLEONIC EUROPE

Men are born and remain free and equal in rights.
—National Assembly of France

Show my head to the people, it is worth seeing.
—George Danton to his executioner

Either you will see me return bathed in glory, or you will have a son who is a worthy citizen of France who knows how to die for the defense of his country.
—A French peasant soldier to his parents

A form of government that is not the result of a long sequence of shared experience, efforts, and endeavors can never take root.
—Napoleon Bonaparte

INTRODUCTION

Without question, the complicated French Revolution is one of the most important events in the history of the world. Its consequences continue to affect the world. In the early twentieth century the Chinese communist leader Chou En-lai was asked what he thought the consequences of the French Revolution were. He responded, "It is too soon to say." And the Italian fascist dictator Benito Mussolini (see Chapter 12) said he stood for a political program that was directly opposed to "the fundamental principles laid down in 1789," the year of the French Revolution.

In the years leading to France's revolution, that country's financial situation grew progressively weaker, largely as a result of constant wars. France's decision to assist Prussia in its aggression against Austria in the **War of Austrian Succession** (1740–1748) was especially fateful for a few reasons. First, in assisting Prussia, France was helping to create another strong power in Europe that would, before long, be a threat to it. Second, France's assistance to Prussia brought Britain into the war. Because France and Britain were global powers, the cost of global warfare was very high. The French monarch's long-standing and growing need for money was a major contributor to the French Revolution.

BACKGROUND

Before the revolution, French society was divided into three classes of people, called "estates." The **First Estate** was composed of the **clergy**, who paid no taxes, although the Roman Catholic Church in France did offer to the government relatively small monetary "gifts." For a long time this did not bother many people. The church kept records of births, deaths, and marriages; it provided assistance to the poor; it established schools; it baptized children, provided the dying with last rites, and presided over the burial of the dead; and it possessed information about eternal life. But by the late 1780s some members of the clergy, especially those of high social rank, had also become arrogant. Initially, many lower-ranking clergy would sympathize with the revolutionaries.

The **Second Estate** comprised the nobility, who were divided into two general categories: the **nobles of the sword** and the **nobles of the robe**. The first group could trace its noble status back for many generations. Though they had social status, not all of them were wealthy. Some had little more wealth than well-off peasants. Nobles of the robe, on the other hand, did not come from a long line of nobles. Instead, many of them had purchased their status, buying (for example) positions in France's high courts, called *parlements*.

Nobles had great influence, paid few taxes, and collected dues from peasants who lived on their lands. Some nobles wanted to see the power of the monarchy diminished in France as it had been in England, while others were opposed to any reforms that might threaten their prestige, privileges, and positions in society. This disagreement among nobles indicates that the ideas of the Enlightenment had been dispersed through upper-class society.

In France's **Third Estate** were all those who did not fit into the other two estates. Among these were relatively wealthy merchants, people whom we would now call middle class, and peasants. The Third Estate's professionals—doctors, lawyers, and bankers, among others—were called the **bourgeoisie**.

By 1789 the bourgeoisie owned about 20 percent of France's land. Many bourgeoisie wanted to rise to the status of noble of the robe, but the offices for sale were often too expensive or there were too few of them to go around. Consequently, many among the bourgeoisie felt thwarted. This is important because the revolution had its start in the Third Estate. It was essentially a middle-class movement.

At the same time, many urban workers—such as gardeners and factory workers—experienced a rapid increase in the cost of living (62 percent between 1785 and 1789), accompanied by a relatively small increase in pay (22 percent) in the same period. The inability of these workers' to meet the basic needs of living would push many of them into sympathizing with the revolution.

While most **peasants** in France were better off than those in other European countries, a majority of them were still poor, and the ideas of the Enlightenment appealed to the better-educated among them. Some peasants owned small plots of land, while many others lived on land they rented from nobles. The bulk of France's tax burden fell on the peasants, who were politically powerless. Peasants paid taxes to the king as well as nonvoluntary **tithes** to the church. Sometimes, food that peasants might have acquired by hunting was taken from them, for nobles held the right to hunt on peasant lands.

Not long before the French revolution began **Abbé Emmanuel Sieyès** (1748–1836) published the pamphlet *What Is the Third Estate?* (1789). The questions Sieyès posed suggest the frustration many in the Third Estate felt. "What is the Third Estate?" Sieyès asked. *"Everything.* What has it been in the political order up to the present? *Nothing.* What does it ask? *To become something."*

THE COMING OF REVOLUTION

By the late 1780s France's financial situation had reached a crisis. Its global war with Britain, called the **Seven Years' War** (1756–1763) in Europe and the **French and Indian War** in Britain's American colonies, had been very costly, as had the assistance France lent the Americans in their revolution against Britain. In early 1787 **Louis XVI** (r. 1774–1792) convened an **Assembly of Notables** to gain the First and Second Estates' consent to a tax on the church and nobility. The Assembly refused to approve the king's plan, and bankers in France began to refuse to lend money to the king. These events suggested that the king's rule was absolute only so long as he kept the wealthy and influential happy. Finally, in August 1788 the king called for the Estates General to convene.

As delegates from throughout France were being chosen to attend the meetings of the three estates, *cahiers de doléances,* or complaint reports, were drawn up. Among many other things, the *cahiers* called for laws to apply to French military personnel the way they did to other Frenchmen, and for no tax to be considered legal "unless accepted by the representatives of the people and sanctioned by the king."

At the convention of the estates at Versailles in May 1789, the some seventeen hundred delegates were politically divided. Many in the First and Second Estates were committed to holding on to their status, and they rejected calls from some in the Third Estate for every delegate to a have a vote, preferring instead that each estate have a single vote. As the Third Estate represented more than 95 percent of France's population, it also called for a doubling of its number of delegates. The king approved this request, though he insisted that each estate continue to vote as a body. This ensured that the first two estates could check the boisterous Third Estate.

The Third Estate's refusal to accept this led to the first act of revolution. Led by Sieyès and **Honoré Gabriel Riquetti, comte de Mirabeau** (1749–1791), the Third Estate renamed itself the **National Assembly** and called on the other two estates to join it. There followed quick reaction and counterreaction: Louis XVI locked the Third Estate out of the hall where meetings were being conducted, so the delegates met instead on an indoor tennis court and there swore not to leave Versailles until they had written a new constitution for France. Though the king soon showed his weak position by ordering the first two estates to join the National Assembly, the **Tennis Court Oath** of June 20, 1789, signaled that revolution had begun.

As this was happening, unrest broke out elsewhere in France. As a result of bad harvests and a slowing economy, bread prices had soared. Riots broke out in many cities, most importantly in Paris. In response to this, Louis XVI sent between seventeen thousand and twenty thousand troops into Paris to support the five thousand already there. And in response to *this,* Parisians attacked the **Bastille**—formerly an arms depot, now a prison and most importantly, a symbol of the king's power. The few prisoners kept there were released; the Bastille's guards were killed, along with about one hundred rioters. The severed heads of several killed guards were paraded through the streets. The king asked an advisor if he had a revolt on his hands. "No," the aide responded, "it is a revolution."

REVOLUTION: PART I

Soon, matters fell beyond the control of any political figure. Rumors in the countryside that nobles were hoarding grain to starve the peasants into submission caused some peasants to take up arms and go on the attack. In this **Great Fear,** nobles' mansions were burned, records destroyed, and properties stolen. Some nobles were killed. Meanwhile, the National Assembly passed laws putting the *ancien regime*—or the old order of kings who ruled absolutely—out of existence.

By the early fall of 1790, nobles and clergy had lost many privileges. The tithe was abolished, as was the exclusive right of the nobility to hunt on land inhabited by peasants. Soon after this nobles lost their titles. Henceforth, all residents of France were *citoyens* ("citizens"). According to the **"Declaration of the Rights of Man and Citizen"** (1789), all citizens were politically equal and enjoyed inherent rights to "liberty, property, security, and resistance to oppression." Like the American **Declaration of Independence** of thirteen years before, the French declaration reflected Enlightenment ideas. But where the American declaration placed power in the hands of individuals who join together in a common cause, the French document claimed that "all authority rests essentially in the nation." It is for this reason that some historians maintain that modern **nationalism** began with the French Revolution.

One manifestation of this new nationalism was the nationalization of the church in France. Before the revolution, the church owned about 10 percent of French land. Now that land was made available to the nation, and the **Civil Constitution of the Clergy** (1790) required clergy to take an oath of loyalty to the nation. It also injected democracy into church politics, requiring bishops to be elected by laymen (that is, nonclergy). This provoked antirevolutionary sentiment among France's devout peasants. About half of France's clergy refused to sign the oath; and the revolutionaries' moves against the church ensured that, before long, many French people who remained loyal to the church would reject the secularizing trends of the revolution.

Though Louis XVI had been greatly humbled, France was still a monarchy, albeit now a **constitutional monarchy**. This meant that the monarch shared power with the National Assembly and could not act beyond the powers granted him by the constitution. According to the French constitution of 1791, the king could choose and dismiss his ministers as he saw fit; he had the power to direct foreign policy and the armed forces; and he could veto legislation from the Legislative Assembly, but (as in the American system) the assembly could override his veto.

While the French Revolution was radical and would grow even more radical, by modern standards it was conservative in some respects. Of France's population of 26 million in 1791, just over 4 million people were eligible to vote—all of them men over the age of 25 years who paid taxes valued at three days' wages. Eligibility for election to serve in the national government was also based on property and wealth. Only about fifty thousand Frenchmen were eligible to be elected. The belief in France, as everywhere else in the Western world that held elections, was that people without property did not have a vested interest in the maintenance of society and thus should not vote, even though their rights to free speech and fair trials were inviolable. In time, restrictions on who could vote fell by the wayside throughout the Western world. They would do so largely in response to the work of political activists. During the early years of the French Revolution, **Olympe de Gouges** (1748–1793) published "**Declaration of the Rights of Woman and Female Citizen**," which called for the political equality of men and women.

In the summer of 1791 the stage was being set for a more radical turn in the revolution. In June of that year, Louis XVI and his family tried to escape France. The king wanted to gain the support of the Austrian emperor **Leopold II** (r. 1790–1792) and to rally the numerous nobles and military officers, called **émigrés**, who had left France when the revolution broke out. About 40 miles short of the Netherlands border, the royal family was arrested and returned to the capital. For the sake of maintaining stability, nonradicals spread the rumor the royal family had been kidnapped. But two months later, the Austrian emperor and Prussia's **King Friedrich Wilhelm II** (r. 1786–1797) declared in the **Declaration of Pillnitz** that their armies would invade France if its royal family were harmed. The radicals in the Legislative Assembly responded to this with a declaration of war. Among these radicals were **Georges Jacques Danton** (1759–1794) and **Jean Paul Marat** (1743–1793). These were members of the group known as the **Jacobin Club**. Long thereafter political radicals were called "Jacobins."

REVOLUTION: PART II

The anxiety and uncertainty stirred by early defeats in battle led to the further radicalization of the revolution. In August 1792 mobs invaded the **Legislative Assembly**, which had taken the place of the National Assembly, and forced it to end the monarchy and to give the vote to all men, regardless of wealth. From that point the revolution fell out of the assembly's hands and temporarily into that of the **Paris Commune**, many of whose members were called *sansculottes* (i.e., people without fine clothing).

Soon the Paris Commune, led by Danton, began executing thousands of people its members deemed antirevolutionary or potentially threatening to the revolutionary cause. In September the new **National Convention** (which had taken the place of the Legislative Assembly) ended France's monarchy. In January of the next year Louis XVI was publicly beheaded on a new device designed to eliminate people quickly, the **guillotine**.

But even the National Convention would soon find itself divided. The **Girondins**, representing the countryside, and favoring a federal system, had been opposed to the elimination of the monarchy; the **Mountain**, representing Paris and a more centralized government, favored it. The radicals in the Paris Commune and their allies in the National Convention began a purge of the leading Girondins. Meanwhile, the region in western France called the **Vendée** revolted against the questionable authority of the National Convention. Calling for an end to a new military draft, for a decentralized form of government, and for the return of the monarchy and the *ancien regime,* inhabitants of the Vendee launched a counterrevolution. And all the while, France remained at war.

The war effort against the combined forces of Austria, Britain, the Dutch Republic, Portugal, Prussia, and Spain was directed by the **Committee of Public Safety**, led by Danton and later **Maximilien Robespierre** (1758–1794). Against these countries, which sought to defeat the revolution and restore the monarchy in France, the committee rallied much of the nation and created Europe's first national army. This meant that nonprofessional soldiers were called to fight, not on behalf of a king or dynasty, but on behalf of France itself. This is another way the revolution helped to create modern nationalism.

To ensure political allegiance to France in a time of stress, the Committee of Public Safety rooted out enemies or potential enemies of the revolution. Olympe de Gouges, whose revolutionary credentials were not beyond suspicion, was executed, as were many Girondins and Queen **Marie Antoinette**. The best-known method of execution was the guillotine, though in Nantes mass drownings on old ships were orchestrated. "By sinking a loaded hulk in a river at night, and then refloating it," writes the historian Norman Davies, the revolutionaries "devised an efficient and inconspicuous system of reusable death chambers." Altogether, between 25,000 and 50,000 French men and women were killed in what has been called the "**Reign of Terror**." The idealism of the Third Estate was long gone. During the Reign of Terror, France was governed by the twelve-man team that composed the Committee of Public Safety.

SECULARIZATION

New laws sought to remove France even further from the *ancien regime*. Churches were closed by the government; monastery libraries (along with libraries owned by nobles) were confiscated and added to the new **National Library**. Antirevolutionary clergy were executed, other clergy were encouraged to abandon their vow of chastity, the word *saint* disappeared from street names, and the cathedral of Notre Dame in Paris was renamed the **Temple of Reason**. Robespierre established a new religion, which he called the "Cult of the Supreme Being." As most French people still considered themselves Catholic, these reforms created more enemies for the revolution.

Even less popular was the **elimination of the Christian calendar**. Gone were festive days celebrating certain saints, and time would no longer be measured from the birth of Christ. France's new calendar began the day the Republic of France was proclaimed, September 22, 1792. (Thus September 22, 1795, was called "year three.") The seven-day week was replaced with a **ten-day week**, the tenth day being a day of rest. The months were renamed, **Thermidor** (heat) being a new summer month. This new calendar never caught on and went out of use entirely in 1806.

By mid-1794 many French people had grown tired of the excesses of the revolution. Now the tables turned on the radicals in the Paris Commune and Committee of Public Safety. Robespierre, who had ordered the execution of Danton in April, was himself executed in July.

THE END OF REVOLUTION

The end of radical revolution came in what is called the **Thermidorian Reaction**, named after the summer month of the revolutionary calendar. Jacobins were purged from political groups, and the influential Jacobin Club of Paris was shut down. Peace was achieved between the Vendée and the central government, and the tables turned on former revolutionaries who now found themselves the targets of persecution. In 1795 the National Convention wrote a new national constitution, establishing a legislature overseen by a **Directory** consisting of five men.

Still, France's political life remained unstable. Challenges from the political left (radicals) and right (royalists) suggested that the Directory would not be able to hold power for long. And still France was at war. It would remain at war almost constantly until 1815.

France's armies faced significant challenges. Many officers, being nobles, were among the *émigrés* or had been executed for their real or potential anti-revolutionary sentiments. This contributed to a lack of leadership in the military. Because the nation was in political upheaval, it was not able to feed and arm soldiers well. And since most French soldiers had been drafted, many of them deserted when they could. At the same time, because of the draft, the French had a vast army of abut 700,000 men. And the French soldiers who remained to fight had a cause to motivate them—the ideals of the revolution.

As this **revolutionary army** took territory in the Netherlands (then governed by Austria), it claimed to be promoting **political liberation** from monarchs. Northern Italy was similarly liberated from Austria in 1797, and the Catholic Church lost many of its privileges in Switzerland as the French moved in. The pope himself fled from the Italian Papal States as the French arrived. Some living in the occupied countries liked the ideas about equality and rights that the soldiers brought with them; others did not. Clearly, the constant warfare stalled industrial investment and advancement on the European continent, allowing the British to move ahead in industry.

THE RISE OF NAPOLEON

By 1799 the only large institution in France that was held in broad esteem was the military. In October of that year Napoleon had returned to Paris, where feelings of discontent were strong because instability was persistent. Not long before Napoleon's return, forces in favor of bringing back the monarchy had attempted to capture the city of Toulouse. What was needed, some thought, was a strong person who could bring stability and order to France.

With the help of conspirators and soldiers, **Napoleon abolished the Directory** and established a three-man consulate to govern France. In fact, though, Napoleon claimed the title of **First Consul**, and the new constitution he drew up made him France's sole ruler. After an attempt on his fife in 1804, Napoleon argued that he needed complete control of France and its empire to maintain order, and he had had himself renamed France's emperor. This was approved in a plebiscite by France's voters.

Napoleon was generally popular, for several reasons. First, he brought order and stability to a weary France. Second, he led a succession of military victories that added to France's wealth and prestige, though they also laid the foundations of future problems (as described later in this chapter).

Third, Napoleon knew about the importance of Roman Catholicism to most French people, recognizing in his constitution that Catholicism was the religion of the majority of Frenchmen and women. Napoleon's **Concordat** with the Roman Catholic Church (1801) gave the pope the power to depose bishops, while Napoleon retained the power to nominate them. In 1806 he abolished the very unpopular and anti-Christian revolutionary calendar.

Napoleon also ensured that advancement in government and the military came by way of merit rather than by status. His **Civil Code** (1804) abolished primogeniture, which required the bulk of a father's property to go to his first-born son. Further, the new code protected personal property. Male peasants were granted rights and were recognized as equal to others in the eyes of the law.

These reforms made Napoleon popular; and to further consolidate his power, he put the majority of newspapers out of business. The newspapers that survived were required to submit articles to government agents for approval before publication. Napoleon was a new kind of "enlightened despot."

INTERNATIONAL CONSEQUENCES OF THE REVOLUTION

The French Revolution's effects on the history of the West would be difficult to overstate. Throughout Europe, as well as in the Americas, reform-minded people looked to Paris as the center of change. Thomas Jefferson, writer of the American Declaration of Independence, mostly approved of the French Revolution, though its excesses concerned him. The **London Corresponding Society** kept up with revolutionary thought, and the anti-British **Society of United Irishmen** appreciated the French Revolution's nationalist sentiments.

At the same time, monarchical governments were disgusted by the revolution and put down pro-revolutionary groups. The Society of United Irishmen was repressed by the British government, and the **Alien and Sedition Acts** passed in the United States were partly designed to prevent French revolutionaries from immigrating to the United States.

France's wars also gave other countries a reason to promote their own sense of nationhood (see the next section). Germany would not become the nation we think of today until the late nineteenth century, but the roots of German nationalism were watered by anti-French feeling. This, combined with reforms learned from the French such as advancement in the military by merit rather than by family prestige, helped especially to make Prussia a formidable military force.

In the 1790s battles were fought in **Poland**, where some sympathized with revolutionary concepts. Revolutionary ideas influential in Poland promoted nationalism and fostered anti-Russian policies. Austria, Russia, and Prussia were eager to gain more territory and to eliminate the possibility of a revolutionary Poland, so in a series of territorial divisions, **Poland was wiped from the map** by these countries between 1793 and 1795. That country would not reemerge as a separate country again until after the First World War.

NAPOLEON THE GENERAL AND NAPOLEONIC EUROPE

As has already been suggested, the most impressive French general of the revolutionary wars was the young man from Corsica named **Napoleon**

Bonaparte (1769–1821). In an effort to weaken Britain's international position, Napoleon occupied Egypt in 1798. This threatened British naval and trade routes to India. France's occupation of Egypt would not last long; the French navy was defeated by the British, commanded by **Lord Horatio Nelson** (1758–1805) at **Aboukir Bay**. But the French presence in Egypt endured long enough to introduce some European reforms into this Muslim country. For example, religious taxes, torture of prisoners, and slavery were abolished. Napoleon also brought many scientists—physicists, chemists, botanists, zoologists, and others—with him. Some of these uncovered the **Rosetta Stone**, named after a town near the discovery site. On the stone were written texts in ancient Greek and Egyptian hieroglyphics. For the first time since ancient centuries, translating hieroglyphics was possible.

The consequences of Napoleon's wars and the reactions of other countries to them were far-reaching. Western civilization emerged from the wars very different from what it had been before. For example, because his wars were costly, Napoleon decided to sell France's **Louisiana Territory°** in the New World to the United States. As a result of this decision, the United States doubled in size and grew substantially in power and wealth.

Other changes were brought by the French military to the regions they conquered and occupied. Throughout western Europe, serfdom was abolished and the concepts of property rights and advancement by merit took hold. Also, nations that sought to resist or to defeat the French were forced to reform. **Prussia** is the best example of this. For one thing, Prussia learned from the French example of a well-trained citizen army in place of mercenary forces. Prussia's privileged **Junker** class of nobles retained significant power, but important reforms were also put into effect: excessive punishment of soldiers was abolished, colleges devoted to the study of war were founded, professional strategists studied war tactics, and patriotism was promoted. Combined with sentiments stemming from the **Romantic** movement (see Chapter 9), which focused on the unique qualities, history, and characteristics of Germans, those reforms contributed to the growth of Prussian nationalism. Napoleon limited the number of Prussia's army to 42,000. But by conscripting a new army each year, Prussia was able by 1814 to have on hand some 270,000 trained soldiers.

In addition to spurring nationalism in some areas, Napoleon's warfare also sparked **guerrilla warfare° in Spain**. Napoleon's army marched through Spain on the way to Portugal. The emperor wanted to stop Portugal from trading with Britain. In response Britain landed forces in Spain that assisted the guerrillas.

Napoleon was not able to pull Portugal out of Britain's orbit, and his efforts against the guerrillas in Spain were very costly.

Napoleon's troops came to even greater hardship in Russia. In 1807 a weary Russia had made concessions of territory to Napoleon in the **Treaty of Tilsit**. But by 1810 that country determined that it would not abide any longer with Napoleon's **Continental System**, which sought to break Britain economically by preventing European trade with it and which provided for commercial laws among European nations that favored France.

At the same time, **Russia** began to prepare for war. In 1812 about one million men under Napoleon's rule invaded Russia. That country's response to the invasion was similar to what it would be in 1940, when Hitler's forces invaded: a **scorched-earth policy**. The Russians backed up, burning crops and towns, including Moscow. This prevented Napoleon's forces from living off the land. And as Napoleon's troops got further from home—as their supply lines grew longer and longer—snow began to fall. As French troops began to retreat in October of 1812, they were harassed by Russians, who were now on the offensive, as well as by freezing temperatures. Just one in six of the French soldiers who went into Russia came out. Napoleon had experienced defeat before. The British Navy had defeated his sailors at **Abaukir** (off the coast of Egypt) in 1798 and again at **Trafalgar** (off the southwestern coast of Spain) in 1805. But never before had Napoleon experienced something like this.

FOR YOUR INFORMATION

Louisiana Territory

The United States purchased Louisiana in 1803. President Thomas Jefferson authorized American agents to purchase only New Orleans. With its rapid expansion westward, the United States wanted unfettered access to the sea out of the mouth of the Mississippi River, where New Orleans was established. Just before, Napoleon's forces had lost a war waged by slaves against their French masters in Haiti. This helped to squelch Napoleon's desire to rebuild an American empire. Now he saw the sale of Louisiana as a way to get money to pay for his wars in Europe. The United States purchased Louisiana for $15 million—along with the U.S. purchase of Alaska from Russia in 1867, one of the best real estate deals in history. Though the number of French-speaking people in Louisiana has declined steadily since that time, French is still spoken in some Louisiana parishes. The census of 1990 recorded that 262,000 Louisiana residents spoke French.

Guerrilla Warfare

Now sometimes called "asymmetrical warfare," guerrilla warfare refers to the methods of fighters using nontraditional means to defeat a stronger enemy. Among the guerrilla's tactics are hit-and-run raids and destruction of supply and communication lines. Guerrilla fighters rarely come out into the open for a large-scale fight. Their goal is to wear an enemy down day by day. The Vietcong and communist North Vietnamese fighters did this to U.S. forces; Afghanis and Muslims did this to Soviet troops in Afghanistan in the 1980s; and partisan groups, especially in eastern Europe, fought this way against the Nazis in the Second World War. In Napoleon's case, the greatest threat from guerrilla fighters was in Spain.

CHAPTER 7

Conservatism, Liberalism, and Revolution

CONSERVATISM, LIBERALISM, AND REVOLUTION

*When ancient opinions and rules of life are taken away, the loss
cannot possibly be estimated. From that moment we have no
compass to govern us; nor can we know distinctly to what port we
steer.*
—Edmund Burke

*The individual is not accountable to society for his actions, insofar as
these concern the interests of no person but himself . . . Liberty consists
in doing what one desires.*
—John Stuart Mill

INTRODUCTION

Until 1940, when Hitler's forces held most of Europe, no European had as
much power as Napoleon. This power was made evident by his defeat of the
great powers of Austria and Russia at **Austerlitz** in central Europe (1805);
by his **Berlin Decrees°** (1806), which forbade countries under his direct and
indirect rule from trading with Britain (this gave rise to the **Continental System** mentioned in Chapter 6); and by one of his acquired titles, **King of Italy**.
But empires do not last forever, and Napoleon's European empire would not
have anything like the endurance of the empires of ancient Rome and Britain,
although France's overseas empire would last well into the twentieth century.
One reason empires do not last is that they give people who do not like to be
controlled something to unite against.

DEFEATING NAPOLEON

By 1813, spurred partly by Napoleon's failed Russian invasion, Russia, Prussia, Austria, and Britain resolved to take the Frenchman on again. The four nations formed the **Quadruple Alliance**. Because many of Napoleon's seasoned troops had died in the Russian campaign, he now commanded less experienced troops. Also, many of his senior officers were weary of war. He suffered a major defeat at **Leipzig** in present-day Germany, and in the spring of 1814 his enemies' troops entered Paris. Napoleon abdicated his throne and went into exile on the island of **Elba** off the Italian coast.

How Europe was to be reorganized after Napoleon's defeat was discussed in Vienna between September 1814 and November 1815. The greatest interest among the powers at the **Congress of Vienna** was preventing any country from dominating the others. New buffer states—Belgium, for example—were established from territories conquered by France. Prussia's territory expanded westward to the Rhine River, and Austria gained control of northern Italy, with both countries acquiring land occupied by the French.

But the Congress of Vienna was not only about reorganizing after war; it was also intended to maintain the peace. This was a new thing in Western history. While France lost territory and was required to restore the monarchy, the peace terms were not burdensome. If they were, the great powers thought, resentment against the victors might spur France to become militant again. The Congress hoped to prevent this by allowing France to join it as a major power. Together, the five powers were called the **Concert of Europe**. Its leading light was the Austrian prince **Klemens von Metternich** (1773–1859).

While the Quadruple Alliance had difficulties, it maintained its alliance when Napoleon briefly presented another threat. Generally, the French army was still loyal to him, and many French people disliked living again in an ineffectual monarchy. Napoleon escaped from Elba, and from Paris promised peace and a constitution that would observe the political rights sought after in the early part of the French Revolution. The Quadruple Alliance did not believe him, however, and in the summer of 1815 Napoleon's forces were defeated at **Waterloo** in Belgium. This time Napoleon was exiled to **St. Helena**, a small island in the Atlantic. He died there six years later. Although France was required to pay the victors an indemnity, or restitution, for some of the costs of the war, the peace settlement was still designed to prevent resentment in France from building. One indicator of the success of the Quadruple Alliance and Congress of Vienna was that **no major Europe-wide war took place until 1914**.

One small though still important war should be mentioned (in addition to the Franco-Prussian War discussed later in this chapter and the Boer War discussed briefly in Chapter 9). The **Crimean War** (1853–1856) pitted Britain, France, and the Ottoman Empire against Russia. The causes for the war were the Ottomans' granting to the French the oversight of **Christian shrines** in the Middle East—a responsibility the Russians thought they should have—and the Russians' occupation of portions of present-day Romania, which threatened France and Britain's interests in the eastern Mediterranean. Most of the war was fought along the coast of the Black Sea. As a result of its loss in the Crimean War, **Russia had to renounce authority over Christian shrines in the Ottoman Empire** and **allow French and British ships to trade in the Black Sea**.

As was the case with most wars before the twentieth century, more soldiers died from disease than from battle wounds in the Crimean War. Many more would have died without the work of **Florence Nightingale** (1820–1910), who called for and received relatively sanitary conditions in the field hospitals. Nightingale also helped to make nursing into a respectable profession for women.

THE RISE OF CONSERVATISM AND LIBERALISM

The French Revolution and the ideas that drove it were hated and feared throughout the upper classes of Europe. The revolution's ideas might seem noble, critics said, but what can freedom mean to a person who has never experienced it? How can a peasant with little experience prevent liberty from descending into anarchy, as happened after the French Revolution? Some of the revolution's foes argued that useful change could only come about as it developed from tradition. Sudden breaks with the past are doomed to fail, they argued, and the established order of things must be respected. Political decisions should be made not only with the living in mind but also bearing in mind the will of the dead and citizens yet to be born. In his *Reflections on the Revolution in France* (1790), the Englishman **Edmund Burke** (1729–1797) wrote, "People will not look forward to posterity who never look back to their ancestors." (Burke is sometimes called the "father of modern conservatism.")

Although **conservatives**, as they would come to be called, valued reason, they did not put unrestrained confidence in it. Nice-sounding ideas can be sincerely wrong, they believed; tradition helps people to determine which ideas are worthwhile and which are not. The *philosophes* and revolutionaries emphasized the importance of the individual and criticism of established religion; conservatives emphasized the importance of traditional communities. Because conservatives considered revolutionary ideas dangerous, some potentially radical books and newspapers were censored throughout Europe.

While conservatism was born in reaction to some of the ideals of the Enlightenment and French Revolution, **liberalism** made some of those ideals more acceptable to Europe's middle classes, referred to by socialists and communists as the **bourgeoisie**. Among the bourgeoisie were people who took advantage of the new economy that industrialization had created, among them bankers, factory owners, exporters, and political office holders. Having tasted some leisure, wealth, status, and political liberty, they wanted more.

This was especially true in England, home of the Glorious Revolution and the philosophy of John Locke, and a shining political example to the French *philosophes*. The best-known liberal work from this period is *On Liberty*, by **John Stuart Mill** (1806–1873). Published in 1859, Mill's influential book argues on behalf of ideas that are now taken for granted by many throughout the Western world. One idea is that so long as people are not making "nuisances" of themselves to others, they should be left alone to pursue their interests. Another of Mill's ideas was that people should keep an open mind about what they believe, for they may find that their beliefs are mistaken. Many of the reformers in the nineteenth and twentieth centuries were influenced by liberal thought. They advocated greater freedom of speech, complete freedom of religion, the vote for all adult men. Some, like Mill, called for women to be given the vote, which would happen throughout Europe following the First World War.

NATIONALISM

As we saw in the previous chapter, the modern idea of the nation was born during the French Revolution. Central to the ideology of **nationalism** is that all citizens are servants of the state. Men serve their country in the military; women can serve their country by raising educated, well-mannered children.

Under nationalism, monarchs and political leaders are subservient to the nation—ideally, their chief purpose is to promote the nation's good. French soldiers and others spread this way of thinking to other regions of Europe, and French domination of Europe gave Prussians, Austrians, and others a force to rally against.

The **Romantic movement** also helped to spur nationalism. This intellectual and artistic movement focused on the unique histories, languages, and customs of different countries. Intellectuals began to think that groups of people, like individuals, possess souls and personalities. For the German writer **Johann Gottfried Herder** (1744–1803), a people possesses its own *Volksgeist*, or "people's spirit." The desire among some individuals to discover, through historical and literary study, the essence of a particular people's soul became part of their political nationalism. Thus, when nationalists appealed to the idea of the nation, they touched people's emotions as well as their reason.

Another important German philosopher of history was **Friedrich Hegel** (1770–1831), whose work is very difficult to understand, though his best-known theory is easy to grasp. According to Hegel, history takes shape as long-held beliefs clash with newly emerging ideas and then, from the clash, a new set of beliefs is formed. For Hegel, his process of a **thesis** (belief) clashing with an **antithesis** (the belief's opposite) and forging a new **synthesis** is the stuff of societal development.

Romantics in England are remembered less for their nationalism and more for their literature. England's chief Romantic writers were **Samuel Taylor Coleridge** (1772–1834), author the "**Rime of the Ancient Mariner**"; **William Wordsworth** (1770–1850); and **Lord Byron** (1788–1824). For these writers nature was a source of inspiration, and the emotions— rather than pure reason, as most *philosophes* suggested—were to be trusted. They believed that city life was emotionally corrupting and mind numbing. The Scottish writer and essayist **Thomas Carlyle** (1795–1881) was heavily influenced by German romanticism and, in turn, influenced one of the major American **transcendentalists**, **Ralph Waldo Emerson** (1803–1882).

REVOLUTIONS

From 1820 through the 1840s liberal, conservative, and nationalistic ideas clashed in several places. Spanish military leaders revolted in 1820 against the conservative rule of **Ferdinand VII** (r. 1814–1833), who ignored Spain's written constitution and disbanded the country's parliament after Napoleon's defeat. The revolt caused Ferdinand to promise to abide by the constitution. In the same year, a revolution in **Naples** led to a constitutional monarchy there.

Radical movements such as those in Spain and Italy made the rulers of Austria, Prussia, and Russia nervous. Organized as the **Holy Alliance**, those three states announced the **Protocol of Troppau** (1820), which empowered them to intervene in the affairs of other countries unable to maintain conservative order on their own.

In 1821 **Austrian troops invaded Naples** and reestablished a nonconstitutional monarchy. **French troops did the same in Spain** in 1823. In neither case was the invading army intent on acquiring territory, as had been the norm before that period in European history. Their purpose now was **restore traditional order**, as the great powers had agreed should be done at Vienna several years before.

More important in the long term was the **Greek Revolution** (1821). Greek liberals and nationalists wanted independence from the predominantly Muslim **Ottoman Empire**. The Greek revolution attracted the attention of influential European liberals and Romantic artists, such as **Lord Byron**, partly because they hoped to see a rebirth of classical Greek democracy.

The Greek Revolution also interested the great powers because it pointed to the so-called **Eastern Question**, which referred to the weakness and instability of Ottoman rule in the Mediterranean region. Among other things, instability in the Mediterranean endangered trade routes important to Britain and France. Thus, in the case of Greece, revolution served the great powers' interests, and Britain, France and Russia sent warships to assist the Greek revolutionaries. Russia, which desired Ottoman territory in the Balkans, also sent troops into present-day Romania. The **Treaty of London** (1830) declared Greece independent and mandated a monarchy there. (In the 1830s **Belgium** similarly gained its independence from the Netherlands.)

Even as Greece was experiencing revolution, Russia's **Tsar Nicholas I** (r. 1825–1855) had to put down the **Decembrist Revolt** of 1825. This effort among nobles and military officers to establish a constitutional monarchy in Russia took place on the first day of Nicholas's rule; his liberal adversaries hoped to take advantage of the transition in government. But the liberals, who had joined political clubs with names such as the **Society of True and Faithful Sons of the Fatherland**, were divided among themselves as to their political ideals. Nicholas, on the other hand, was resolute. The revolt's leaders were executed.

FRANCE: REVOLUTION, EMPIRE, AND DEFEAT

Perhaps not surprisingly, revolution also broke out in France. Since the end of Napoleon's regime in 1815, France had been ruled by a very conservative monarchy that favored the nobility and Catholics. Through the late 1820s, with the approval of **Louis XVIII** (r. 1814–1824) and **Charles X** (r. 1824–1830), Protestants and liberals were harassed and sometimes killed by **ultraroyalists**—people interested in returning France to the days of the *ancien regime*. In 1829, after liberal reformers had won a majority in the **Chamber of Deputies**, Charles X dissolved that legislative body, censored newspapers, and restricted the franchise to men with significant property. This sparked riots that Charles was unable to control, and he abdicated the throne. In his stead the liberals placed **Louis Philippe I** (r. 1830–1848) in control of France.

Louis Philippe was open to reform. The number of men eligible to vote doubled during his reign, and Catholicism was removed as France's official religion. But the new king was certainly not sympathetic to radical ideas. In 1848, when crowds of demonstrators appeared in the streets of Paris calling for the widening of the franchise and for government assistance to small businesses, the king's **National Guard** opened fire, killing about forty. As in 1830, barricades went up in the streets and, as before, the king abdicated rather than try to regain control.

The **provisional government** established by the Chamber of Deputies comprised nine men, among them republicans and socialists. One of their leaders, **Louis Blanc** (1811–1882), established government-run shops to provide employment, and the vote was soon given to all men.

The days of this new government were numbered, however. French people living in the country or who simply were not sympathetic to radical ideas elected a majority of conservatives to the new **National Assembly**. The government workshops were closed, and some of their laborers were drafted into the military. More riots broke out, though this time the government put them down. Some fifteen hundred radical demonstrators were killed and about four thousand were exiled, while others, such as Blanc, fled to England. This French **Revolution of 1848** came to an end with the ascension to the presidency of Napoleon's nephew, **Louis Napoleon Bonaparte** (1808–1873). Bonaparte had earlier attempted to take over the French government (in 1836 and 1840). After years of waiting in England, he won the presidency in an election.

Louis Napoleon benefited from his name and, like his uncle, he had little use for democracy—at least when it caused him trouble. In 1851 the National Assembly refused to amend the constitution to allow Louis Napoleon to stand for reelection. Consequently, he seized power, used troops to disperse the assembly, and called for new elections. About two hundred Frenchmen who resisted this were killed, and ten thousand were exiled to Algeria in North Africa. Like his uncle before him, Louis Napoleon held a **plebiscite** to ask for the people's approval of his new position. More than 7 million voters gave him their approval, but some 600,000 did not. Perhaps more would have voted against Louis Napoleon if they could do so without fear. The following year Louis Napoleon took the title **Emperor Napoleon III** (not Napoleon II, in deference to Bonaparte's son, who had died). This too was approved in a plebiscite.

As one might expect of an emperor, Napoleon III sought to expand French influence and power, though he was not always successful. In 1858 he promised the prime minister of Piedmont-Sardinia, **Count Camillo Benso di Cavour** (1810–1861), that he would assist the Italian provinces of Lombardy and Venetia in their attempts to break free from the Austro-Hungarian Empire.

Napoleon withdrew his troops from battle before both provinces could gain their independence, however. In doing so Napoleon managed to anger both French liberals (who supported the Italians' desire for independence) and conservative Catholics (who were unhappy to see their country at war with Catholic Austria).

Four years later the French went to war in **Mexico**, capturing Mexico City and seating a prince there, **Maximilian** (r. 1864–1867). France's reason for going to Mexico initially had been to collect debts owed to French citizens. Following the American Civil War, Napoleon III feared war with the United States, which was not happy to see France in control of Mexico. Thus the emperor withdrew his forces by 1867. Meanwhile, France acquired other colonies in Africa and Asia. It maintained control over those colonies through the mid-1900s.

Napoleon III's greatest defeat came at the hands of the Germans in the **Franco-Prussian War** of 1870. Despite lasting just six months, the war was important and, for the French, humiliating. Napoleon III himself was captured, and his army was quickly defeated, with 100,000 of his soldiers taken prisoner at **Sedan**. Paris was besieged for four winter months, during which time starvation threatened. German troops paraded through Paris, and France was required to pay indemnities that amounted to twice what the war had cost Germany.

As a result of the **Treaty of Frankfurt** (1871), France lost its eastern territories of **Alsace** and **Lorraine** to Germany. With this land went important iron mines and cloth mills. Its loss came as a deep blow to the proud spirit of the French people. Earlier the remaining French government had declared the country a republic. The age of the Napoleons had ended. Following the Franco-Prussian War, France was never again the dominant European power. But the anger it felt toward the Germans would have far-reaching consequences in a later war (see Chapter 10).

NATION BUILDING: ITALY

The most outspoken Italian nationalist of the nineteenth century, **Giuseppe Mazzini** (1805–1872), spent most of his life in exile on account of his radicalism. From platforms in Switzerland, France, and England he agitated for the unification of the Italian states. Mazzini's **Young Italy** movement constantly failed in its attempts to spur revolution, but it also fed the heightened aspirations of a growing number of Italians. Mazzini, who felt no loyalty to the pope, hoped for Rome to become the capital of a united Italy. He is the best-known radical advocate for the movement known as the *Risorgimento* ("Resurgence").

In the first half of the nineteenth century Italy's nationalists faced numerous obstacles. For example, portions of northern and southern Italy were under Austrian control, and the **Papal States** were governed by the Catholic Church. As elsewhere in Europe in 1848, the Austro-Hungarian Empire, ruled by the **Hapsburg** dynasty, experienced revolution. Protestors rioted in the streets of Vienna, leading to the dismissal from office of Metternich by **Ferdinand I**. Metternich went to England in exile.

In the spring of 1848 radicals in Milan and Venice agitated for independence from foreign domination, and protestors in the Papal States, Piedmont, Tuscany, and Naples called for, and received, written constitutions. At the same time, **Charles Albert** (r. 1831–1849), king of **Piedmont-Sardinia**, declared war on Austria. In the short term, though, the **inability of various Italian groups and states to work together**, along with the strength of the Austrian army, led to the defeat of Italian nationalism.

The seeds of unification had been planted, however, and a constitution Charles Albert wrote for Piedmont-Sardinia would later serve as a model for the Italy's national constitution. Before long, nationalism would prevail in Italy as a result of both revolution and the work of moderate political figures— chiefly, **Count Camillo Benso di Cavour**.

In 1848 Cavour was elected to Piedmont's Chamber of Deputies. Soon after, the king, **Victor Emmanuel II** (1820–1878), made Cavour his minister of agriculture and trade. At first Cavour's main interest was to increase Piedmont's power. Cavour needed international friends, and he was able to gain Britain and France as potential allies when he brought Piedmont into their war with Russia (the Crimean War described earlier in the chapter). This led to Britain's condemnation of Austrian interference in Piedmont's affairs and to a closer political relationship between Piedmont and France, though, as previously discussed, France backed out of its commitment to help Italian provinces defeat the Austro-Hungarian Empire in the **Austro-Piedmontese War** of 1859.

The entry onto the public stage of **Giuseppe Garibaldi** (1807–1882) brought Italy closer to unification. Garibaldi had led volunteers into battle in the war of 1859, and beginning in the next year he and about one thousand of his soldiers, called "**Red Shirts**," began a campaign of conquest in southern Italy. Soon, Garibaldi's men, bolstered by locals who joined them, had conquered Sicily and established a new government in Naples. Cavour, meanwhile, sent troops south to occupy the Papal States under the pretext that he was protecting them from Garibaldi. Victor Emmanuel II also went south to meet Garibaldi, but rather than wage more war, Garibaldi handed control of the territory he had conquered to the king. The **Kingdom of Italy** was established in 1861. Cavour was its first prime minister. He died two months after the kingdom was established.

NATION BUILDING: GERMANY

In terms of global consequences, the creation of **Germany** must be considered more important than the creation of Italy. The twentieth century's two global wars are unimaginable without Germany.

By the 1850s Germany's important states enjoyed a form of free trade called the *"Zollverein."* Railroads provided for easy travel and economic ties among the states. The result was a strong sense of community among German speakers who shared a common general culture.

Of the German states, **Prussia** was the powerhouse, and **Kaiser Wilhelm I** (r. 1861–1888) was committed to building a stronger military. Prussia's parliament, dominated by liberals, was opposed to this. A standoff ensued, and the kaiser called on **Otto von Bismarck** (1815–1898) to resolve it.

Earlier Prussia's ambassador to France and Russia, Bismarck was appointed by Wilhelm I to be Prussia's prime minister in 1862. Bismarck was a Prussian patriot of intense will, energy, and practicality. He had little use for idealism. "The great questions of the day will not be decided by speeches and majority decisions," he said, "but by iron and blood." A word often associated with him is *realpolitik*—politics based on what was possible, not on appealing theories.

Early on, Prussia's parliament was not interested in going along with Bismarck. The elections of 1863 kept the liberals in power. Bismarck would have to go around them. One way he did this was by waging war against Denmark, which had formally annexed the northern, partly German duchies of **Schleswig** and **Holstein**. Bismarck's easy victory increased his popularity and authority.

As a result of that war, Austria was given governance over Holstein and Prussia over Schleswig. The arrangement led to disputes, and Bismarck was eager to show which of the two German nations was most powerful. Bismarck encouraged Prussian troops to be troublesome to Austrians. The resulting **Seven Weeks' War** (1866) led to the clear defeat of Austria. Now Prussia was the unquestioned dominant force in central Europe. Consequently, the city of Frankfurt and the German states of Hanover, Hesse, and Nassau were annexed by Prussia in retaliation for their support of Austria. This created the **North German Confederation**. The **Reichstag** (or parliament) was formed, though it had little power. All power resided in Bismarck, now referred to as the

chancellor, and the kaiser. The confederation was dominated by the military, and a majority of patriotic and nationalistic Germans approved.

The **Franco-Prussian War** (1870–1871) was also instigated by Bismarck, who edited a telegram sent from the kaiser to him to make it seem that the kaiser had insulted the French. Around the same time tensions were high because the French feared that a German would become king of Spain following a military coup in that country in 1868. France declared war in June 1870, and the southern German states joined the Confederation in its war against France. As noted earlier in this chapter, the decisive battle came at Sedan (near the France-Luxembourg border). The southern states, which allied themselves with Bismarck, remained in the country he had created. The Germany we think of today was born.

FOR YOUR INFORMATION

Berlin Decrees

The Berlin Decrees, and the Continental System that came from them, involved cutting off Britain's trade. One problem for France was that, after the American Revolution, trade between Britain and the United States was brisk. France's desire to stop this trade led to an undeclared war with the United States. By mid-1797, about three hundred American ships had been seized by the French. Meanwhile, the French threatened to arrest the envoy the Americans sent to Paris. That year, too, American officials in Paris were told that if they wished to meet the French foreign minister to discuss the difficulties between the two countries, they would first have to pay a heavy bribe. Called the "XYZ Affair" (after the three Frenchmen who had approached the American officials), this led to calls for open warfare with France. The war remained undeclared and was fought mostly in the West Indies. Between 1798 and 1800, American sailors captured about eighty French warships, though hundreds of American ships were taken by the French.

CHAPTER 8

The Second Industrial Revolution and Shifting World Views

THE SECOND INDUSTRIAL REVOLUTION AND SHIFTING WORLD VIEWS

*Man with all his noble qualities . . . with his godlike intellect
which has penetrated into the movements and constitution of the
solar system . . . still bears in his bodily frame the indelible stamp
of his lowly origin.*
—Charles Darwin

*Physical concepts are free creations of the human mind, and are
not, however it may seem, uniquely determined by the external
world.*
—Albert Einstein

At bottom God is nothing other than an exalted father.
—Sigmund Freud

The two great European narcotics, alcohol and Christianity.
—Friedrich Nietzsche

INTRODUCTION

The late nineteenth century was a time of fundamental change in Europe and, consequently, in much of the world. Students in public schools still focused their studies on mathematics, history, and Latin, as students had done for a long time, but the science they learned in 1899 was much different from what their parents had learned in 1859. People born in 1840 who were still alive in 1910—and because life expectancies were rising, there were many of them—may or may not have liked the change they witnessed, but they could not have missed it. As mentioned in the previous chapter, many people's identities were altered by nationalistic feelings, either in support of major states (e.g., the newly created Germany under Bismarck) or of linguistic and ethnic minorities within nations and empires (e.g., the Welsh, Irish, and French Canadians).

Within that lifetime people saw the pace of travel quicken and transportation become more comfortable. By the end of the nineteenth century, trains criss-crossed western Europe and North America, and by 1909 the American automaker Henry Ford made his factories so efficient that his **Model T** automobile was affordable to most consumers.

At the end of the nineteenth century, the German engineers **Gottlieb Daimler** (1834–1900) and **Karl Benz** (1844–1929) perfected the **internal combustion engine**. Another German invented the diesel engine in 1897. Automobiles produced their own pollution, but many people preferred that to the tons of horse dung that littered big-city streets every year.

Within that lifetime as well a person could be presented with several sophisticated worldviews that challenged the opinions prevalent, if not universally embraced, in Western civilization since ancient times. As discussed later in this chapter, for the first time average Europeans were told that they descended from lower life forms (**Darwinism**), that most human mental processes are unconscious and irrational (**Freudian psychology**), and that the Bible was like other ancient books: full of wisdom but historically unreliable (**Higher Criticism**). For many, the main figure in the New Testament, Jesus of Nazareth, ceased to be God in human form and became a notable good-deed-doer, a great moral philosopher, the ultimate philanthropist. Heaven lost its appeal for some; these advocates of a **social gospel** wanted to build a kingdom of God on earth. Given the incredible advances in so many fields that people experienced in the late nineteenth century, this belief was not so crazy—at least until after the First World War.

Among those who emphasized both religious and social salvation were the members of the **Salvation Army**, founded by **William** and **Catherine Booth** in 1878 and still a major distributor of help to the poor, especially in the United States, Canada, and Britain. Declaring war on the work of the devil in modern cities, the Salvation Army's mission has always been to help drug addicts, prostitutes, the homeless, and others in need.

THE TRIUMPH OF INDUSTRY

While large corporations—the British East India Company, for example—had existed since the early modern period, mega-businesses as we think of them today came into existence in the late nineteenth century. That was true throughout Western civilization but especially in the United States, to which millions of **Europeans emigrated** in the late nineteenth century. (Between 1846 and 1932, more than 50 million Europeans emigrated, the overwhelming majority to the Western Hemisphere—especially the United States, Canada, Argentina, and Brazil.) In the 1890s **Standard Oil**, owned by the American industrialist **John D. Rockefeller** (1839–1937), monopolized more than 75 percent of U.S. **oil**, which was vital to the growth of industry. (Oil was a key strategic concern among combatants of the First World War—one reason the war spread to the Middle East.)

Although the United States was the world's industrial powerhouse, western European industry grew phenomenally as well. In 1882 there were about 205,000 German factories with more than 100 employees each; by 1907 the number of factories had risen to 879,000. These factories produced necessities and luxury items, which were marketed to the public with increasing sophistication. Typewriters, bicycles, and sewing machines were produced by the millions.

Along with oil, the most important commodity of the Second Industrial Revolution was **steel**. In 1860 Europe's major powers produced about 125,000 tons of steel; by 1913 some 32 million tons were being produced. That steel was put to use building **ships**, **trains**, **bridges**, and **weapons** of war. Advances in chemical production made laundry soap and plastics available to ordinary Europeans. And by the end of the nineteenth century, many ordinary Europeans enjoyed **electrical lighting** in their homes, electricity-powered **subways**, and **streetcars**.

In the late nineteenth century daily **newspapers** replaced the pulpit as the public's main source of news about the world, partly because fewer people were going to church, partly because the **penny press** newspapers were inexpensive. Newspapers could print news about the previous day's events around the world because **telegraph** wires linked the globe. The first **intercontinental cable**—between North America and Britain—was laid in 1867.

By 1900 the **telephone**—invented in 1876 by **Alexander Graham Bell** (1847–1937)—was almost taken for granted in big cities; and in 1901 **Guglielmo Marconi** (1874–1937) sent the first **radio waves** across the Atlantic. In 1900 the **zeppelin°** airship made air travel possible. Three years later the first **airplane** took to the skies, albeit very briefly.

URBANIZATION

These inventions, and many others, would have made the late nineteenth century a period of great change. But European society was altered in even more fundamental ways. Most jobs linked to the Industrial Revolution were in urban factories, and the factories' rapid and inexpensive production often put slower, rural producers out of business. Consequently, in the late nineteenth century western Europeans, and to a lesser extent eastern Europeans, moved to cities by the millions. In 1800, 40 percent of Britain's population was urban; by 1900 that figure had grown to 80 percent. In 1800 the population of **London** stood at about 1 million; a century later it had grown to 6.5 million. In the same period the population of **Berlin** grew from some 172,000 to 2.7 million.

The growth of cities made urban development necessary. Formal **police departments** were organized; **departments of health** sent out agents to ensure sanitary conditions in apartments; and **organized hospitals**, staffed by **professional nurses and doctors**, became the norm. The availability of **gas heating** made indoor hot baths possible. Complicated sewage systems made **indoor plumbing** possible. Human refuse could now be flushed out of sight rather than dumped in the street, an alley, or a nearby river. Britain's **Public Health Act** (1875) made it illegal to construct new buildings without plumbing.

All the while the number of men who could vote in Western civilization expanded. In 1884 the liberal British prime minister **William Gladstone** (1809–1898) presided over the passing of a **Reform Act** that gave the vote to 60 percent of Britain's adult men.

While the living conditions of many city dwellers were abysmal by contemporary standards and drew much criticism at the time, it was still true that industrialization had caused most people's living standards to rise. Because urban workers labored only 10 to 12 hours a day, six days a week (more or less), they had more **leisure time**. By the end of the 1880s there were roughly five hundred music halls in London. **Tourism** as we know it took hold during the period—an indication of growing wealth. Organized team sports and athletic events provided athletes and spectators with entertainment, churches competed with popular amusements held on Sundays. Another sign of a more leisurely way of life was the fad for **bicycles** that spread across the Western world. Little did people know that the rubber their bicycle tires were made of could have come from the Congo, where Belgian taskmasters often brutalized the natives. Joseph Conrad's novel *Heart of Darkness* (1902) takes place in the Congo.

MODERNIZATION

For the first time, churches also found themselves competing with an array of opposing worldviews. Challenges to traditional religious views had existed in Europe for a long time. But the general population was much better educated in the late nineteenth century than it had been in the early modern period. Austria, for example, had made primary education compulsory in 1869, France did the same in 1882, and primary education was required throughout Britain by 1902. The curriculum of many schools was quite rigorous by modern standards, emphasizing ancient and modern languages, history, science, and mathematics. (Even the public school in the small, isolated Alaskan town of Nome required its students to study Latin.) And while the number of Europeans and Americans attending universities remained very small by current standards, more were seeking higher education than ever before.

One result is that by 1900 illiteracy among adults was all but eliminated in Britain, Scandinavia, Germany, and France. (In Eastern Europe, where education was not emphasized, the story was different. In 1900, 79 percent of Russians could not read.) The demand for newspapers and other publications, rose dramatically. Mass-circulation newspapers increasingly emphasized **sensationalism**, but they still contributed to a greater awareness of scientific discovery and of alternative views to Christianity.

By 1900 Europeans could know that the Frenchman **Louis Pasteur** (1822–1895) had discovered that the source of contagious diseases is bacteria, not water, air, or odor. Also thanks to Pasteur, people throughout Europe could benefit from disinfected milk—that is, milk that had been *pasteur*ized. They might have read in the papers that the German professor of public health

Robert Koch (1843–1910) had isolated the **tuberculosis** bacillus. Beginning in the late nineteenth century childbirth became less painful for some women as **anesthetics** began to be used. Around the same time the Austrian monk **Gregor Mendel** studied inheritance traits in generations of peas, and as a result of his work he came to be called the "father of genetics."

In the last quarter of the nineteenth century, deaths from disease in Europe decreased by 60 percent. To be sure, disease remained a serious problem: several thousand Europeans died from **measles** each year; and in 1918 a flu epidemic killed some 600,000 Americans—more than three times the number killed in World War I, which ended in the same year. But there remained a growing sense among people living in the West that human reason was slowly but surely conquering nature.

Meanwhile, certainties about the workings of the world began to shift once again—as they did during the Scientific Revolution, especially regarding questions about the nature of matter. In 1895 the **X-ray** was discovered and led many to question prevailing views about the solidity of matter. In 1898 the chemist **Marie Curie** (1867–1934), with her husband, Pierre, discovered radium, which did not act according to prevailing theories. For their work, the Curies won the Nobel Prize in 1903. In 1905 **Albert Einstein** (1879–1955) published an article in which he stated his **theory of relativity**. To the standard view of the universe—that it had the three dimensions: height, width and depth—Einstein added a fourth dimension: time.

Reason was employed to challenge scientific theories that had earlier seemed quite reasonable. At the same time, the value of human reason came to be questioned in the late nineteenth century. Intellectuals who would help to create the disciplines we now call **sociology**, **psychology**, and **anthropology** began to speak and write about the irrational forces—emotions, symbols, myths, and unconscious thought processes—that shaped human behavior. Perhaps the best known of these intellectuals is the Austrian **Sigmund Freud** (1856–1939), considered the founder of psychoanalysis. Essentially, Freud taught that what humans are conscious of is just a small fraction of their mental lives. Beneath consciousness lies the vast unconscious where irrational, violent, and self-destructive desires prevail. One way into the unconscious, wrote Freud, was through dream interpretation. He published his hugely influential book *The Interpretation of Dreams* in 1900. While most of Freud's theories have been rejected in recent decades, many of the concepts he developed, such as the various **defense mechanisms**° people use, are worthwhile. Freud also made a significant contribution to **secularization**—the process of becoming more interested in worldly, material things and less interested in spiritual things—by arguing that God is merely a person's "projection" into the heavens of a father figure.

A greater challenge to Christianity was the theory of evolution put forward by **Charles Darwin** (1809–1882) in *On the Origin of Species* (1859) and *The Descent of Man* (1871). Darwin benefited from the earlier work of **Charles Lyell** (1797–1875) whose *Principles of Geology* (1830) argued that the earth could not be six thousand years old, as a literal reading of the first few chapters of Genesis (in the Bible) would require. Also influential to Darwin was the work of **Thomas Malthus** (1766–1834), who maintained that all species, including humans, produce more offspring than can survive due to inevitable food shortages. By implication, those who survive are the winners in the unending struggle that life is.

Darwin's theory rests on two basic ideas. The first, **variation**, concerns usually minor differences among organisms that give some an advantage in life—for example, the giraffe with the slightly longer neck who can eat leaves from trees other cannot reach, or the somewhat cleverer female who knows how to avoid trouble with problematic mates. These variations provide their possessors advantages, and over time, through the process of **natural selection** (Darwin's second key idea), such traits become more dominant. In the long run intelligence wins out over stupidity and, for giraffes, long necks win out over short ones. In the very long run, according to Darwinism, new species evolve while others become extinct.

For many Christians, Darwinism challenged not only a literal reading of the Bible's creation story but also the view that the world, and especially the people inhabiting it, was under the loving direction of God. Now nature, where all was struggle and gradually changing, seemed brutal and indifferent. At the same time, other Christians accepted and adopted Darwinism, claiming that God had presided over the evolutionary process and that the most morally fit—like the most physically fit—would inherit the earth. Thus Darwinism spurred both religious doubt and moral activism.

Among the other challenges to Christianity in late nineteenth century Europe were the writings of **Friedrich Nietzsche** (1844–1900). Nietzsche, who made famous the phrase "God is dead," hated Christianity for its emphasis on self-sacrifice. He encouraged readers instead to exercise a "will to power."

Nietzsche also criticized the West's emphasis on reason. Instead, he wrote, more attention should be given to raw human impulses, the irrational and the emotional. For Nietzsche the minority of the strongest should rule. There was little room in his philosophy for compassion or pity.

Oddly, in time both Nietzsche and church ministers who wished to help the poor could be called **Social Darwinists**. Formulated by the British philosopher **Herbert Spencer** (1820–1903), social Darwinism applied some of Darwin's basic ideas to individuals, societies, and nations. Spencer made popular the phrase "**survival of the fittest**" and argued that the most fit had a moral duty to rule the weak. Many imperialists would take this to heart and treated natives in Africa and Asia with contempt. Others, such as the British poet **Rudyard Kipling** (1865-1936), spoke of the "**white man's burden**"—that is, his obligation to uplift the colonized.

Others, quite differently, came to believe that the best and brightest had an obligation to help the less bright reach their potential. The American multimillionaire **Andrew Carnegie** (1835–1919) promoted a **gospel of wealth**, arguing that the rich should help the poor to help themselves. Among other things, Carnegie built libraries in communities across the United States.

Because social Darwinian thought became so pervasive, the late nineteenth and early twentieth centuries were characterized by competition—individuals against individuals, businesses against businesses, ethnic groups against ethnic groups, countries against countries. The race to see who was "fittest" was on, and it would have dramatic consequences.

FOR YOUR INFORMATION

Zeppelin

In 1937 the first transatlantic zeppelin, the German *Hindenburg*, caught fire while it was landing in New Jersey. The disaster was captured on film and radio. As was the case after the World Trade Towers in New York were targeted by terrorists in September 2001, people could watch those caught in the tragedy jumping to their deaths. At the time, airplane travel was not considered safe; most people still preferred trains. The graphic loss of the *Hindenburg* also caused many to decide that travel by zeppelin was not safe, either. Save for a small number of zeppelins that fly over sporting events for marketing purposes (such as the Goodyear Blimp), that mode of travel came and went rather quickly.

Defense Mechanisms

According to Freud, the "ego," a person's conscious mental life, has to protect itself from the impulses of the "id," the part of the human psyche that contains the dark passions. One way the mind does this, Freud argued, is by employing defense mechanisms. For example, think of someone you know who refuses to acknowledge that he or she has a problem. Freud calls this **denial**. When a man kicks a safe object, like his cat, instead of the less safe object he is actually angry at (like his boss), he is employing the defense mechanism of **displacement**. Have you ever covered your dislike for another person by convincing yourself that he or she did not like you? That is **projection**—the projection of your feelings onto another person. These are just a few of the many defense mechanisms Freud described.

CHAPTER 9

Imperialism, Nationalism, and Socialism

IMPERIALISM, NATIONALISM, AND SOCIALISM

I desire to encourage and foster an appreciation of the advantages which will result from the union of the English-speaking peoples throughout the world.
—Cecil Rhodes

The greatest of our evils and the worst of our crimes is poverty.
—George Bernard Shaw

IMPERIALISM

In the late nineteenth century a process that had begun centuries before was completed. Most of the globe was directly controlled or economically and politically dominated by Western nations. Britain, most of all, was the world's dominant power. This influence was achieved and bolstered by that country's formidable navy. Much smaller than the state of California, Britain at the beginning of the twentieth century held sway over 20 percent of the world's population. The well-known saying was true: **The sun never set on the British Empire.** (Neither, in fact, did it set on the French Empire.) Not since the Roman Empire had the world seen such an achievement, the consequences of which endured into the twenty-first century. One legacy of the British Empire is the famous **Rhodes Scholars** program for study in Oxford, England. It is named after **Cecil Rhodes** (1853–1902), who was a key figure in British South Africa and who wanted to see select students in the colonies gain British educations in England and return to their countries as further agents of British civilization. The African country Rhodesia, now called Zimbabwe, was also named after Rhodes.

Another legacy of European imperialism is the many Bibles translated into native languages. Often, because **"the Bible follows the flag,"** missionaries were a strong presence in the colonies. The Bible, or portions of it, was usually the first book translated into local languages.

Some of the troubles African nations continue to experience partly stem from the fact that very hostile groups with very different customs and cultures live within national boundaries invented by Europeans. At the same time, much of the freedom that exists in the world—in, for example, **India, Jamaica**, and **Hong Kong**, not to mention the United States—is the product of the British Empire.

Britain's empire—including Canada, India, Australia, New Zealand, and present-day Kenya, South Africa, Sudan, and Nigeria—was the largest in the world. At the same time, France held **Indochina** (present-day Vietnam) and large portions of north and east Africa (by 1945 a million people of French ancestry lived in Algeria); the Netherlands governed present-day Indonesia; and, as a result of its victory in the **Spanish-American War** (1898), the United States held Guam, the Philippines, and Puerto Rico, in addition to Samoa and Hawaii. Even Portugal held African colonies—for example, present-day Mozambique.

NATIONALISM

Although personal geographic loyalties had fairly narrow definitions in the early 1800s, by the end of the 1800s national governments and economies had become stronger. That strength was both a cause and an effect of **nationalism**. Before 1860 Americans spoke of the United States in the plural ("the United States *are* about to do such and such"). After 1865, the year the American Civil War ended, Americans began to speak of the United States in the singular. Loyalty to state governments had given way to loyalty to central government. Meanwhile, in many places in Europe, as well as in Canada, **linguistic minorities** saw their identities challenged by the greater, more powerful identities of the nations in which they resided. Consequently, nationalist and regionalist movements sprang up in Wales, Scotland, and Ireland (against the English); in Brittany (against the French); in Quebec (against the English-speaking majority in Canada); and most consequentially, among Serbs and other Slavs in the Austro-Hungarian empire.

SETTING THE STAGE FOR WAR

The social Darwinian struggle for national fitness led Europe's key powers to compete for colonies, international prestige, influence, and economic power. In time, the inevitable tensions between the powerful countries led not only to nationalism but also to a massive, self-destructive, and global war. That war set the stage for the even more massive Second World War, which in turn paved the way for the global dominance of two non-Western European powers—the United States and the Soviet Union. What began as a struggle to see which European nation was fittest, ended with the eclipse of European power and influence.

The late nineteenth and early twentieth centuries were rife with war talk. In 1902, for example, ships from Britain, Germany, and Italy blockaded Venezuela and seized its warships to force the collection of money owed to the Europeans. Events like this led the United States to rattle its sabers, since it considered the Western Hemisphere off-limits to the European colonial powers.

The origins and causes of the First World War are complicated and still debated among historians. What is clear is that long-standing tensions and suspicions created an atmosphere that made war acceptable in 1914.

The **Berlin Conference** (1885), which divided Africa among the Europeans and contributed greatly to what was called the **"Scramble for Africa,"** was designed to prevent war. But Germany's leadership later came to believe that it had not received its fair share, and among the causes of the war was the desire of Germany under **Kaiser Wilhelm II** (r. 1888–1918) to acquire African colonies. Wilhelm also wanted to prevent Britain from building a railroad from Cairo in North Africa to the Cape of Good Hope in South Africa. In the mid-1880s Germany thwarted Britain's ambition by acquiring African territory in east and west Africa that would become the nations of Namibia, Togo, Cameroon, and Tanzania.

In the early twentieth century, meanwhile, Germany sought to build a powerful railroad of its own from Berlin to Baghdad in present-day Iraq. In the British government's view, this was a threat to Britain's interests in the Middle East. Germany also sought to influence the affairs of Morocco, which was in France's sphere of influence. In 1905 **Germany's government publicly favored Moroccan independence**. In 1911 it sent the warship *Panther* to the Moroccan coast following an uprising there against the French. This suggested to the French and British that Germany was still interested in inserting itself into North African affairs.

These threats to French and British prestige and influence drove the two governments together, and they shared a common concern about Germany's intentions. At the same time **Germany's support of Austria-Hungary** in its attempts to keep control of its Slavic minorities put **Germany at odds with Russia**, which supported the aspirations of the Slavs to leave the Austro-Hungarian Empire. By 1914 Germany faced powerful enemies to the west and east. By 1914 Austria-Hungary was the only dependable ally Germany had left.

The following list of alliances and/or international agreements of friendship points to the mistrust among Europe's leading nations that would lead to global conflict:

- Three Emperors' League (1873): Germany, Austria, and Russia
- Dual Alliance (1879): Austria and Germany
- Triple Alliance (1882): Germany, Austria, and Italy
- Franco-Russian Alliance (1894)
- British-Japanese Alliance (1902)
- Entente Cordiale (1902): Britain and France
- Triple Entente (1907): Britain, Russia, and France

Of these, the most consequential were the **Triple Alliance** and the **Triple Entente**. It was these two alliances that went to war in 1914, though Italy soon changed sides, and the Ottoman Empire (the heart of which is present-day Turkey) fought alongside Germany and Austria-Hungary. The Ottomans, Austrians, and Germans had a common enemy in Russia.

THE HAPSBURG EMPIRE

To people living in Australia, California, Canada, Scotland, and Bermuda in 1900, it might have been hard to believe that events in eastern Europe could trigger a global war. Yet eastern Europe's problems would become Europe's problems—and then the world's. The key power in eastern Europe was the **Hapsburg Empire**, after 1867 referred to as the **Austro-Hungarian Empire**. One man, **Francis Joseph**, ruled the empire from 1848 to 1916. He had little interest in encouraging industrialization or political liberalization. His

German-speaking government, based in **Vienna**, presided over numerous linguistic and ethnic groups. And while Francis Joseph presided over both Austria and Hungary, the latter country enjoyed considerable independence, especially in internal affairs. The central government controlled foreign affairs and matters of defense. Austria-Hungary was also called the **Dual Monarchy**.

Within Hungary were linguistic and ethnic groups who wanted a relationship with Hungary similar to the one between Hungary and Austria—that is, a relationship characterized by considerable liberty to direct their own affairs. Czechs, for example, wanted a high degree of autonomy. Francis Joseph was sympathetic to the idea of a Triple Monarchy, but Hungary, fearing other groups would follow the Czechs' example, was opposed to it.

As the nineteenth century wore on, nationalistic feeling within Austria-Hungary grew stronger, and schools taught students in regional languages. Others who identified with nations or groups living outside Austria-Hungary— among them Poles, Italians, and Romanians—argued that they should break away from the empire. Some of these, along with other Slavic peoples such as the Ukrainians, looked to **Russia** as a potential national liberator. The nation of **Serbia** also sought to bring the Serb lands of Austria-Hungary within its borders. As discussed in the next chapter, these interests would trigger a global war.

SOCIALISM

Along with, and related to, the other great change that came to Western civilization in the late nineteenth and early twentieth centuries was socialism. Between 1700 and 1800 factory and urban workers rioted, or threatened to riot, to bring about reform. But by the late nineteenth century some workers (though never a majority) were banding together in labor unions and **left-wing°** political parties, propelled by a belief in liberal reform and/or socialism. They were assisted by the work of journalists and authors such as **Henry Mayhew** (1812–1887), who wrote *London Labour and the London Poor* (1851) to stir the English to "improve the condition of a class of people whose misery, ignorance, and vice, amidst all the immense wealth and great knowledge of [London] is a national disgrace."

Labor unions, organizations in which workers join together to protect themselves from exploitation, became legal in Britain in 1871, in France in 1884, and in Germany by 1891. The central concerns of labor unions were better pay, reduced mandatory work hours, and improved workplace conditions. Many things twenty-first-century workers take for granted—required breaks after a set number of hours at work, paid vacations, workers' compensation for injuries, and so on—were fought for by early labor unions. Unions were most successful in Britain, which had long been Europe's most industrialized and liberal major country. Eventually, workers at mines, railways, and docks were launching major strikes.

Europe's first political party devoted to the interests of the labor movement was Britain's **Labour Party**, which sent twenty-nine members to Parliament in 1906. Though the Labour Party soon attracted Socialists, it did not begin as a socialist party.

Some of Britain's genuine early Socialists could be found among the writers and members of high society who formed the **Fabian Society**, which advocated gradual societal evolution in the direction of socialism. Perhaps the Fabian Society's best-known members were **H. G. Wells** (1866–1946) and **George Bernard Shaw** (1856–1950).

Among the reforms Britain experienced as a result of the work of Socialists and liberals was the **National Insurance Act of 1911**, which made unemployment benefits and modest health care° available to workers. Financing this kind of program required new taxes. The legislation and new taxes combined meant that government would grow and become an ever-greater presence in the economy.

A significant spur to socialist thinking was the *Communist Manifesto* (1848) by **Karl Marx** (1818–1883), though many of the specifics of Marx's ideas were not put into wide practice in western Europe. Whereas Marx called for revolution, western Europe experienced gradual reform; whereas Marx claimed to have discovered a scientific and thus irrefutable approach to politics, most Socialists were more practical in their outlook.

Marx believed that the Utopian future of humankind depended on the new industrial working class—the **proletariat**—liberating itself from the oppression of the capitalist system—a system in which the few (**capitalists**) most benefited from the labors of the many. Following the overthrow of the capitalist system, a new economic system void of economic classes and property would become a reality.

Marxism was a belief system that required great faith in the wonderful world to come; the widespread failure of communist societies in the late twentieth century show that many lost faith in Marxism. One reason Marxism failed is that it predicted that misery would grow and grow until the proletariat rebelled and the **bourgeoisie** (middle class) was put in its place. But industrialization gave rise to an ever-growing middle class that experienced more leisure, not less. Some prominent Socialists such as the German **Eduard Bernstein** (1850–1932) noticed this flaw in Marxist doctrine and came to believe that communism could be achieved slowly but surely through democratic means. Socialists like Bernstein were called **revisionists**.

Some radicals in Britain and France, including Marx, formed the **First International** in 1864. Its successor, the **Second International**, was formed in 1889. These organizations were devoted to revolution. However, as previously noted, the Socialists' approach in Britain was one of gradual reform. French politics were more influenced by radical thought—not a surprise given France's political history since 1789. By 1914 France's Socialists held the second-greatest number of seats in **Chamber of Deputies**, and radicals periodically threatened the government. But France never experienced a communist revolution.

Nor did **Germany**, even though its **Social Democratic Party (SDP)** was western Europe's most influential socialist political organization. From its beginning in 1875 the SDP was divided between revolutionaries and reformers. Germany's chancellor **Otto von Bismarck** was friendly to neither group, and antisocialist laws passed in the Reichstag suppressed socialist newspapers and meetings. This did not prevent the SDP from growing as a political party, however, and Bismarck came to believe that the influence of the Socialists could be diminished if he instituted reform himself. Laws providing for modest **health and accident insurance**, along with **pensions** for the elderly, were passed in the Reichstag (parliament) in the 1880s. The Socialists spurred one of Europe's great anti-Socialists to action.

As discussed in the next chapter, the one European country that did experience communist revolution was Russia. In the late nineteenth and early twentieth centuries Russia experienced industrialization, which was promoted by that country's finance minister **Sergei Witte** (1849–1915). Under Witte's direction, the length of Russia's train tracks nearly doubled to 60,000 miles between 1890 and 1904. Steel and coal production increased dramatically, as well.

At the same time, however, industrial work in 1900 was as difficult in Russia as it had been in England seventy years before. Also, unlike many western Europeans, most Russians did not see industrialization improve their lives. Labor unions were illegal and taxes high. A very rapidly growing population—from 50 million to more than 100 million between 1860 and 1914—put pressure on farmlands and led to hunger. In response to these conditions, reformers and revolutionaries formed the **Social Revolutionary Party** and **The Constitutional Democratic Party**. But because Russia was ruled by a tsar, there was no system for these parties to work in, and their leaders had to operate in exile outside Russia. The most important Russian radical, who is highlighted in the next chapter, was **Vladimir Lenin** (1870–1924).

Though **anarchists**, people who advocate the elimination of government, were never as successful as the Socialists and Communists were, they did cause a great deal of turmoil, particularly by assassinating American and French presidents (William McKinley and Marie François Sadi Carnot, respectively) and high-ranking leaders in Italy, Austria, and Russia.

FOR YOUR INFORMATION

Left Wing

Why are people of liberal political views sometimes described as "left wing"? At the beginning of the French Revolution, the members of the Third Estate sat on the left side of the National Assembly, while those in the First Estate sat on the right. Since the Third Estate was where support for revolution and political innovation was strongest, people in favor of rapid political change have been linked to the left, while conservatives are said to be on the right.

Health Care

Beginning in the 1930s, during the Great Depression, government involvement in the Western economies grew dramatically, and sometimes in unexpected ways. In that decade France began paying French couples who had more than one child, and for many couples that was a major source of income. The Swedes were the first to establish a state-run, **tax-funded health care system**, which is now the norm throughout the West, except in the United States. Even in America, however, the poor, the elderly, and military veterans can receive government-funded medical care. Outside the United States, many Westerners were glad to pay high taxes in exchange for government services. But by the late twentieth century economies that were sluggish because of high tax rates, along with expensive services, led many European countries to cut back on government programs. The British prime minister **Margaret Thatcher** (b. 1925) is especially remembered for cutting government expenses and programs.

CHAPTER 10

The First World War

THE FIRST WORLD WAR

From that moment, all my religion died. All my teaching and beliefs in God had left me, never to return.
—British survivor of the Battle of the Somme (1916)

It must be a peace without victory . . . Only a peace between equals can last.
—Woodrow Wilson

We shall now proceed to construct the socialist order.
—Vladmir Lenin

INTRODUCTION

Between 1914 and 1918 some 8 million men died in Europe's most devastating war to that time. Total casualties of the First World War—killed, wounded, missing—came to 37 million. Among the consequences of the First World War were the emergence of the United States as a global power, the emergence of Russia as a center of global communism, the undermining of the view that Europeans were morally superior to other peoples, a growing sense of philosophical pessimism and religious doubt, and significant cultural change. The single greatest consequence of the First World War was its offspring, the even more devastating Second World War (1939–1945). It would take these two mammoth wars—and the millions of deaths they represent—to cause Europeans to seek other ways to resolve significant political differences. In the early twenty-first century, the thought of warfare between, say, England and Germany was unthinkable.

ORIGINS OF THE WAR

Probably the most important long-term cause of the war was Germany's concern for its security. This concern had roots in experiences of war going back hundreds of years. In modern times, Germany faced a large potential enemy to the east, Russia, and a large potential enemy to the west, France. As long as he was Germany's chancellor, **Otto von Bismarck** maintained a workable diplomatic relationship with Russia. This alliance offset Germany's concerns about a potentially troublesome France. But when the brusque and reckless **Kaiser Wilhelm II** dismissed Bismarck in 1890, Germany's diplomatic relationship with Russia deteriorated, and Russia became allied with France. Feeling hemmed in by two large enemies (Russia and France), Germany forged a fateful alliance with the Austro-Hungarian Empire. By 1914 this alliance was offset by another alliance between France and Russia.

A further cause of the war was the race for national prestige that had existed in Europe from the sixteenth century. As discussed in earlier chapters, monarchs had financially supported scientific work and established observatories, partly to bolster national prestige. Also, since the early 1500s European powers had competed for overseas colonies and the wealth and preeminence they brought. As noted in the previous chapter, this competition came close to disintegrating into conflict, as when Britain and France nearly went to war over the possession of the Sudan in 1899 in what was called the **Fashoda Crisis**. By 1914 the European powers had also been engaged in an arms race for several years. As Germany's navy grew, for example, the British strove to maintain superiority. This international competition was partly spurred by **social Darwinism**. In August 1914 war broke out in Europe long after many came to believe that it was inevitable.

Another cause of the war was the fact that Europe had not seen a lengthy and costly war since the final defeat of Napoleon in 1815. Prussia and France had fought a war in 1870 (the **Franco-Prussian War**), but it ended quickly and did not cause loss of life on a scale anywhere near what Europe would experience in the early twentieth century. Britain's war against the **Boers** of South Africa was costly, but it was also far removed from Europe. This meant that, for many, war had become romanticized. In 1914 it seemed a good way for a young man to bring glory on himself, to have a good time, to be a hero. When war was declared in August 1914, middle-class young men throughout Europe enthusiastically volunteered to fight, believing that the war would be over by Christmas. At the same time, many Europeans feared that their populations were growing morally soft, that they simply enjoyed the fruits of the empires their fathers had built. A little war, many thought, would be a good way to toughen up the young.

Still another very important cause of the war was **nationalism** in central Europe. Germany's main ally, the Austro-Hungarian Empire, comprised not only speakers of German and Magyar (Hungarian) but also Czechs, Slovenians, and Serbs who wanted independent nations. The nation of Serbia sympathized with and assisted Serb nationalists in Austria-Hungary.

This brings us to the trigger of the First World War: the assassination of the Austrian **Archduke Franz Ferdinand** (1863–1914) by **Serbian nationalists**. Austria believed that the assassins had been assisted by Serbia, and when Serbia declined to meet Austria's demands (which essentially would have placed Serbia under Austrian control), Austria declared war on Serbia (July 28). Russia, which saw itself as a defender of Slavic peoples, rallied to Serbia's defense and declared war on Austria. Germany, Austria's ally, declared war on Russia (August 1) and then on France (August 3). Britain, standing by its pledge to defend the **neutrality of Belgium** (which the Germans invaded on August 1), declared war on Germany (August 4). Germany and its comrade nations were called the **Central Powers**. Russia, France, and Britain were the **Allies**.

GERMAN STRATEGY AND THE WESTERN FRONT

Germany now faced what Bismarck had feared: a war on two fronts—against the French and British to the west and against the Russians to the east. Germany's strategy, summarized in the **Schlieffen Plan**, had a few components: First, avoid France's defenses along the Franco-German border. Second, smash through Belgium, enter northeastern France, and quickly capture Paris. (This would knock France out of the war and, the Germans hoped, not allow Britain time to mobilize.) Third, with France defeated, Germany could turn its attention to defeating Russia. The Schlieffen Plan depended on speed, and the Germans were speedy. But their supply line became too stretched out, and the French and British troops already deployed were able to stop the Germans short of Paris.

Rather than retreat, both forces simply dug in. In time a series of trenches stretched from the coast of Belgium to the border of neutral Switzerland (about 300 miles). From that time until 1918, warfare on this **western front** was characterized by armies hurling themselves against a defender's artillery, trenches, and machine guns. The body count was massive. For example, on the single morning of July 1, 1916, the beginning of the **Battle of the Somme**, the British suffered nearly sixty thousand casualties; at the end of the day, the British had nothing substantial to show for it. This kind of experience helped to create the so-called **Lost Generation**—the young people who came of age during and soon after the war.

The horrors of trench warfare on the **western front** was described in the powerful poetry written by soldiers like England's **Wilfred Owen** (1893–1918), who was killed in battle. In his most-remembered poem, "**Dulce et Decorum Est**," Owen describes the soldiers' plight: "Bent double, like old beggars under sacks / Knock-kneed, coughing like hags. . .Drunk with fatigue, deaf even to the hoots / Of disappointed shells that dropped behind." He also refers to the "green sea" that sometimes enveloped the **Great War's** soldiers— that is, poison gas. Following the war, the Western powers agreed not to use poison gas in future conflicts. This was one important step the West took in an effort to civilize war.°

In 1918, after Russia had left the war (see Chapter 11), the Germans were finally able to break through the Allies' trenches and come dangerously close to Paris. But before Paris came under attack, American troops were engaged in combat and helped to push the Germans back.

According to President Woodrow Wilson, the Americans had entered the war primarily because of Germany's **unrestricted submarine warfare** on all ships destined for the British Isles. The best-known noncombatant ship sunk by the Germans was the *Lusitania,* sent to the bottom of the Atlantic in 1915. About 1,200 people aboard died, including 128 Americans.

In 1917 the Germans made an even worse mistake. A German message to the Mexican government, called the **Zimmermann Telegram**, was intercepted by the British and passed to the United States government. In case the United States entered the war, the telegram said, Mexico should ally itself with Germany. Once the war was done, the telegram continued, Mexico would obtain New Mexico, Arizona, and Texas. This scheme, which now seems crazy, stirred American sentiment against Germany. The United States entered the war in 1917 and its combat troops saw less than a year of action. But there is no question that the Allies benefited significantly from America's belated involvement. By the fall of 1918 Germany knew that it could not win the war, and it sued for peace.

A TROUBLED PEACE

Before the war had ended, President Wilson had called for "peace without victory." In other words, he did not want Germany to be kicked when it was down. Looking back, it is difficult not to wish that the French, represented at the peace talks at **Versailles** near Paris by **Georges Clemenceau** (1841–1929), and the British, represented by **David Lloyd George** (1863–1945), had taken Wilson's advice. But at the same time, it was easy for Wilson to say what he did: the war had not touched American soil. Eastern France, on the other hand had been devastated; France had lost about 5.5 million men. And while Lloyd George was not as eager for revenge as the French were, he famously said that he would squeeze Germany "until the pips squeak."

The **Versailles Treaty**, which would humiliate Germany and motivate **Adolf Hitler** to seek his own revenge, was tough. It was also both understandable (given France's experience) and regrettable (given the consequences). Germany had to acknowledge its full responsibility for the war and pay **reparations** to the Allies—that is, the Germans had to repay the Allies for the cost of the war (about $31.5 billion in 2004 dollars). All of Germany's colonies (in Asia and Africa) were lost and placed under the control or supervision of the Allies. **Alsace-Lorraine**, which Germany had taken from France after the Franco-Prussian War, was returned to France. The German army was limited to a 100,000-man defensive force, and it was not allowed to have any warplanes or tanks. The coalfields of Germany's Saar region were to be occupied by the French for fifteen years.

The roots of the Second World War partly lie in the Versailles Treaty—or, perhaps more accurately, in what Hitler believed about the treaty. In 1941, when Germany controlled most of western Europe, Hitler said that he had freed Germany "from the death sentence of Versailles."

THE WAR AND SOCIAL CHANGE

The "Great War," as it was called, was the first international **total war**. Seemingly every citizen had a role to play. In Britain, about 40 percent of soldiers examined for military service were rejected for health reasons, but they could do important jobs—making munitions or uniforms in factories, or growing food (the average soldier in combat needs about 4,000 calories a day to function well). More than at any time before, **governments took increasing control of their economies**: labor strikes were banned, natural resources such as coal were rationed, and prices were controlled. As millions of men were serving in the various nations' militaries, women took their places in factories and at other jobs. This set the stage for women gaining the vote (**suffrage**) soon after the war—in Britain in 1918, in Germany in 1919, and in the United States in 1920. (At that time, even the pope declared his approval of giving women the vote.) Some women in these countries had been agitating for the vote for years. Perhaps the best-known British "suffragette" was the radical **Emmeline Pankhurst** (1858–1928), who led the **Women's Social and Political Union**, which led large, noisy, and sometimes violent demonstrations.

The First World War was also the first chance for governments to employ large-scale **propaganda**. One thing that had turned Americans against Germany by 1917 was a very effective anti-German campaign waged by the British. Posters and newspaper advertisements depicting the Germans as apes, rapists, baby killers, and library burners were easy to find. (Early in the war German troops had committed some atrocities against Belgians, and the university at Louvain was sacked. But the propaganda made it seem that this was routine behavior for the Germans, or the **Hun** as some called them.)

Propaganda was used to attract men to serve in the military. This was needed by the British because, after the initial rush of enthusiasm at the beginning of the war, fewer men voluntarily enlisted without encouragement. Australian recruitment posters depicted Germans shooting unarmed women and Britain's speakers of Welsh (an ancient Celtic language) were appealed to in their own language. In most of the countries at war, **conscription** had to be employed to keep the number of troops up.

Propaganda also helped to sell war bonds—called "**victory bonds**" in the English-speaking countries. In exchange for the promise of a return on the bond's price plus interest, people bought victory bonds as a patriotic act.

Soon after the First World War dress among Westerners began to become more **casual**, though it would not be until the 1980s that jeans at church services and T-shirts on public airplanes would be the norm. During the 1920s skirts became shorter and slip-on shoes became fashionable among urban young people, along with **jazz** music, a dance called the jitterbug, and trendy women smoking in public. The war experience also encouraged new art forms such as **cubism**, which emphasized the fragmentation of human experience. Probably the best-known cubist painter is **Pablo Picasso** (1881–1973).

FOR YOUR INFORMATION

Civilizing War

Beginning in 1864, Western nations have signed agreements called the **Geneva Conventions**. Signatories to the Geneva Conventions agree to care for wounded enemies and not to torture or deprive them of basic necessities while in captivity. Nations that abide by the Geneva Conventions further agree to make the identities of enemy dead known to the enemy government so information can be provided to the dead soldier's family. Also, medics, hospitals and transportation vehicles clearly marked with medical symbols—especially a red cross—are not valid targets of war. Neither can they be used to hide weapons or for covert military actions.

CHAPTER 11

The Russian Revolution and the Early Soviet Union

THE RUSSIAN REVOLUTION AND THE EARLY SOVIET UNION

The dictatorship of the Communist Party is maintained by recourse to every form of violence.
—Leon Trotsky

You cannot make a revolution with silk gloves.
—Joseph Stalin

INTRODUCTION

The First World War changed all the countries that fought in it, but it changed some more than others. The British Empire grew smaller as Ireland became the **Irish Free State** (1921). Greater freedom for Ireland—or **Home Rule**—was agreed to in 1914, though the war postponed its implementation. During the war, in 1916, nationalists in the **Irish Republican Army**, led by **Eamon de Valera** (1882–1975), sparked a civil conflict called the **Easter Rising**. This attack on the government in a time of war led many in England to want to be rid of the Irish. In 1949 the government of Ireland declared itself a completely independent republic (it had remained neutral during the Second World War). The six mostly Protestant northern counties of Ireland, called **Ulster**, continued to be part of Britain, and conflict there between republicans and Northern Irish loyal to Britain continued through the twentieth century.

Much more drastically, following the Great War the **Austro-Hungarian Empire ceased to exist**. From it emerged Czechoslovakia (currently the Czech Republic and Slovakia), Yugoslavia, Hungary, and Austria. In the east, the **Ottoman Empire also went out of existence**. From it emerged Turkey, Syria, Iran, and Iraq.

The Russian Empire, too, was fundamentally altered. As a result of Russia's peace agreement with Germany, the **Brest-Litovsk Treaty** (March 1918), Russia surrendered most of its western territory, including present-day Finland, Estonia, Lithuania, and Poland. Of greater international consequence, the hardships of war helped to push Russia into revolution. Russia's communist revolution of 1917 is easily one of the most important events of the twentieth century.

THE RUSSIAN REVOLUTION

By early 1917, after three years of war, Russia was ripe for revolution. Less industrialized than other warring countries, Russia was not able to arm its soldiers adequately. Sometimes men were sent into combat without weapons; they were told to pick up rifles from dead or wounded comrades. The loss of millions of working men to the war led to a decline in farm production. This meant underfed troops as well as hunger in Russia itself. In early 1917 riots erupted in Russian cities.

Meanwhile, Tsar **Nicholas II** was away at the front trying to direct the war. Consequently, some blamed him for the devastating losses Russian soldiers faced. About two million Russians died in the war. Back in St. Petersburg, Nicholas's wife was under the influence of a bizarre "holy man" and unwashed peasant named **Rasputin**, who cared for her unhealthy son.

Another problem was that the Russian Empire included more than one hundred linguistic groups, many of whom held more closely to ethnic identities than to a sense of Russian nationality. Also important was the war that vast Russia had lost to little Japan in 1905. The **Russo-Japanese War** concluded with the first military loss of a European power to an Asian country.

By early 1917 discontent in Russia had reached the point where citizens were willing to risk being injured challenging the government. In a demonstration twelve years before, in 1905, thousands of Russians marched to the seat of government, the **Winter Palace**. They were fired on by soldiers, and nearly one hundred were killed. When soldiers joined demonstrators in March 1917, Nicholas II had no choice but to give up power.

Immediately a **provisional government** was organized, comprising leaders who had served in the Duma, the nearly powerless legislative assembly that had been established by Nicholas after the events of 1905. In the provisional government were political moderates who wished to see Russia evolve into a socialist or democratic state. It immediately enacted laws providing for universal suffrage, an 8-hour workday, and political equality for all.

Opposed to the provisional government were radicals in the Soviets, the local communist councils established throughout Russia, which later gave their name to the Soviet Union. (In time, Russian communists would sometimes be simply referred to as Soviets.) The soviet in St. Petersburg, or Petrograd as it came to be called, was dominated by radicals. Leading the radicals was **Vladimir Lenin** (1870–1924), who had been in exile in Switzerland for many years. Because an unstable Russia was in Germany's interest while the war was still going, Germany helped Lenin return to Russia.

Whereas the provisional government wanted Russia to keep its commitments to its allies and remain in the war against Germany, the Soviets called for withdrawal from the conflict. And whereas the provisional government wanted to pass legislation making the confiscation of the Tsar's lands legal, the Soviets advocated simply seizing the land. The Soviets' slogan, "**Peace, land, bread**" appealed to soldiers who were tired of war, to peasants who wanted more land, and to many who did not have enough to eat. Another slogan, "**All power to the Soviets**," seemed to promise influence to the powerless.

By the summer of 1917, soldiers in the Russian army were abandoning the front and seizing property from landowners. By October the number of Bolshevik Party members had grown from about 50,000 to some 240,000 members. Though Lenin had many enemies, he also had the help of the highly skilled and organized **Leon Trotsky** (1877–1940). Together they plotted the overthrow of the provisional government, which took place on November 6-7,1917. Immediately, the results of elections held earlier were made null, whatever small steps toward democracy Russia had taken were eliminated, and a dictatorship was installed. Lenin claimed to have seized power from the wealthy **bourgeoisie** on behalf of the lower-class and poor **proletariat**, though Lenin and his close associates would rule absolutely. In the first six years of Bolshevik rule, Lenin's secret police, the **Cheka**, executed 200,000 people (compared with about 14,000 Russians executed in the fifty years preceding the Bolsheviks).

Soon, the Bolsheviks withdrew from the war, declared all land national property (this rubber-stamped the seizure of lands that had taken place shortly before) and handed control of factories over to workers. The world's first large-scale experiment in communism had been born.

In 1919 the Soviets founded the **Third International** (its forerunners were discussed in Chapter 9), also called the Comintern. This institution provided rules for Socialists throughout Europe to follow. Among its **Twenty-one Conditions** was the **rejection of all political forms that called for the institution of communism through gradual means**. The conditions also required strict allegiance to Moscow as the center of revolution. Some Socialists in western Europe abided by this and looked to Russia as the model country. This stoked fears in Europe that Russia was bent on fostering revolution outside its own borders. These fears led many to join radical anticommunist parties, such as the Fascists in Italy and the Nazis in Germany.

CIVIL WAR AND ITS AFTERMATH

The Bolsheviks established their government in the name of the people, but before long they had established a government much more tyrannical than what Russia had experienced under the Tsars. Lenin's excuse for dictatorship was that, since Russia's peasants were not ready for socialism, they needed to be led to Utopia by the Bolshevik **vanguard**—that is, by those on the revolution's cutting edge. Before long the euphemism used to justify dictatorship in the name of freedom was "**Revolution from above**." As **George Orwell** (1903–1950) satirically put it in his outstanding political novel *Animal Farm* (1945), "All animals are equal, but some animals are more equal than others."

Soon after the Bolsheviks took power, civil war broke out between **Red Russians** (Bolsheviks) and **White Russians**—all those opposed to the Bolshevik regime, such as liberals and monarchists. The civil war provided the Bolsheviks with an occasion to eliminate all potential threats.

During the civil war fourteen countries—including Japan, Britain, France, and the United States—sent troops to various parts of the Russian Empire in support of anti-Bolshevik forces. They were ineffective, but they did give the Bolsheviks a great opportunity for propaganda. Russians had to rally behind the government because their country was threatened by foreigners.

To prosecute the Reds' war against the Whites, Lenin instituted "**war communism**," which sent food from the countryside into the cities, where many potentially anti-Bolshevik residents faced starvation. This led to starvation in the country. Also, farmers who were not able to sell their goods for a profit produced less. This led to further deprivation. Large strikes occurred in 1920 and 1921, along with the mutiny of part of Russia's fleet at **Kronstadt**. Meanwhile, resistance to Soviet agents carrying off grain for strangers to consume suggested that many did not appreciate the promised land toward which Lenin and his followers were marching. Indeed, by 1921 many in Russia were experiencing **famine**. That forced Lenin to institute his **New Economic Policy**, which allowed peasants to sell some of what they produced. Communism would be saved by making a concession to capitalism. In response to this measure of freedom allowed them, farmers increased production, and famine conditions subsided.

Lenin's New Economic Policy was not embraced by all, and his death in 1924 led to a power struggle within the Soviet government. The two key players were **Leon Trotsky** and **Joseph Stalin** (1879–1953). Trotsky advocated government control of all farms and paying for industrial growth with funds gained from selling farm products. He also called for the freedom of party members to criticize the government and believed that revolution outside Russia was vital to the success of the revolution inside Russia. Opposite Trotsky was Stalin, who had on his side the newspaper *Pravda,* which means "truth." Stalin called for a continuation of the New Economic Policy and for "**socialism in one country**," a slogan suggesting that Russia's revolution could succeed without outsiders' help. Trotsky lost the contest for power, was exiled to Siberia, and was eventually murdered in Mexico by Soviet agents.

STALIN'S REGIME, 1927–1939

In terms of numbers killed, Joseph Stalin must be remembered as one of the greatest murderers of all time. (His greatest competition in this category was China's Mao Zedong, another communist.) Historians disagree about how many died as a result of Stalin's desire to rid the Soviet Union of people he considered potential troublemakers, but all recent estimates are in the tens of millions. Stalin was paranoid, brutal, lacking in conscience and fully in command—the worst possible combination.

Stalin is also remembered as the person who presided over the great **industrialization** of Russia. Beginning in 1928 he turned away from the New Economic Policy and toward a series of **five-year plans**. These plans called for quotas of industrial goods to be produced in a systematic fashion; they emphasized the production of **steel**, **iron**, **electricity**, and heavy **tools** such as tractors.

Clothing, meanwhile, was hardly produced at all. As part of the five-year plans, workers were moved from rural areas into industrial towns and cities, where health and work conditions were worse than what was experienced in England decades before. That was ironic because since Marx had been motivated by the wretched conditions of England's factories.

As the 1930s progressed the Soviet industrial workplace became more and more oppressive. Workers who were fired also lost their apartments and access to rationed food, and perhaps one-quarter of construction work was done by **political prisoners**. Some workers did succeed within the system, gaining higher wages and status; but doing so almost required eliminating one's own personality.

All things were done for the good of the nation, and the good of the nation was defined by Joseph Stalin. During the Great Depression (1929–1940), the **Soviet Union** (also called the **Union of Soviet Socialist Republics, or U.S.S.R.**) experienced full employment, while unemployment in the United States rose to 25 percent. In those years the U.S.S.R.'s industrial production also rose by 400 percent, while American production declined.

An effective **propaganda** campaign put on by the Soviet government made many Russians feel that they were doing something important and were on the cutting edge of progress. But if given the option, few people in Britain, Canada, or France would have traded places with Soviet factory workers. And, when the Second World War began, the Soviet Union had to rely on the United States for assistance.

In those years Stalin also collectivized agriculture, meaning he ended the free commerce of the New Economic Policy and brought all farming under strict government control. Those farmers, called *"kulaks,"* who had grown prosperous within the earlier system were now to be executed or otherwise disposed of. Shortly, all farmers and peasants who resisted **collectivization** by burning their crops and slaughtering their animals came to be called *kulaks* and they, too, were marked for elimination or removal from politically correct society. An uncertain number of *kulaks* were killed, and millions more were removed from farms; some were sent into exile, others to collective farms. Not surprisingly, famine broke out again. Between 5 million and 7 million people died.

So long as the murdered were peasants or strangers without power, the Soviet leader class could rest easy. But the **Great Purges** began in 1934. Many of those who had worked hard to achieve political status in the Soviet Union became the victims of Stalin's paranoia. Two-thirds of the elected members of the Communist Party's Central Congress were arrested and shot; the assassination of the chief of Leningrad's Communist Party, **Sergei Kirov** (1886–1934), was used as a pretext to purge the party throughout the Soviet Union. **Show trials** attended by journalists from around the world condemned Soviet leaders to death. Among those executed were high-ranking military officers, including nearly sixty of the Soviet Union's eighty corps commanders. In time the purge was transformed into a general witch hunt. Germany and Japan were growing in military power, and in 1936-1937 food production was in steep decline (due to bad weather). Someone needed to become the scapegoat, and old priests, suspicious neighbors, and anyone who might ever have been critical of the communists became targets.

Around one million people—men and women—were killed. Millions more were exiled to **Siberia** and elsewhere.

Partly because some believed that dangerous people had been removed from Soviet society, partly because the elimination of so many created job opportunities for those who remained, and partly because those not targeted were glad to be alive, the purges enjoyed popularity in the Soviet Union. Of course, it wasn't possible for anyone who wanted to live in peace to show anything other than approval; and Stalin posters and statues throughout the Soviet Union made it seem that he was everywhere.

Quite unlike Lenin, Stalin promoted nationalism. References to Russia as the "motherland" and "fatherland" became common in public life. Non-Russians— Ukrainians, for instance—had to play along or face punishment. To ensure a future supply of communist true believers, Stalin promoted higher birth rates by making abortion illegal and providing payments to pregnant women. Italy's **Benito Mussolini** and Germany's **Adolf Hitler**, introduced in the next chapter, also promoted high birthrates, at least among the favored segments of their nations' populations.

STALIN AND THE ROAD TO WAR

In 1936 a civil war broke out in Spain between a government composed of socialists and communists, called the **Popular Front**, and antisocialist forces led by military officers, their leader being **Francisco Franco** (1892–1975). Although Spain would remain neutral during the Second World War, the **Spanish Civil War** helped to prepare the stage for that conflict. Stalin was a Russian nationalist (though he was actually a Georgian), but he thought it important to provide aircraft and tanks to the Popular Front, which had been elected in 1931. Socialists and Communists from throughout the Western world also assisted the Spanish republicans by creating brigades that went into combat. The nearly three thousand Americans who went to Spain formed the **Abraham Lincoln Brigade**. At the same time Mussolini and Hitler assisted Franco's forces. Their militaries gained experience that would be useful during the war to come. In the end, which came in March 1939, Franco's forces won. Franco remained Spain's dictator into the mid-1970s.

Although the Soviet Union and Hitler's Germany were at odds indirectly in Spain, in 1939 neither wanted a direct conflict. In August 1939 the Soviets and Germany's Nazis signed a **nonaggression pact**, also called the **Molotov-Ribbentrop Pact**. The pact publicly declared that the two countries would not go to war against one another. Secretly, it provided that Germany and the Soviet Union would divide Poland between them after Germany attacked it the following month. The pact also called for the return of much of the territory lost to Russia as a result of the Brest-Litovsk Treaty of 1918. Hitler had no intention of keeping his promise not to attack the Soviet Union, but for the moment he wanted to keep the U.S.S.R. at bay.

CHAPTER 12

The Second World War

THE SECOND WORLD WAR

*We shall fight on the beaches, we shall fight on the landing
grounds, we shall fight in the fields and in the streets; we shall
fight in the hills. We shall never surrender.*
—Winston Churchill, June 4, 1940

Believe, obey, fight.
—Italian fascist slogan

*In the whole history of the German nation, of nearly 2,000 years,
it has never been so united as today and, thanks to
National Socialism, it will remain united in the future.*
—Adolf Hitler, December 11, 1941

*More than an end to war, we want an end to the beginning of
all wars.*
—Franklin D. Roosevelt, April 13, 1945

INTRODUCTION

Some hoped that the First World War would "make the world safe for democ-racy." The irony is that after the war many Europeans turned away from democ-racy toward one-man or one-party rule. In the years between the two world wars, Italy, Spain, Portugal, Austria, Germany, and other European countries became dictatorships. Some dictators were popularly elected. For example, **Adolf Hitler** promised that if he and his National Socialist, or **Nazi**, Party were democratically elected, he would end democracy in Germany. He kept his promise.

The reason many turned away from democracy was that it did not seem to work. Until **Benito Mussolini** (1883–1945), also called *Il Duce* ("the leader"), won power in Italy and Hitler in Germany, both countries experienced political instability.

THE ROAD TO WAR: MUSSOLINI'S ITALY

Many of Benito Mussolini's supporters were war veterans who felt that Italy had not gotten its share of the Austrian Empire's spoils following the First World War.

Italy's **Fascist Party** was antidemocratic. Its members believed—and many in Italy since before the First World War agreed with them—that democracy did not work, or at least that its reliance on compromise and negotiations weakened the country. As evidence they could point to the results of the elections of 1919. In that year the **Socialist Party** and the **Catholic Popular Party** did well in elections, although neither gained a governing majority. Because the political habits that make democracy possible—such as patience, a willingness to compromise, and trust of strangers—were not part of Italy's experience, and because the two parties were so different, they could not work together. The result was political deadlock. The fascists promised to end gridlock. They were also **anticommunist**. This appealed to businessmen and property owners.

Further, the Fascists were fiercely nationalistic. For them, what mattered most was not the people (as liberals said) or laborers (as Socialists and Communists said) or traditions (as conservatives said). What mattered was the Italian nation.

Finally, like Social Darwinists throughout Europe, Fascists believed that violence and warfare cleansed and fortified the body politic. As a matter of policy, Fascists would break up socialist meetings and beat up those in attendance.

Thus Mussolini's Fascists appealed to nationalism, racial pride, and a sense of postwar grievance. By promising order and secure employment to angry workers and jobs for the unemployed, Mussolini also appealed to laborers who might otherwise be attracted to socialism, as he himself had been earlier in life.

Mussolini's rise to power was dramatic. He formed the Fascist Party in 1919. Three years later, when thousands of his followers marched on Rome in what was called the "**Black Shirt March**," the king, **Victor Emmanuel III** (1900–1946), declined to break it up. Indeed, he asked Mussolini to become prime minister. In 1924 the Fascists were voted into power, and soon thereafter all other parties were made illegal. The Fascists' appeal, in addition to their threats of violence, brought them into power.

By 1926 Mussolini was in complete political control. His **Lateran Pact** of 1929 with the Catholic Church further consolidated his power. Mussolini himself was an atheist, but he knew that most Italians were Catholics. Thus getting the church's stamp of approval was important to him. In the pact Mussolini declared Catholicism Italy's official religion, recognized the church's authority over the **Vatican**, made church lands tax exempt, and al-lowed the church to oversee rules regarding marriage. In return the church recognized Mussolini's status as ruler of Italy.

Among Mussolini's other appeals was his vision of reestablishing the Roman Empire. A good way to start was by expanding Italian holdings in North Africa. Italy's invasion of **Ethiopia** in 1935 also had to do with overcoming the humiliation of Italy's defeat by the Ethiopians at the **Battle of Adowa** in 1896. Italy was the only European nation to have been defeated by Africans in war.

The invasion of Ethiopia is of great importance for a few reasons. First, the world saw in 1935 and 1936 what it would see on a much greater scale a few years later: the massive **bombing of civilian population centers**. Next, it revealed the **weakness of the League of Nations**, which protested Italy's invasion and placed embargoes on some goods but not sufficiently to harm Italy's war effort. The League of Nations, an international organization formed after the First World War, was designed to prevent wars of aggression. The U.S. President Woodrow Wilson proposed the idea, though the Senate voted against the United States joining the league. Finally, the league's failure to prevent Mussolini from continuing his invasion of Ethiopia showed Hitler that he too could get away with aggression.

THE ROAD TO WAR: HITLER'S GERMANY

The Nazi Party was as small and unimportant when it took shape in 1921 as Mussolini's Fascist Party had been in 1919. At that time its leader, Adolf Hitler, was a political nonentity who had been imprisoned for several months in 1923 for trying to seize the government of the German state of Bavaria in what was called the **"Beer Hall Putsch."** Hitler's trial provided him with publicity, and by the end of that year the party had about seventy thousand members. During his time in prison, Hitler wrote his political memoir *Mein Kampf* ("My Struggle").

In Hitler's favor was the political instability of Germany's **Weimar Republic**, which had been established near the end of the First World War as a result of liberal, socialist, and communist agitation and demonstrations. **Hitler's hatred of Communists** stemmed from his belief that this new government stabbed Germany in the back by surrendering to the Allies in 1918. His hatred of Jews was stoked by the knowledge that several communist and socialist leaders were Jewish. And the Weimar government was an easy target. Many teachers, judges, and other professionals did not believe in democracy, especially if it placed Socialists in power. Nor did the German military favor the government.

Also on Hitler's side in the early 1920s was an economy in collapse. German workers, widows, and elderly lost their bank savings, and Germany's currency became all but worthless. In the early 1930s, as a result of the **Great Depression**, unemployment in Germany skyrocketed. Germans who were out of work, angry about their lot in life, frustrated over Germany's weakness, or just looking for something to do were attracted to the Nazi Party, which provided young people with a sense of purpose, uniforms, and enemies to blame—most of all, the Jews.

Anti-Semitism had been common in Europe since Roman times, and the Jews were singled out for persecution by great powers long before the Roman Empire. No other group of people has faced harassment from so many directions for so long. This is not to say that Jews faced constant pressure in Europe. The British prime minister **Benjamin Disraeli** (1804–1881), for example, was a Jew, although he had converted to Christianity. Generally speaking, however, anti-Jewish feeling was the norm. In the early nineteenth century, for example, Napoleon placed restrictions on Jews' movements within France, and the **Dreyfus Affair** (1895) revealed that anti-Semitism was still quite alive in the late nineteenth century. **Alfred Dreyfus** was a French military officer of Jewish stock who was found guilty of selling military secrets, though his prosecutors appeared to have been driven more by anti-Semitism than by a commitment to justice. The French writer **Émile Zola** (1840–1902) made this point powerfully in an essay that repeated the phrase *J'accuse* ("I accuse"). In 1906 evidence appeared that led to Dreyfus's full exoneration. In the early twentieth century, anti-Semitism was fiercest in central and eastern Europe, where most Jews lived. Hitler absorbed it in its most rabid form as a young man.

Adolf Hitler was able to gain complete power largely because many German people believed he would restore Germany's dignity and strength. Rather than allow Germany to be dictated to by foreign powers or the League of Nations, he asserted his own will—and he remained unchecked by outside forces. In 1933 Hitler claimed that a **fire at the Reichstag** was started by communists and, capitalizing on the fear of communism among many Germans, he used the fire as an excuse to take complete control of Germany. Soon thereafter, Hitler **withdrew Germany from the League of Nations**. In the same year he began to **conscript large numbers of young men into the German military**. This directly conflicted with post-First World War agreements, but Hitler despised those agreements, and the Germans who agreed to them.

In 1936 Hitler sent military forces into the Rhineland, near France's eastern border, and another postwar agreement went up in flames. That year Hitler also allied himself with Mussolini's Italy in the **Rome-Berlin Axis**. Two years later the Versailles Treaty (signed at the end of the First World War) was trashed again when Hitler's forces occupied Austria and absorbed that country into the new German empire, or Reich. The union of the two countries was referred to as **Anschluss** ("joining"). Soon thereafter Hitler demanded that the German-speaking western part of Czechoslovakia called the **Sudetenland** be included in his growing empire.

By that time war seemed imminent. The British prime minister **Neville Chamberlain** (1869–1940) at **Munich**, in the German state of Bavaria, and the French prime minister Edouard Deladier agreed to allow Hitler to occupy the Sudetenland. Chamberlain returned to England promising **"peace in our time"** and encouraging Britons to sleep well. Hitler prepared for war.

THE FIRST YEAR

War came on September 1, 1939, when Hitler's fast-moving tanks, well-trained troops and air force, or **Luftwaffe**, invaded Poland. For the first time, the world saw **blitzkrieg** ("lightning war") in action. Unable to stand against Germany's war machine, the Polish army collapsed within a month. Within a few days of Hitler's invasion of Poland, France and Britain declared war on Germany. Russia, meanwhile, invaded Poland from the east.

After several weeks the guns of war fell silent; Hitler made no more aggressive moves until the spring of 1940. This quiet period is referred to as the **"phony war."**

During those quiet months many Europeans wondered if large-scale war could still be averted. The answer to that question came in April of 1940 when, in rapid succession, Hitler's forces overran Belgium, the Netherlands, Norway, and Denmark. France, which imagined itself secure behind a series of defenses called the **Maginot Line**, fell into Nazi hands within six weeks. Northern France was occupied by the Germans until the summer of 1944; southern France was ruled by the **Vichy Regime**,° a government supervised by the Nazis. Some Allied troops later died combating Vichy French forces in North Africa. The **Free French**, those who had fled France with the intention of fighting the Nazis another day, along with Frenchmen from France's colonies, were led by General **Charles de Gaulle** (1890–1970), who was based in London.

As France was being defeated, nearly 200,000 British troops in France, along with about 140,000 French troops, were evacuated at **Dunkirk** on the coast of Belgium. Every type of British boat available was put to work taking those troops across the English Channel to Britain.

Earlier, Hitler had hoped that Britain would determine that prosecuting the war was not in its own best interest. Partly because Hitler considered the British to be similar to the Germans—English, for example, is a Germanic language—Hitler would have preferred not to fight them. But Britain's new prime minister, **Winston Churchill**, was in no mood to appease Hitler. And even as German bombers set British cities aflame, Churchill challenged the British people to courageously endure the **Blitz**, the bombing of Britain's cities. (British aircraft, meanwhile, also bombed German cities.) In the **Battle of Britain**, Germany had the advantage of a large air force, while Britain had the advantage of **radar** (which detected incoming planes). The British had also broken Germany's secret code, encrypted on a machine called **Enigma**, and they often knew in advance what the enemy intended to do.

ANGLO-AMERICAN ALLIANCE

From the outset, Churchill knew that **the British Empire could not withstand the challenges of world war without the assistance of the United States**. Among other problems, much of Britain's heavy weaponry had been left on the beaches of Dunkirk. Since the mid-1930s, however, the U.S. Congress had passed several **neutrality acts** designed to keep the United States out of any foreign war. In 1940 American public opinion decisively favored Britain, but that did not change the fact that most Americans wanted nothing to do with Europe's war.

This view of things changed at the end of 1941, when Germany's ally, Japan, attacked the American Pacific fleet at Pearl Harbor in Hawaii. Still, months before the attack at Pearl Harbor, Churchill had convinced the U.S. government to provide Britain with old warships in exchange for U.S. military bases on British possessions in the Western Hemisphere (e.g., Newfoundland and the West Indies). Churchill also persuaded the United States to supply Britain with all necessary war supplies, promising to pay for them after the war. The **Lend-Lease Act** passed by the U.S. Congress made this possible. Thus, while America remained formally neutral, it actively assisted Britain and the Canadians, whose fleet was indispensable. Hitler knew this, and by mid-1941 an undeclared war at sea had begun between American and German vessels. In late October, for example, the *U.S.S. Reuben James* was sunk off the coast of Iceland, with the loss of more than one hundred U.S. sailors.

The United States formally entered the war against Hitler's ally, Japan, on December 8, 1941, the day after Japan's surprise attack on Pearl Harbor. A few days later Hitler declared war on the United States. In his speech Hitler said that Germany, Italy, and Japan, the main players among the **Axis** powers, would "wage the common war forced upon them by the U.S.A. and England."

Together, Britain's victory over Germany's Luftwaffe (air force) in the Battle of Britain and the entry of the United States into the war played a major role in the defeat of Hitler. Through the war, the relationship between the United States and Britain would always be sound, even if it was not always easy—something that remained true into the early twenty-first century. The United States provided much of the industrial material, manpower, and firepower the **Allies**—Britain and the America—needed to defeat Hitler in North Africa, Italy, and western Europe.

STRATEGY, THE RUSSO-GERMAN WAR, AND VICTORY

Rather than invade France early in the war, as another member of the Allies, the Soviet Union, wished, the United States and Britain decided first to attack the Axis powers' "soft underbelly." The Anglo-Americans first saw major action together in North Africa, winning victories against the Vichy French, Italians, and Germans in Morocco, Algeria, Tunisia, Libya, and Egypt. A major victory against the German field marshal **Erwin Rommel** (1891–1944), who would later be implicated in a plot to assassinate Hitler, was gained by the British general **Bernard Montgomery** (1887–1976) at **El Alamein** in Egypt in October 1942. This victory kept the **Suez Canal** in the Allies' hands.

Following the defeat of the Axis in North Africa, the Allies invaded **Sicily** with the goal of controlling the Mediterranean. The capture of Sicily led the Italian king to dismiss Mussolini as prime minister, and in September 1943 the new Italian government declared war on Germany. Italian troops, along with civilian fighters (called **partisans**), joined the Allies in their fight against the German troops occupying Italy. Through the last two years of the war, Italy served as a base from which Allied planes bombed Axis sites. In April 1945 Mussolini was captured and executed by antifascist Italians.

Britain was the staging ground from which the **D-Day** invasion of German-occupied France was launched on June 6, 1944. This massive invasion, involving two million men and five thousand vessels, was a great success, though some invaders had it easier than others. The U.S. soldiers who first landed at **Omaha Beach** (a code name) on the coast of Normandy faced devastating losses; many, weighed down with more than fifty pounds of equipment, drowned when they stepped off their landing craft. Others were gunned down before they left their boats. But Omaha Beach was taken, and along the coast of Normandy the British, Americans, and Canadians established beachheads and began the slow but sure process of pushing the Germans back into Germany.

Hitler's forces put up a stiff resistance. In December they launched a serious counterattack in Belgium, which has come to be called the **Battle of the Bulge** because it forced the Americans to retreat, thus causing a "bulge" in the Allies' line of defenses. This was the deadliest battle in American history, but by early January the Germans were once again backing up.

Another key factor behind the defeat of Hitler was his own attack on Russia in late June 1941. Before the war (as discussed in the previous chapter), the Soviet Union and Germany had signed the **Molotov-Ribbentrop Pact** (also called simply the **Nazi-Soviet Pact**), which made them allies for a short time. Together Russia and Germany carved up defeated Poland. But Hitler never intended to leave Russia in peace.

In June 1941 Hitler's forces plunged deep into Russia, arriving at the outskirts of **Stalingrad** and Leningrad and to within 20 miles of Moscow. But the Russians' great manpower reserves and fierce resistance—put up by soldiers and civilians alike—along with the **Germans' thin supply lines** and the severe Russian winter stopped the German invasion, and by early February 1943 the Germans were retreating. In the battle for Stalingrad—a city Hitler wanted because it was a center for rail transportation and provided access to oil fields—some 260,000 Germans died and another 110,000 were captured. Incredibly, the Soviets sustained the loss of nearly 800,000 soldiers and civilians. At the battle of **Kursk** in July 1943, the Germans lost 300 tanks. From that point, the Germans fell back. The Russians captured Berlin in the spring of 1945. German civilians, especially women, suffered greatly at the hands of the Russians. All war is brutal, but the war fought between the Germans and Russians was especially so, with horrendous atrocities committed by both sides.

V-E Day (for "victory in Europe") arrived on May 7, 1945, when what was left of the German army surrendered unconditionally. A week earlier Hitler had committed suicide, but not before encouraging his followers one last time to continue the war against Jews. "Above all," Hitler wrote in his last political statement, "I charge the leadership of the nation and their followers with the strict observance of the racial laws and with merciless resistance against the universal poisoners of all peoples, international Jewry."

Just before the end of the Second World War the Allied leaders met at **Potsdam**. Divisions between the Americans and Soviets that soon developed into a "cold war" came to the surface at the Potsdam Conference. U.S. President Truman correctly accused the Soviet leader, Stalin, of wanting to make satellite states of the East European countries Soviet forces had liberated from the Nazis. Also at Potsdam, Truman revealed to the Soviets and the British that the United States possessed a new weapon vastly more powerful than any seen before. Four days after the end of the conference, on August 6, 1945, that the United States dropped an **atomic bomb** on Hiroshima. Japan surrendered after Truman ordered a second bomb to be dropped on Nagasaki.

THE HOLOCAUST

Through the 1930s the Nazis had put increasing pressure on Germany's Jews. After the war began, Hitler briefly thought that he might exile Europe's Jews to Madagascar, but that was impractical. Later he arrived at his **Final Solution°**: the extermination of Europe's Jews, better known as the **Holocaust**. In charge of this program was **Heinrich Himmler** (1900–1945), head of the Nazi *Schützstaffel* ("protective force"), better known simply as the **SS**. An element of the SS, the *Einsatzgrüppen*, comprised mobile units of killers who murdered women, children, and the elderly. The regular army, or **Wehrmacht**, sometimes helped to round up Jews. The SS was also assisted in eastern Europe by Ukrainians, Lithuanians, and Latvians.

Death camps were established in eastern and central Europe. The camp at **Auschwitz**, about 40 miles from Cracow, Poland, was the largest built by the Nazis. Well over one million Jews, Poles, Gypsies (or Roma), and Soviet prisoners were killed there. Among its roles was putting prisoners to forced labor before exterminating them. Those not fit for work when they arrived at the camps were immediately executed in gas chambers. Most of the rest died within a few months of their arrival. Some were experimented on by ruthless doctors. Gold was extracted from the mouths of prisoners and stored in banks. In the end about six million Jews were exterminated. Ninety percent of Jewish children in lands occupied by the Nazis died. Along with them, **gypsies, Christians who had resisted Nazism or helped Jews to hide**, and **developmentally disabled** people were murdered.

Little better than the Jews in Nazi's eyes were the **Slavs**—Poles, Russians, and others who were considered to be *untermenschen* ("subhumans"). Russian and Polish prisoners of war were frequently executed, tortured, starved to death, or made into slaves. Of the 5.5 million Russian prisoners taken by the Germans, 3.5 million died. Slavic civilians were also sent as slaves to Germany. Intellectuals, priests, and professionals were murdered. Schools and churches used by Slavs were closed.

Perhaps the most disturbing fact about the Nazi death machine is that it was run by well-educated people whom we would otherwise consider civilized. They enjoyed classical music and wanted what was best for their own children. Many of them felt no guilt after the war. At the **Nuremberg War Crimes Trials** after the war, some excused their work by saying that they were simply following orders. Some continued to believe that they had done the world a favor.

It is a "disturbing psychological truth," wrote one student of the death camps, that "ordinary people can commit demonic acts."

Into the early twenty-first century Germans and their allies linked to Nazi war crimes were tracked down, arrested, tried, and executed or imprisoned. One Nazi criminal, **Adolf Eichmann** (1906–1962), lived for years in Argentina before he was captured by Israeli agents and put on trial in Jerusalem. In her famous book *Eichmann in Jerusalem* (1961), the Jewish intellectual **Hannah Arendt** (1906–1975) argued that Eichmann seemed hardly demonic; indeed, he appeared as a mere bureaucrat who became part of a death machine he was not very interested in. He was a careerist who saw carrying out Germany's deadly policies as a way to advance himself.

One partial consequence of the Holocaust was the establishment of Israel as a nation. The roots of modern Israel extend to the ancient times, but after the war there was a sense that the Jews, who had been dispersed around the world since the first century, should have a homeland. An important early advocate of **Zionism**, or Jewish nationalism, was **Theodore Herzl** (1860–1904). In 1897 the **First Zionist Congress** met in Basel, Switzerland, and called for a Jewish homeland in Palestine. That hope was realized in 1948. The **United States was the first nation to recognize Israel as a nation**. Since that time, the United States has been involved, to one extent or another, in Middle Eastern affairs.

FOR YOUR INFORMATION

Vichy Regime

Hitler was eager for revenge against France, which had humiliated Germany with the Versailles Treaty at the end of the First World War. In the Second World War, France surrendered to the Germans after about a month of combat. Northern France was occupied by Nazi troops until the fall of 1944. Southern France was governed from the town of Vichy by Marshall **Petain**, a hero of the First World War. In 1942 all of France was occupied by the Nazis. Through the war years, some French people resisted the Nazis by cutting communication wires, killing soldiers on patrol, sabotaging vehicles and so on. Nazi reprisals against the Resistance, or the **Maquis**, were fierce. Other French people actively assisted the Germans in fighting the Allies and rounding up Jews for elimination. Most did little to assist either side.

Final Solution

While the Nazis were the most efficient mass killers the world has seen, they were not the only ones to have systematically eliminated millions of people. During the First World War 2 million Armenian Christians in Turkey died as a result of Turkish oppression. While many had forgotten this by 1939, Hitler had not. "I have sent my Death's Head units to the east with the order to kill without mercy men, women, and children of the Polish race or language," Hitler said. "Who, after all, speaks today of the annihilation of the Armenians?" Incredibly, in terms of body count, Hitler cannot compete with the Soviet Union's communist dictator, Joseph Stalin (discussed in Chapter 11).

CHAPTER 13

The Cold War

THE COLD WAR

From Stettin in the Baltic to Trieste in the Adriatic, an iron curtain has descended across the [European] Continent...This is certainly not the liberated Europe which we fought to build up.
—British Prime Minister Winston Churchill, March 5, 1946

The Marshall Plan will go down in history as one of America's greatest contributions to the peace of the world.
—U.S. President Harry S. Truman, 1955

I like Mr. Gorbachev. We can do business together.
—British Prime Minister Margaret Thatcher, 1984

OVERVIEW

In 1950 the **United Nations** (UN), which replaced the failed League of Nations, authorized a conflict against communist forces from North Korea and China. The charter of the UN asserted that the organization was "determined to save succeeding generations from the scourge of war." One lesson of the inter-war years, however, was that sometimes long-term peace can only be gained through conflict in the immediate term. The main non-Korean, anticommunist combatant in Korea was the United States, though Great Britain, Turkey and Australia, among other nations, also sent a small number of troops there. The UN had been formed shortly before the end of the Second World War. One of its purposes was to pick up where the League left off.

The origins of the UN are in a document called the **Atlantic Charter**, drawn up by Franklin Roosevelt and Winston Churchill in 1941. Though the UN's responsibilities would extend beyond disarming aggressor nations, that would be one of its founding ideas. And partly in recognition of the status of the United States as a new world power, the UN's headquarters were based, and remain, in New York. Another signal of American power was the **Bretton Woods Agreement** of 1944, which made the U.S. dollar the world's reserve currency.

The **Korean War** (1950–1953) ended almost where it began: the armistice line of June 1953 straddled the thirty-eighth parallel, which, after the Second World War, had divided communist North Korea from noncommunist South Korea. Still, into the early twenty-first century, the war had not formally ended. The boundary between the Koreas remained the most heavily militarized in the world. The Korean War was one of many conflicts of the **Cold War** (1945–1991).

The term *Cold War* usually refers to a decades-long struggle for global mastery between the two major powers to emerge from the Second World War—the United States and the Soviet Union—along with their allies. (Countries that resisted alignment with either power were referred to collectively as the **Third World**.) More broadly, it refers to a global war between the ideologies of communism and democracy, though anticommunists who gained the support of the United States were frequently not interested in democracy. The Cold War world was a nasty one; the United States felt compelled to ally itself with unsavory regimes whose only virtue was their anticommunist politics.

The standoff between the United States and the Soviets began in the immediate aftermath of the war (though the roots of the Cold War go back much further). The **Soviets had captured Berlin** and occupied East Germany, losing tens of thousands of soldiers in the process. The Allies—the British (including the Canadians), **Free French**, and Americans—occupied West Germany, and as part of an agreement among the Allies they also acquired occupation zones in Berlin. It was clear that the Allies intended to see Germany become a democratic state.

Soon it also became clear that the Soviets intended to occupy East Germany indefinitely. It became even more clear that the Soviets intended to establish puppet governments throughout eastern Europe. The nations of Poland, Czechoslovakia, Hungary, Romania, and Bulgaria, along with East Germany and the many small states absorbed earlier by the Soviets (such as Lithuania and Latvia), would be controlled by the Soviets. In 1955 they formed the **Warsaw Pact**, the counterpart to **NATO** (the North Atlantic Treaty Organization), which had been created in 1949, as a military alliance. Among the early members of NATO were the United States, Great Britain, France, Spain, Portugal,

Italy, Iceland, Norway, Canada, and West Germany. After the end of the Cold War, many countries previously in the Warsaw Pact joined NATO.

BEGINNINGS OF THE COLD WAR: 1945–1949

Following the Second World War, Communist parties in several western European countries were strong. Having been opposed to fascism since the early 1930s, Communists could say they had always been right. Also, in devastated regions of Europe, some people were open to the radical political views communism presented. In France and Italy, especially, it seemed that **Communist parties might gain significant political power**. Soon after the war, moreover, **civil war erupted in Greece**. It appeared that Western civilization's cradle of democracy and classical education might turn to communism. Meanwhile, it became clear that eastern Europe, including the eastern portion of Germany occupied by the Soviet Union, would remain under Soviet control for an indefinite period.

The United States, as the strongest of the Allies at the end of the war, was in a position to prevent the spread of communism into western Europe. One way it did so was by providing a group of European nations more than $12 billion of economic assistance from 1948–1951. Formally called the **European Recovery Program** and better known as the **Marshall Plan** (named after the U.S. secretary of state George Marshall), the funds it provided helped Europeans to rebuild their countries. The Marshall Plan, which was implemented by the **Organization for European Economic Cooperation**, also brought western Europe under a stronger political influence from the United States (though no formal strings were attached to the funds). Finally, the Marshall Plan helped to ensure that the U.S. economy would remain strong. By getting Europe going economically, the plan made it possible for Europeans to buy American imports.

To assist the anticommunists in the **Greek Civil War**, which immediately followed the global conflict, as well as anticommunists in Turkey, the United States provided the Greeks and Turks with roughly $400 million in economic and military aid. This came as a result of the **Truman Doctrine**. "I believe it must be the policy of the United States," President Truman said in 1947, "to support free peoples who are resisting attempted subjugation by armed minorities or by outside pressures." And to prevent all of Berlin from falling into the hands of the Soviets, who in 1948 blockaded the corridor connecting West

Berlin to West Germany, the Allies flew goods into West Berlin for a year. At its peak the **Berlin Airlift** flew about 13,000 tons of supplies into West Berlin daily. This demonstrated the extent of the Allies' air power, as well as their resolve to keep West Berlin out of the Soviets' hands. After a year, the Soviet Union relented, and the corridor connecting the city with West Germany was reopened. For the first time, the Soviets and Allies (mainly the United States) had faced off, and the Soviets had backed down. To reduce American influence in East Germany, and to prevent people living in Soviet-occupied countries from traveling to the west, the Soviets built the **Berlin Wall** in 1961. The best known gate that passed through the wall from West to East Germany was called **Checkpoint Charlie**.

GLOBALIZATION OF THE COLD WAR: 1950–1989

The second face-off came when the Soviets were given a deadline by the U.S. president **John F. Kennedy** to halt the building of missiles on Cuba, which had experienced a communist revolution in 1959 and was only 90 miles from the U.S. coastline. The **Cuban Missile Crisis** (1962) marks the period when the two world superpowers came the closest to war. Had Kennedy invaded Cuba, Soviet leader **Nikita Khrushchev** (1894–1971) probably would have attacked the United States with short-range nuclear missiles. If Khrushchev had not agreed to halt production of missile sites on Cuba, and to remove the missiles already there, war probably would have resulted.

From one point of view the U.S. policy of "**containment**" of the Soviet Union seemed to be working. Then again, it is very likely that the United States later removed missiles from Turkey to compensate the Soviets for their earlier concession. A sense had developed in the great powers that there could be no winners in a nuclear war. To prevent such a war from happening accidentally or as the result of a rogue military leader, in the early 1960s the United States and the Soviet Union established an emergency communications system that put the nations' leaders into immediate contact with one another.

Communism and capitalism are both expansionistic. Capitalists seek new resources and customers; Communists seek converts to a political creed that promises, ultimately, a global Utopia of selfless workers. After 1949, the main combat zones between the two ideologies were in Asia. In that year, **China**, the world's most populous nation, became communist. As mentioned at the beginning of this chapter, in June the following year, with the consent of the Chinese and apparently of the Soviet Union, soldiers from communist **North Korea** invaded noncommunist South Korea.

No sooner had shooting stopped in Korea (in 1953) than attention was shifted to French **Indochina**, present-day **Vietnam**, Cambodia, and Laos in Southeast Asia. Prior to the war Indochina had been a French colony, and it was returned to the French after the war. But many Vietnamese, especially those favoring communism in the country's north, were tired of their country being occupied, and the French suffered a major defeat in Vietnam at **Dienbienphu** in 1954. It seemed to the western democracies, and especially to the United States, that Vietnam would become communist. If it did so, according the **Domino Theory** then prevalent, the other Southeast Asian nations would also fall to communism. The U.S. believed itself obligated to prevent this from happening and, beginning in the late 1950s, U.S. military advisors, weapons, troops, and funds were sent to Vietnam.

Intense U.S. involvement in Vietnam began in 1964. By 1973, after a series of military defeats and domestic protests, the U.S. concluded that it should remove its troops from Vietnam. By the end of 1975, all of Vietnam had become communist. Laos and Cambodia also became communist. Thailand did not. The conflict in Vietnam was very controversial, both in the United States and abroad. Many in the western democracies saw the United States as a bully, picking on a small country whose people did not want American help.

The Soviet Union faced its own "Vietnam" in the 1980s in the rugged land of Afghanistan. All the reasons the Soviets, now led by Leonid Brezhnev, invaded Afghanistan are not completely clear. One certain reason is that the Soviet Union wanted to maintain a pro-Soviet government in that country. Thus the invasion was spurred by a variation on the **Brezhnev Doctrine** of 1968, in which Soviets reserved to themselves the right to interfere in the domestic politics of communist nations.

For a decade beyond its invasion in 1979, the **Soviet-Afghan War°** sapped the morale of the Soviet military. About two thousand Soviet soldiers were killed each year the Soviet Union occupied Afghanistan, and there seemed to be no way to conquer and pacify that undeveloped country. During the war Afghan fighters were provided with weapons by the United States and China, which were funneled through Pakistan, and the Soviets withdrew completely from Afghanistan in 1989. In the late 1990s and into the early twenty-first century, some countries that had received U.S. assistance would become enemies of the United States by aiding and harboring radical Muslim terrorists.

THE SPACE RACE

Throughout the Cold War the United States and the Soviet Union vied for dominance in outer space. In 1956 the Soviets were the first to launch a satellite—called *Sputnik*—into space. That alarmed Americans who believed that the launch indicated the Soviets had gained technological superiority. Thus President Kennedy's appeal to land Americans on the **moon** was widely embraced. The U.S. flag was planted on the moon in 1969. When Neil Armstrong stepped out of his spacecraft he said, "That's one small step for a man; one giant leap for mankind." From that point on, U.S. dominance in space was unquestioned.

THE END OF THE COLD WAR

From early in the Cold War, the Soviet Union faced challenges to its dominance in Eastern Europe. The Soviet premier following Stalin, **Nikita Khrushchev**, held power from 1956 through 1964. Best known to Americans for being opposite President Kennedy during the Cuban Missile Crisis, Khrushchev allowed for a little more freedom in the Soviet Union. He eliminated restrictions on small private farms and allowed the publication of the novel *One Day in the Life of Ivan Denisovich*, which criticized some elements of Soviet life. The novel's author was **Aleksandr Solzhenitsyn** (b. 1918), who later lived in the United States. Among Americans, Solzhenitsyn was the best-known critic of the Soviet Union. In 1956 Khrushchev gave a **speech at the Twentieth Congress of the Communist Party**. The speech, which denounced Stalin and some of his tactics, was supposed to remain secret, but it was soon made public.

This apparent openness encouraged reform-minded Communists in **Poland**, led by **Wladyslaw Gomulka** (1905–1982), to reduce restrictions against the Roman Catholic Church in Poland and to seek greater political independence from the Soviet Union. That in turn encouraged reformers in **Hungary**, most importantly **Imre Nagy** (1896–1958), to call for Soviet troops to leave their country and for Hungary to leave the Warsaw Pact. Those movements were met with force, however, and much of whatever openness might have developed was stopped. The point was made again in 1968 when reformers in **Czechoslovakia** launched the so-called **Prague Spring**, which sought to make the political culture less repressive. As in Hungary in 1956, Soviet troops moved in, replaced the reformer **Alexander Dubcek** (1921–1992), and ended political liberalization.

Lasting reforms, leading ultimately to the collapse of the Soviet Union, began to take hold in the late 1980s. The Soviet-Afghan War, like the U.S. war in Vietnam, brought criticism of the Soviet Union from around the world. But whereas the Vietnam conflict did not immediately contribute to the military decline of the U.S., the **war in Afghanistan played a major role in bringing about the end of the Soviet Union**. Among other things, it was expensive and unpopular at home. The Soviet economy and a commitment among Soviet people to the cause of communism were waning.

The Soviet leader who presided over the end of the U.S.S.R. was **Mikhail Gorbachev** (b. 1931). Gorbachev was a reformer who believed that communism was the best system possible but that, in practice, it had been hijacked in the U.S.S.R. by corruption. Using as slogans the words *perestroika* ("restructuring") and *glasnost* ("openness"), Gorbachev allowed more political liberty. Censorship became less severe and political prisoners were freed. Gorbachev was willing to be criticized publicly and, following the model of Lenin's New Economic Policy, he allowed for private property (see Chapter 10). In 1988 Gorbachev introduced a new constitution and called for a **Congress of People's Deputies**. Many reformers and government critics were elected to it.

Soon, however, Gorbachev lost control of reforms. The Soviet media began to criticize the military actions in Afghanistan and against rebellious ethnic groups in the U.S.S.R. The budget of the very expensive military was cut, further demoralizing the Soviets' armed forces.

Meanwhile in Soviet-dominated Poland, the labor organization **Solidarity** was challenging the Communists for political power. As in the Soviet Union, the communist government in Poland had allowed greater freedoms since the early 1980s. As a result the Communists lost overwhelmingly in the elections of 1989. That led to the appointment of a noncommunist prime minister and to the international fame of Solidarity's founder, **Lech Walesa** (b. 1943).

Also in 1989 the East Bloc country of **Hungary** opened its borders with noncommunist Austria. This made it possible for people living behind the **Iron Curtain** (a term made famous by Winston Churchill after the Second World War) to get to the West. At the same time Hungary made noncommunist political parties legal and large anticommunist demonstrations broke out in **East Germany**. Before the end of the year, the great symbol of the Cold War, the **Berlin Wall**, was torn down. In December the playwright and anticommunist dissident **Václav Havel** (b. 1936) was elected president of **Czechoslovakia**.

Change in communist Europe was coming about faster than most people could have imagined. It succeeded largely because Gorbachev refused to stop it. Repudiating the old **Brezhnev Doctrine** (1968), which announced the Soviet Union's right to interfere in the internal affairs of communist countries, Gorbachev withdrew Soviet troops from eastern Europe.

The U.S.S.R. itself held together a little longer. Gorbachev hoped to maintain the communist system but recognized that political competition could be good for the government. Among Gorbachev's opponents was the powerful president of Russia, **Boris Yeltsin** (b. 1931), who favored movement toward capitalism. At the same time anti-Soviet nationalist movements broke out in other countries within the U.S.S.R.—Latvia, Lithuania, and Estonia in particular—and anti-Soviet feeling became public in the Islamic states bordering Afghanistan and Iran, such as **Azerbaijan**. A **failed coup** against Gorbachev by communist hardliners in 1991 indicated that his reforms would hold but his government was unstable. **Yeltsin,** the most public and dashing resister of the coup, emerged a hero. Gorbachev was humiliated by "the knife plunged in his back" by his own appointees. He resigned on Christmas Day 1991. That same day the Soviet Union ceased to exist. In its place arose the **Commonwealth of Independent States**. The Cold War was over, and this dramatic change spurred reform in other parts of the world. In 1993 the South African government's policy of strict racial segregation, called **apartheid**, was abolished.

FOR YOUR INFORMATION

The Soviet-Afghan War

The American war in Vietnam and the Soviet war in Afghanistan have much in common. Both were civil wars, with the United States supporting anticommunist Vietnamese and the Soviets supporting procommunist Afghans. Both wars took a heavy psychological toll on the superpowers' soldiers as they confronted unfamiliar terrain and weather. Both wars became unpopular on the superpowers' home fronts. There were huge anti-war protests in the United States and, following Gorbachev's reforms, in the Soviet press as well. The United States was internationally criticized for its actions in Vietnam, and the Soviet Union was widely condemned for its invasion of Afghanistan. In Vietnam, the U.S.S.R. indirectly fought the United States by supplying the North Vietnamese; in Afghanistan the United States indirectly fought the U.S.S.R. by supplying the Afghans. Until 1970 the North Vietnamese and Vietcong (communist South Vietnamese) had a safe haven in Cambodia; the Afghans always had a safe haven in neighboring Pakistan. Vietnamese and Afghan strategy involved wearing the enemy down; both societies were accustomed to hardship and war. But Soviet and U.S. soldiers were not accustomed to the adversities they would face. The Vietnamese and Afghanis knew their terrain much better than the forces of the superpowers. Both were more resistant to illnesses and diseases common to their areas. For example, a problem the Soviets faced was altitude sickness, the symptoms of which are headaches, nausea, vomiting, dizziness, malaise, insomnia, and loss of appetite. It was impossible in both wars for soldiers of the superpowers to distinguish between friend and foe. Thus a general mistrust and hatred of all Vietnamese and Afghanis arose. Children from Vietnam and Afghanistan were used as combatants or to lure soldiers into ambushes.

CHAPTER 14

Western Culture and Politics Since 1945

WESTERN CULTURE AND POLITICS SINCE 1945

Unless we get off our fat surpluses and recognize that television in the main is being used to distract, delude, amuse and insulate us, the television and those who finance it, those who look at it and those who work at it, may see a totally different picture too late.
— Television and radio broadcaster Edward R. Murrow

It is the duty of Muslims to prepare as much force as possible to terrorize the enemies of God.
— Anti-American terrorist Osama bin Laden (1998)

POST-SOVIET RUSSIA AND EASTERN EUROPE

Post–Soviet Russia was the largest and most powerful of the Commonwealth states. **Boris Yeltsin** was its leader from 1991 to January 2000, though he faced a significant challenge against his authority in 1993. In that year he suspended Russia's parliament, and then the parliament declared him deposed. The military sided with Yeltsin, however, and he remained in power. All along, observers wondered whether Russia would really become a democratic state with a prosperous economy. By the early twenty-first century Russia was challenged by political and business corruption and a lack of economic growth.

Russia was also challenged by a civil war with separatists in Muslim **Chechnya**. This was among the greatest challenges faced by the second Russian president, **Vladimir Putin**. The Chechnyan fighters, who wished to create their own nation independent of Russia, were aided by radical Muslims from around the world. Fighters connected to the **Taliban**, which took charge of Afghanistan after the Soviet defeat there, and financed by wealthy radicals such as **Osama bin Laden**, assisted the Chechnyans in their cause.

Following massive terrorist attacks on the United States on September 11, 2001, the United States went to war with the Taliban and Osama bin Laden's terrorist network, **Al Qaeda**, which took responsibility for the attacks. The United States and Russia thus had common cause against radical Muslim terrorists, although the two countries continued to be at odds over many important issues. In 2003 the United States followed up the short war called "**Operation Desert Storm**" (1991), which was sparked by Iraq's annexation of Kuwait, with an invasion of **Iraq**. The United States feared, incorrectly, that Iraq held **weapons of mass destruction**. It was also clear that Iraq's leader, **Saddam Hussein**, favored anti-American terrorism. Russia protested the U.S. invasion vigorously, as did many other countries, including France and Germany.

Following the collapse of the Soviet system, civil war broke out in **Yugoslavia**. The same eastern European country that had seethed before the First World War boiled again after the death of its strong leader, **Marshal Tito** (1892–1980), who had been a leader of Yugoslavia's anti-Nazi resistance movement. Within Yugoslavia's borders were ethnic groups of different religions who had mistrusted one another for centuries—Serbs, Bosnians, Albanians, Croats, Montenegrins, and Macedonians. War began in the summer of 1990 when **Slovenia and Croatia declared their independence from Yugoslavia**. In the course of the war the Serbs followed a policy of "**ethnic cleansing**," eliminating thousands by killing and forcibly removing Muslims from Serbia. The Serbs' leader, **Slobodan Milosevic**, was tried for war crimes at an international criminal tribunal established by the United Nations. The **Dayton Accord** (1995) followed NATO bombing strikes against Serbian targets. As a result of the agreement, Bosnia gained its independence and NATO troops remained in the Balkans into the twenty-first century.

Haiti, meanwhile, continued to experience the chaos that had been customary there for decades, and American and French troops went to the island republic in 2004 to reestablish order. Also in the early 2000s the United Nations tried to bring peace to **Sudan**, a former British possession that had experienced decades of war.

DECOLONIZATION

As described in the previous chapter, in the early 1950s many Vietnamese were eager to kick the French colonists out of their country. Anticolonial sentiment such as this was widespread in the decades following the Second World War. Many countries that had entered the modern world because of European influence and direction now wanted to assert their independence from Europeans. In 1956—the year of Sputnik, Khrushchev's secret speech, and the uprisings in Hungary and Poland (see the previous chapter)—Egypt's leader **Gamal Abdal Nasser** (1918–1970) declared his country's complete control of the **Suez Canal**. This threatened English and French interests, especially their access to oil in the Middle East. A war between Israel and Egypt in the same year gave England and France a pretext for sending troops into the canal zone. But the United States and the Soviet Union refused to recognize the legitimacy of that move, and the canal went back into Egyptian control. Elsewhere in North Africa, **Algerians** fought for their independence from France, which they gained in 1962 after a bloody war.

By 1970 most of Africa's nations were independent: **Nigeria** and **Kenya**, for example, gained their independence from England in 1960 and 1963, respectively. More than a decade before, in 1947, Britain kept the promise it made before the Second World War to let go of **India**, long its most important colony. On the eve of the twenty-first century, Britain said good-bye to **Hong Kong**, another important colony, which is now under Chinese rule. The **Falklands War** (1982) pitted Britain against Argentina and showed that the United Kingdom would still fight for territory far beyond its shores—in this case, small islands off the east coast of South America.

But by the late twentieth century the days of colonialism were long over. In the early twenty-first century many questioned whether the United States was an imperial power. But if it was, its influence was symbolized more by fast food, rock music, and business interests than by weapons, although U.S. troops were stationed around the world—in Germany, Korea, Japan, Saudi Arabia, and many other countries.

SOCIAL AND POLITICAL TRENDS

Though **Portugal** and **Spain** remained dictatorships for many years after the Second World War, the general story in Western civilization was ever-increasing freedoms. Freedom of religion was the norm as was, increasingly, freedom *from* religion.

As more and more young people attended colleges and universities, students became more influential. In the 1960s and early 1970s **student demonstrations** contributed to the U.S. troop withdrawal from Vietnam; and in 1971 an amendment to the U.S. Constitution gave the right to vote to eighteen-year-olds. Student demonstrations in France in 1968 nearly toppled the government of **Charles de Gaulle** (1890–1970), leader of the **Free French** during the Second World War. One French protest poster depicted de Gaulle with his hands over a young person's mouth saying, "Sois jeune et tais toi" ("Be young and be quiet").

Increasingly, women left behind traditional roles and took on careers, and many children spent much of their early years in day-care centers. Marriage itself became less common as couples decided to live together without the formality of a ceremony and without the explicit blessing of churches or governments. Birth rates throughout western Europe plummeted. In 2003 the population of Italy could not replace itself. Like other places in western Europe, it depended on immigrants to do much of its poorly paid labor.

With the advent of **rock-and-roll** music and widespread **television** viewing in the 1950s, youth culture—especially in the United States—came to dominate popular culture. Young people had their own music, their own manner of dress, and their own ways of speaking. Young intellectuals were influenced by the **existentialist** writings of **Albert Camus** (1913–1960) and **Jean-Paul Sartre** (1905–1980). Existentialism is difficult to define, but it stresses the individual's responsibility to make life meaningful for him or herself, even in the face of life's apparent absurdity. In time, existentialism would give way to another difficult-to-define outlook called **postmodernism**, which emphasizes suspicion toward all claims to truth and authority. For instance, a postmodernist might be reluctant to say that Shakespeare is better literature than comic strips, which leaves open the question why anyone should bother paying attention to writers posing as postmodernist authorities.

Young people also rallied to the cause of environmental protection. *Silent Spring* (1962) by **Rachel Carson** (1907–1964) is credited with launching the global environmental movement. Throughout western Europe **Green parties** formed to promote environmental protection. Often by allying themselves with other left-wing parties, the Greens were able to influence government. An accident at a nuclear plant at **Chernobyl** in Ukraine in 1986 and the fear among many of the world's scientists that industrial emissions were causing **global warming**, which could wreak havoc on the world's ecosystems, spurred many to become more conscious of the environment.

Many members of the Green parties could be included in the **New Left** that emerged in the 1950s and 1960s. While holding to socialist and, sometimes, Marxist doctrines, the New Left rejected the authoritarianism of the Soviet Union, calling instead for socialist reform within the existing democratic systems in place. Also among the New Left were feminists who wished to reform society. In *The Second Sex* (1949) the French feminist **Simone de Beauvoir** (1908–1986) argued that womanhood was largely a construction of a male-dominated culture. "One is not born a woman," she wrote, "one becomes one."

In the 1960s change came as well to one of Europe's conservative institutions, the Roman Catholic Church. The **Second Vatican Council** significantly altered some Catholic forms and beliefs. The council permitted Mass to be said in local languages rather than in Latin, as the custom had been for centuries. It also acknowledged that sexual relations within marriage were not only for procreation, and it recognized that parents might have good reasons to limit the number of children they have, though the church continued to be opposed to artificial **birth control**. Some traditions held firm, however: only men could be priests, and priests were still required to remain celibate.

Also beginning in the 1960s mass **immigration** to European countries from former colonies was altering western Europe's ethnic and religious makeup. Fueled by immigration from North Africa, France's Muslim population grew dramatically. In 2000, more Muslims went to mosques each week in France than French men and women attended churches.

Politically, the western countries began to pull closer together. In 1957, as a result of the **Treaty of Rome**, the **European Economic Community** (EEC), also called the **Common Market**, was formed. The western nations in the market eliminated tariffs on goods from other member states.

The EEC grew over time. In 1982 the former dictatorships of Spain and Portugal joined it. In 1991 the **Treaty of Maastricht** called for a common currency to be used throughout western Europe. By 2001 most of western Europe had adopted the new currency, called the **euro**.

Called the **European Union (EU)** since 1993, many of the less prosperous eastern European nations, along with Turkey, wanted to join the community of nations. The EU would set conditions for membership. In the early twentieth century, for example, Turkey was required to abolish the death penalty as a condition for membership. Some western Europeans worried about mass immigration from poorer eastern European countries.

By 2005 it seemed obvious that the large U.S. troop presence that had marked the German landscape since the end of the Second World War would disappear. Its purpose had been to prevent Soviet aggression. Facing a very different threat from terrorists elsewhere in the world, the United States could take its troops out of Europe. Some Americans feared that Germany would again build a large military.

CONCLUSION

Western civilization in the early twenty-first century was obviously a fundamentally different milieu from what it had been during the period discussed at the beginning of this text.

Messages that would have taken months to deliver in 1500 could be delivered in a few seconds by email. In 1648 most of the nations that compose Western civilization in 2000 did not exist, partly because the concept of a nation did not yet exist. In 1648 the majority of people shared a basic view of the world: God controlled all things. In the early twenty-first century, Western people could choose from a bewildering array of philosophies, theologies, and political points of view.

In 1648 people in western Europe did not have much time for entertainment. In the early twenty-first century some Europeans would have up to six weeks of paid vacation each year. Teachers and college professors were paid twelve-month salaries for eight months of work. The average American watched more television than anyone else in Western civilization—in 2000, about four hours a day—but entertainment and American popular culture pervaded societies across the globe.

At the beginning of the twenty-first century, western Europe was not a serious military power, although the United States alone accounted for half of the world's spending on defense. But the ideas born in Western civilization were the dominant ideas around the world. Cuba, China, and Vietnam were communist countries, and communism was born in Western civilization. Around the world everyone used the language of democracy, even if they had no real interest in it—and democratic language was born in Western civilization. Television, automobiles, computers, and radios were born in Western civilization. People from around the world went to universities in Western countries because there were considered the best in the world.

In the early twenty-first century, many believed that Western civilization was in decline, that some other power or collection of powers would overtake it within a few decades. The future cannot be known. But what could be said with certainty at the beginning of the third millennium was that Western civilization had been the most influential civilization the world had ever seen.

PRACTICE TEST 1

CLEP Western Civilization II

Also available at the REA Study Center (*www.rea.com/studycenter*)

This practice test is also offered online at the REA Study Center. Since all CLEP exams are computer-based, we recommend that you take the online version of the test to simulate test-day conditions and to receive these added benefits:

- **Timed testing conditions** – helps you gauge how much time you can spend on each question
- **Automatic scoring** – find out how you did on the test, instantly
- **On-screen detailed explanations of answers** – gives you the correct answer and explains why the other answer choices are wrong
- **Diagnostic score reports** – pinpoint where you're strongest and where you need to focus your study

PRACTICE TEST 1

CLEP Western Civilization II

(Answer sheets appear in the back of the book.)

TIME: 90 Minutes
120 Questions

DIRECTIONS: Each of the questions or incomplete statements below is followed by five possible answers or completions. Select the best choice in each case and fill in the corresponding oval on the answer sheet.

1. Who among the following invented a calculating machine?

   (A) Pascal
   (B) Descartes
   (C) Leibniz
   (D) Zwingli
   (E) Leonardo da Vinci

2. Which of the following monarchs did NOT gain the approval of prominent French *philosophes*?

   (A) Louis XIV
   (B) Joseph II
   (C) Frederick the Great
   (D) Catherine the Great
   (E) William III of Orange

3. Who among the following is most associated with early modern dissection of human cadavers?

   (A) Paracelsus
   (B) Vesalius
   (C) Brahe
   (D) Kepler
   (E) Harvey

4. Each of the following terms is directly related to Napoleon Bonaparte's biography EXCEPT

   (A) Elba
   (B) King of Italy
   (C) Continental System
   (D) "first among equals"
   (E) Berlin Decrees

5. The belief that monarchs rule as agents of God is referred to as the concept of

   (A) constitutional monarchy
   (B) anarchy
   (C) laissez-faire
   (D) mercantilism
   (E) divine right

6. After the English Civil War, Oliver Cromwell

   (A) was elected president
   (B) was declared England's new monarch
   (C) rejected politics and returned to his farm
   (D) invaded France
   (E) presided over a military dictatorship in England

7. Nobles of the robe were

   (A) wealthy Frenchmen who had purchased their nobility
   (B) wealthy Frenchmen who were nobles because of their family trees
   (C) mostly poor Frenchmen who remained nobles because they kept the king's favor
   (D) Englishmen who held seats in the House of Lords
   (E) Englishmen who served as the monarch's ministers

8. "We [are] determined to save succeeding generations from the scourge of war, which twice in our lifetime has brought untold sorrow to man kind…" This statement comes from which of the following texts?

 (A) Charter of the United Nations
 (B) National Assembly's "Declaration of the Rights of Man and Citizen"
 (C) U.S. Constitution
 (D) Edmund Burke's *Reflections on the Revolution in France*
 (E) Bishop Bossuet's *Politics Drawn from the Very Words of Holy Scripture*

9. "To emancipate woman is to refuse to confine her to the relations she bears to man, not to deny them to her; let her have her independent existence and she will continue none the less to exist for him also." Who wrote these lines?

 (A) Catherine Booth
 (B) Florence Nightingale
 (C) Simone de Beauvoir
 (D) Mary of Guise
 (E) Hannah Arendt

10. "A dream, then, is a psychosis, with all the absurdities, delusions, and illusions of a psychosis." Who wrote these words?

 (A) Henry Mayhew
 (B) Sigmund Freud
 (C) Percy Bysshe Shelley
 (D) John Stuart Mill
 (E) Rudyard Kipling

11. "After [March 31,1920] the total number of effectives in the Army of the States constituting Germany must not exceed one hundred thousand men, including officers and establishment of depots." These words appeared in what document?

 (A) Maastricht Treaty
 (B) Treaty of Rome
 (C) Paris Peace Treaty
 (D) Treaty of Ryswick
 (E) Versailles Treaty

12. The French writer who criticized the French king for waging wars against its neighbors was

    (A) Bossuet
    (B) Fenelon
    (C) Chateaubriand
    (D) Sartre
    (E) Camus

13. All the following are causes of the Crimean War EXCEPT

    (A) U.S. interests in the Black Sea
    (B) French oversight of Christian shrines in the Middle East
    (C) Russian occupation of parts of Romania
    (D) the growing weakness of the Ottoman Empire
    (E) British and French interests in the eastern Mediterranean

14. The philosopher John Locke is best known for writing that all people possess rights to

    (A) "liberty, equality, fraternity"
    (B) "life, liberty, and the pursuit of happiness"
    (C) "life, liberty, and property"
    (D) "peace, order, and good government"
    (E) "a free public education"

15. The period following the republic in England is known as the

    (A) Troubles
    (B) Reign of Terror
    (C) Age of Anxiety
    (D) Restoration
    (E) Renaissance

16. Which of the following statements is most true of Louis XIV?

    (A) He moved France toward constitutional monarchy.
    (B) He substantially increased French territory.
    (C) He increased the hunting rights of peasants.
    (D) He lost control of the reforms that led to revolution.
    (E) He brought peace between Catholics and Huguenots.

17. Which of the following countries least benefited economically from the persecution of the Huguenots?

    (A) England
    (B) Holland
    (C) Prussia
    (D) France
    (E) Britain's American colonies

18.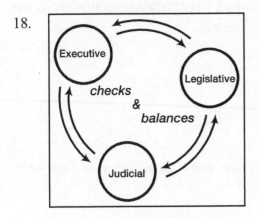

    The American founders who argued for a system of checks and balances in government, as illustrated above, were most indebted to whom among the following?

    (A) Machiavelli
    (B) Monteverdi
    (C) Michelet
    (D) Mendel
    (E) Montesquieu

19. When Catherine the Great of Russia heard that Diderot faced trouble because of his writings, she

    (A) invited him to Russia
    (B) employed Russia's police to help track him down
    (C) made his writings illegal in Russia
    (D) banned his writings from Russia's public schools
    (E) compared him unfavorably to Russia's best philosophers

20. Which of the following cities was called the "Athens of the North"?

    (A) Dublin
    (B) Frankfurt
    (C) Copenhagen
    (D) Amsterdam
    (E) Edinburgh

21. Generally speaking, leaders of France's Enlightenment most admired the political system of which of the following?

    (A) England
    (B) Sweden
    (C) Austria
    (D) Prussia
    (E) Russia

22. The "Declaration of the Rights of Man and Citizen" stemmed from what movement?

    (A) English Revolution
    (B) American Revolution
    (C) Russian Revolution
    (D) Greek Revolution
    (E) French Revolution

23. The map of Africa below illustrates the consequences of which of the following?

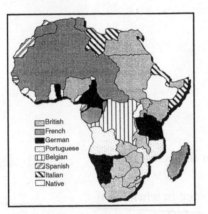

British
French
German
Portuguese
Belgian
Spanish
Italian
Native

(A) socialism
(B) anarchism
(C) industrialism
(D) imperialism
(E) liberalism

24. Guerrilla warfare, as modern people think of it, first emerged in what country?

(A) Ireland
(B) Russia
(C) Spain
(D) France
(E) Netherlands

25. The British writer of the late eighteenth and early nineteenth centuries, Thomas Malthus,

(A) theorized that Europe was heading toward overpopulation
(B) wrote that, eventually, all Europe would become one nation
(C) was a prominent member of the Fabian Society
(D) urged Britain to fight on the side of the Confederacy during the American Civil War
(E) was one of Britain's first prominent factory owners

26. The author of *The Interpretation of Dreams* was

    (A) Friedrich Nietzsche
    (B) Sigmund Freud
    (C) Carl Jung
    (D) Abraham Maslow
    (E) Carl Rogers

27. The year 1848 is remembered as

    (A) a year of unusual peace
    (B) the year of Britain's first major industrial reforms
    (C) a year of revolutionary fervor
    (D) the year Germany defeated France in a brief war
    (E) the year Napoleon was finally defeated and sent into exile

28. In the late nineteenth and early twentieth centuries, heads of state in the United States, Italy, France, and Austria were assassinated by

    (A) anarchists
    (B) Communists
    (C) monarchists
    (D) Social Darwinists
    (E) liberal reformers

29. In 1914 Austria-Hungary

    (A) was at war with the Ottoman Empire
    (B) annexed northern Italy
    (C) agreed to allow its population of Serbs and their land to become part of Serbia
    (A) was absorbed by Nazi forces
    (E) was Germany's one strong ally

30.

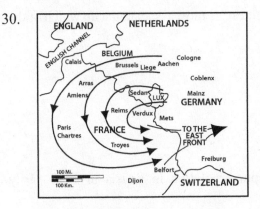

The map above depicts a strategy put into effect at the beginning of which war?

(A) War of 1812
(B) First World War
(C) Franco-Prussian War
(D) Seven Years' War
(E) Crimean War

31.   Wilfred Owen's poem *"Dulce et Decorum Est"*

(A) describes some of the horrors of the First World War
(B) is one of Britain's best-known nationalist works
(C) was used by the British government to encourage enlistment into the military
(D) suggested that British women should be given the vote
(E) played a major role in encouraging British economic reform

32.   The agreement that ended conflict between Germany and Russia in 1918 was the

(A) Paris Peace Treaty
(B) Versailles Treaty
(C) Brest-Litovsk Treaty
(D) Berlin Conference
(E) Munich Conference

33. The idea of the "survival of the fittest" is most associated with which of the following?

    (A) communism
    (B) *laissez-faire*
    (C) mercantilism
    (D) social Darwinism
    (E) anarchism

34. Vladimir Lenin was able to spur revolution in Russia in 1917 partly because

    (A) he had been in hiding in St. Petersburg for several years
    (B) British forces brought him to Russia via the Arctic
    (C) he was Tsar Nicholas II's close associate
    (D) the Austrians helped him to escape to Russia from France
    (E) the Germans sent him to Russia on a train from Switzerland

35. The theory of the "divine right" of kings is elaborated in which of the following?

    (A) *Politics Drawn from the Very Words of Scripture*
    (B) *Leviathan*
    (C) *Essay Concerning Human Understanding*
    (D) *Wealth of Nations*
    (E) *Decline and Fall of the Roman Empire*

36. Which of the following peoples lived in a republic in the seventeenth century?

    (A) Dutch
    (B) French
    (C) Spaniards
    (D) Portuguese
    (E) Prussians

37.

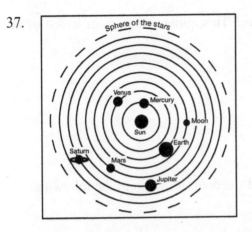

In this depiction of the universe, the sun is placed at the center of the universe. Which of the following was the first to discover this fact about the universe?

(A) Galileo
(B) Newton
(C) Brahe
(D) Copernicus
(E) Kepler

38. The inductive method of scientific reasoning is most associated with which of the following?

(A) Descartes
(B) Pascal
(C) Bacon
(D) Newton
(E) Locke

39. Which of the following ended the Thirty Years' War?

(A) Treaty of Versailles
(B) Warsaw Pact
(C) Paris Peace Treaty
(D) Edict of Nantes
(E) Treaty of Westphalia

40. "During the time men live without a common power to keep them all in awe, they are in that condition which is called *war;* and such a war, as is

of every man, against every man." This quote comes from which of the following?

(A) Hobbes
(B) Locke
(C) Mill
(D) Montaigne
(E) Erasmus

41. The Edict of Nantes gave limited freedoms to which of the following?

(A) Puritans
(B) Lutherans
(C) Huguenots
(D) *sans-culottes*
(E) *politiques*

42. The view that each human being has an inherent right to life, liberty, and property is associated with which of the following?

(A) Cromwell
(B) Locke
(C) James I
(D) William III of Orange
(E) Richelieu

43. *"Cogito ergo sum."* That famous statement is associated with what kind of thought processes?

(A) deductive reasoning
(B) dialectical reasoning
(C) calculus
(D) theory of gravity
(E) inductive reasoning

44.   Galileo wrote, "Philosophy is written in this grand book." To which of the
      following was he referring?

      (A) Copernicus's *Revolutions of the Heavenly Spheres*
      (B) the New World
      (C) the universe
      (D) his own book *The Starry Messenger*
      (E) Pascal's *Pensées*

45.   Who among the following revoked the Edict of Nantes?

      (A) James I
      (B) Henry of Navarre
      (C) Charles II
      (D) Louis XIV
      (E) William III

46.   The year 1688 is notable for which of the following events?

      (A) England's Glorious Revolution
      (B) execution of Charles I
      (C) establishment of colonies in North America by Puritans
      (D) Ireland's independence from England
      (E) Publication of Thomas Hobbes' political work *Leviathan*

47.   England's civil war pitted

      (A) Calvinists against Lutherans
      (B) Cavaliers against Roundheads
      (C) Huguenots against *politiques*
      (D) English against French
      (E) American colonists against the British monarchy

48.   Which of the following nations was the first to have a bill of rights?

      (A) United States
      (B) France
      (C) Italy
      (D) Belgium
      (E) England

49.

This image symbolizes which of the following monarchs?

(A) Charles I
(B) Cromwell
(C) Frederick the Great
(D) Louis XIV
(E) Bossuet

50. Who among the following is recognized as an important mathematician, philosopher, and theologian?

(A) Pascal
(B) Galileo
(C) Locke
(D) Oliver Cromwell
(E) Marie Curie

51. Political revolution was experienced in each of the following countries during the nineteenth century EXCEPT

(A) Spain
(B) Italy
(C) Greece
(D) Belgium
(E) Britain

52. "The source of all sovereignty resides essentially in the nation." This quote comes from which of the following texts?

    (A) "Declaration of the Rights of Man and Citizen"
    (B) English Bill of Rights
    (C) *The Social Contract*
    (D) U.S. Constitution
    (E) *The Prince*

53. Olympia de Gouges was

    (A) Louis XIV's key supervisor at Versailles
    (B) the first woman accepted into the First Estate
    (C) a French revolutionary and early feminist
    (D) an antirevolutionary defender of the church
    (E) a prominent Huguenot refugee to England

54. Who argued that space and time are not absolute but relative to the position of the observer?

    (A) Freud
    (B) Pasteur
    (C) Einstein
    (D) Koch
    (E) Curie

55. Who among the following is remembered as an "enlightened despot"?

    (A) William III of Orange
    (B) Peter the Great
    (C) Joseph II
    (D) Louis XVI
    (E) George III

56. All the countries below experienced *blitzkrieg* EXCEPT

    (A) Sweden
    (B) Poland
    (C) Belgium
    (D) France
    (E) Netherlands

57. The Enlightenment belief that after God created the world and natural laws he stepped back and let the universe run on its own is called

   (A) deism
   (B) Arminianism
   (C) Anabaptism
   (D) Quakerism
   (E) positivism

58. The editor of the first modern encyclopedia was

   (A) Rousseau
   (B) Descartes
   (C) Voltaire
   (D) Diderot
   (E) Condorcet

59. Cesare Beccaria's best-known work advocates which of the following?

   (A) Governments should not control economies.
   (B) The universe is like a grand watch created by a "Great Watchmaker."
   (C) English Catholics should be able to hold seats in parliament.
   (D) Prisons should be places of reform as well as of correction.
   (E) Monarchs should share power with elected officials.

60. The publication *What is the Third Estate?* appealed most to France's

   (A) bishops
   (B) middle classes
   (C) king
   (D) high-ranking military officers
   (E) impoverished peasants

61. In Bolshevik terms, the "vanguard" referred to

   (A) machine gunners in the Russian civil war
   (B) small farms
   (C) communist leaders
   (D) capitalists
   (E) pacifists

62. Which of the following institutions is most closely related to the Reign of Terror?

    (A) National Assembly
    (B) National Convention
    (C) Girondins
    (D) Directory
    (E) Committee of Public Safety

63. French clergy, nobles, and others opposed to the French Revolution who fled France were called which of the following?

    (A) Émigrés
    (B) Refugees
    (C) Bourgeois
    (D) *Sans-culottes*
    (E) Jacobins

64. Napoleon's army faced devastation from military action and winter cold in which of the following countries?

    (A) Belgium
    (B) Britain
    (C) Prussia
    (D) Russia
    (E) Spain

65. Napoleon's economic warfare led to an undeclared war at sea between France and which of the following nations?

    (A) Belgium
    (B) United States
    (C) Prussia
    (D) Austria
    (E) Spain

66.

Political revolution broke out in each of the cities on the map above in which of the following years?

(A) 1688
(B) 1789
(C) 1848
(D) 1917
(E) 1989

67. Which of the following countries twice defeated invading armies partly by retreating and burning its own country's farmland?

(A) Finland
(B) Netherlands
(C) Prussia
(D) Denmark
(E) Russia

68. During the First World War, which of the major countries among the Allies was unable to provide its troops with adequate food and weaponry?

(A) Britain
(B) Australia
(C) Bulgaria
(D) Russia
(E) Ireland

69.   The provisional government of early 1917

(A) united Britain's political factions
(B) sought to establish a nonradical reformist government in Russia
(C) was based in Rome and called for Italy's occupation of Vienna
(D) was favored by the young Adolf Hitler
(E) brought independence to Ireland

70.   The Treaty of Brest-Litovsk

(A) led to significant losses of Russian territory
(B) led to significant gains of Russian territory
(C) led to the independence of Norway from Sweden
(D) led to U.S. involvement in the First World War
(E) was the result of Russia's defeat by Japan in 1905

71.   The New Economic Policy

(A) was accepted by all radical communists
(B) was championed by Leon Trotsky
(C) allowed Russian farmers to sell their produce at the market for a profit
(D) took all land out of the hands of individuals
(E) caused famine in the Ukraine

72.   Who among the following had significant influence over the household of Tsar Nicholas II?

(A) Joseph Stalin
(B) Kaiser Wilhehm II
(C) Voltaire
(D) Diderot
(E) Rasputin

73.   The dominant first leader of the Bolsheviks was which of the following?

(A) Karl Marx
(B) Vladimir Lenin
(C) Rasputin
(D) Joseph Stalin
(E) Nicholas II

74.

On the left is Adolf Hitler, on the right is Joseph Stalin. This cartoon was published in what year?

(A) 1917
(B) 1923
(C) 1930
(D) 1939
(E) 1945

75. Aside from the German and Austrian empires, what other large empire among the Central Powers ceased to exist after the First World War?

(A) British Empire
(B) Empire of Scandinavia
(C) Ottoman Empire
(D) U.S. empire in the Pacific
(E) Belgium's African empire

76. The two key Western powers in the Middle East following the First World War were

(A) Britain and Germany
(B) Britain and France
(C) France and Italy
(D) United States and France
(E) United States and Israel

77. Middle Eastern lands placed under the authority of Western countries were called

    (A) mandates
    (B) colonies
    (C) associates
    (D) dependencies
    (E) dominions

78. Which of the following was an important trade and communication link in the Middle East throughout the twentieth century?

    (A) Berlin to Baghdad Railway
    (B) Cape to Cairo Railway
    (C) Panama Canal
    (D) Suez Canal
    (E) Siberian Railroad

79. Sixteenth century "privateers" were

    (A) advocates of free trade between nations
    (B) pirates who plundered with their government's implicit or explicit approval
    (C) laborers employed with the British East India Company
    (D) free-lance contributors to daily newspapers
    (E) intellectuals who advocated separation of church and state

80. Joseph Stalin's five-year plans

    (A) eliminated the monarchy in Russia
    (B) allowed farmers to sell their produce for a profit
    (C) led to the rapid industrialization of Russia
    (D) sparked the Russian Civil War
    (E) were a complete failure

81. The main result of the United States, Britain, Japan, Czechoslovakia, and other countries sending troops into Russia during its civil war was

    (A) the defeat of communist revolution in Russia
    (B) the end of the First World War
    (C) the beginning of the Second World War
    (D) a propaganda victory for the communist "Red" Russians
    (E) the formation of the League of Nations

82. As a result of the "Beer Hall Putsch," Adolf Hitler

    (A) was named leader of the Nazi Party
    (B) sent troops into the Rhineland
    (C) was imprisoned for several months
    (D) formed an alliance with Italy
    (E) was named chancellor of Germany

83.

This photograph illustrates *Anschluss*, which refers to

    (A) Germany's occupation of Austria in 1938
    (B) a nonaggression agreement between Russia and Germany
    (C) Italy's invasion of Ethiopia in 1935
    (D) the German conscription laws instituted in 1933
    (E) a conversation between Hitler and the British prime minister Neville Chamberlain in Munich in 1938

84. The Molotov-Ribbentrop Pact concerned

    (A) Germany's occupation of Austria in 1938
    (B) a nonaggression agreement between Russia and Germany
    (C) Italy's invasion of Ethiopia in 1935
    (D) the German conscription laws instituted in 1933
    (E) a conversation between Hitler and the British prime minister Neville Chamberlain in Munich in 1938

85. Near the end of the First World War, who called for "peace without victory"?

    (A) Woodrow Wilson
    (B) Georges Clemenceau
    (C) David Lloyd George
    (D) Kaiser Wilhehm II
    (E) Vladimir Lenin

86. Which powerful country did NOT join the League of Nations?

    (A) France
    (B) Germany
    (C) Britain
    (D) Japan
    (E) United States

87. As a result of the Lateran Pact

    (A) Mussolini gained the formal recognition of the Catholic Church
    (B) the Fascists closed most of Italy's schools
    (C) Italy formed an alliance with Germany and Japan
    (D) Germany agreed to limit its army to 100,000 men
    (E) France promised to defend Poland if Germany attacked it

88. After his conference with Hitler at Munich in 1938, the British prime minister Neville Chamberlain

    (A) called on Parliament to prepare for war
    (B) agreed to allow Hitler to militarize the Rhineland
    (C) promised war if Hitler's troops occupied Austria
    (D) said that he believed war was not on the horizon
    (E) agreed to allow Hitler's troops to occupy Poland

89. The concept of separation of church and state was at the heart of which of the following?

    (A) Treaty of Versailles
    (B) Treaty of Westphalia
    (C) Proclamation of 1763
    (D) Torquemada
    (E) Council of Trent

90. The *philosophes* were

    (A) members of the anti-Nazi French resistance
    (B) members of the English Parliament opposed to James I
    (C) French writers and intellectuals who promoted political reforms
    (D) influential French university professors
    (E) Huguenots exiled in England

91. John Locke is to the idea of individual rights what Bossuet is to the idea of

    (A) divine right
    (B) dream analysis
    (C) socialism
    (D) anarchism
    (E) communism

92. The most opulent monarch's household in seventeenth-century Europe was at

    (A) London
    (B) Versailles
    (C) St. Petersburg
    (D) Berlin
    (E) Madrid

93. Charles Darwin benefited from the earlier work on geology of

    (A) Herbert Spencer
    (B) Friedrich Nietzsche
    (C) Albert Camus
    (D) Charles Lyell
    (E) Gottlieb Daimler

94. The Vichy Regime refers to

    (A) the rule of Louis XIV
    (B) the Nazi puppet state in southern France
    (C) France's rule in Vietnam
    (D) an international organization formed after the First World War
    (E) an international organization formed after the Second World War

95.   The Glorious Revolution was glorious partly because it

(A) was bloodless
(B) eliminated Catholic political power in Germany
(C) led to a republic in England
(D) placed Britain in control of India
(E) led to the defeat of Napoleon

96.   Postmodernism emphasizes all the following EXCEPT

(A) the belief that Western civilization is not superior to other cultures
(B) ultimate truths cannot be known by human beings
(C) historical education should emphasize the works of key leaders
(D) there is no real way to judge between "good" and "bad" art
(E) most perceived differences between men and women are the
      result of social forces

97.   The undeclared war between the United States and France, 1798–1800,
      was fought mostly in

(A) Europe
(B) Canada
(C) Asia
(D) the West Indies
(E) the North Pacific

98.   The economic outlook that emphasized a nation hoarding gold and pro-
      moting exports was

(A) *laissez-faire*
(B) mercantilism
(C) utopianism
(D) communitarianism
(E) bimetallism

99. This anti-Semitic photograph, which depicts a protest against the Versailles Treaty, was taken in which of the following periods?

Source: United States Holocaust Memorial Museum

(A) 1880–1900
(B) 1905–1915
(C) 1925–1939
(D) 1940–1945
(E) 1950–1960

100. Until the 1990s Sarajevo was best known as

(A) the birthplace of Hitler
(B) the site of Franz Ferdinand's assassination
(C) the site of the Battle of Waterloo
(D) the place of German surrender in 1918
(E) a holiday resort for monarchs

101. The region coveted by France and Germany in the nineteenth and early twentieth centuries was

(A) Alsace-Lorraine
(B) Belgium
(C) English Channel
(D) Haiti
(E) Morocco

102. In the late nineteenth century, what replaced the pulpit as the primary source of information about the world?

(A) television
(B) radio
(C) newspapers
(D) public speeches
(E) telephones

103. Suffragettes of the nineteenth and early twentieth century primarily wanted

(A) an end to the consumption of alcohol
(B) all shops closed on Sundays
(C) the elimination of political parties
(D) an end to war
(E) the right to vote for women

104. In the late twentieth century,

(A) Europeans migrated in large numbers to the United States
(B) Europeans migrated in large numbers to former colonies
(C) residents in former colonies migrated in large numbers to Europe
(D) population stability led to little overall migration
(E) the earlier trend of urbanization began to reverse

105. At some point in the late nineteenth and early twentieth centuries, Germany was allied with all the following EXCEPT

(A) the Ottoman Empire
(B) Russia
(C) France
(D) Italy
(E) Austria

106. The first European nation to be defeated by an African nation in modern times was which of the following?

(A) Russia
(B) Spain
(C) Italy
(D) Belgium
(E) Portugal

107. Which nation most assisted the American colonies in their war of independence against Britain?

(A) France
(B) Spain
(C) Canada
(D) Mexico
(E) Netherlands

108. Christina of Sweden

(A) was an absolute monarch opposed to reform
(B) was a patron of intellectuals, artists, and scientists
(C) took the throne of England in 1688
(D) paid mercenary armies to defeat Napoleon
(E) attacked Catholicism more ferociously than any other European monarch

109. The first European to write out a theory of gravity was

(A) Newton
(B) Galileo
(C) Kepler
(D) Vesalius
(E) Pascal

110. Gibbon's *Decline and Fall of the Roman Empire*

(A) was the first work of history published since ancient times
(B) explained history without reference to the will of God
(C) combined historical study and theological reflection
(D) was not published until long after the author's death
(E) was a forgery of a document written in the eighth century

111. Which of the following is most associated with the first Industrial Revolution?

(A) gold
(B) oil
(C) sugar
(D) tea
(E) cotton

112. France's National Assembly originated in a declaration

    (A) from Louis XVI
    (B) from the Third Estate
    (C) from the Paris Commune
    (D) in the Civil Constitution of the Clergy
    (E) of the National Convention

113. In the early twentieth century, high school education in the industrialized countries of the Western world emphasized

    (A) subjects related to farming
    (B) Latin, mathematics, history, and science
    (C) business and economics
    (D) the Bible and public speaking
    (E) socialism and current events

114. The North Atlantic Treaty Organization was founded after the Second World War to

    (A) end famine in Africa
    (B) rebuild Europe
    (C) promote decolonization
    (D) provide a common defense against the Soviets
    (E) defeat North Korean communists

115. The modern belief that there is nothing inherently right or wrong is referred to as

    (A) deism
    (B) existentialism
    (C) relativism
    (D) cubism
    (E) absolutism

116. In 1968, what almost toppled the government of France?

    (A) war in Algeria
    (B) war in Vietnam
    (C) war in the Ivory Coast
    (D) student demonstrations
    (E) riot following a Jimi Hendrix concert

117. In the late twentieth century, what did Basques, Quebecers, and Chechnyans have in common?

    (A) Their countries hosted the Olympics.
    (B) They were at war with more powerful states.
    (C) They desired to create independent nations.
    (D) They wished to join more powerful nations.
    (E) Their governments joined NATO.

118. Following the First World War, dress among Westerners became increasingly

    (A) casual
    (B) formal
    (C) monotone
    (D) homemade
    (E) dirty

119. Which response BEST describes the great dictatorships of the twentieth century?

    (A) Despite themselves, they always had to accommodate a free press.
    (B) They never officially outlawed religion.
    (C) They were never as repressive as Louis XIV's France.
    (D) They were the most repressive regimes in history.
    (E) They eliminated radio and television.

120. Which of the terms below best describes Oliver Cromwell?

    (A) Lutheran
    (B) Anglican
    (C) Catholic
    (D) Anabaptist
    (E) Puritan

PRACTICE TEST 1

Answer Key

1.	(A)	31.	(A)	61.	(C)	91.	(A)
2.	(A)	32.	(C)	62.	(E)	92.	(B)
3.	(B)	33.	(D)	63.	(A)	93.	(D)
4.	(D)	34.	(E)	64.	(D)	94.	(B)
5.	(E)	35.	(A)	65.	(B)	95.	(A)
6.	(E)	36.	(A)	66.	(C)	96.	(C)
7.	(A)	37.	(D)	67.	(E)	97.	(D)
8.	(A)	38.	(C)	68.	(D)	98.	(B)
9.	(C)	39.	(E)	69.	(B)	99.	(C)
10.	(B)	40.	(A)	70.	(A)	100.	(B)
11.	(E)	41.	(C)	71.	(C)	101.	(A)
12.	(B)	42.	(B)	72.	(E)	102.	(C)
13.	(A)	43.	(A)	73.	(B)	103.	(E)
14.	(C)	44.	(C)	74.	(D)	104.	(C)
15.	(D)	45.	(D)	75.	(C)	105.	(C)
16.	(B)	46.	(A)	76.	(B)	106.	(C)
17.	(D)	47.	(B)	77.	(A)	107.	(A)
18.	(E)	48.	(E)	78.	(D)	108.	(B)
19.	(A)	49.	(D)	79.	(B)	109.	(A)
20.	(E)	50.	(A)	80.	(C)	110.	(B)
21.	(A)	51.	(E)	81.	(D)	111.	(E)
22.	(E)	52.	(A)	82.	(C)	112.	(B)
23.	(D)	53.	(C)	83.	(A)	113.	(B)
24.	(C)	54.	(C)	84.	(B)	114.	(D)
25.	(A)	55.	(C)	85.	(A)	115.	(C)
26.	(B)	56.	(A)	86.	(E)	116.	(D)
27.	(C)	57.	(A)	87.	(A)	117.	(C)
28.	(A)	58.	(D)	88.	(D)	118.	(A)
29.	(E)	59.	(D)	89.	(B)	119.	(D)
30.	(B)	60.	(B)	90.	(C)	120.	(E)

PRACTICE TEST 1

Detailed Explanations of Answers

1. **(A)**   Pascal invented a calculating machine thirty years before Leibniz. Pascal was a mathematician, theologian, and philosopher. Descartes was another mathematician and philosopher who, like Pascal, believed there were good philosophical reasons to believe in God. Descartes invented analytical geometry and promoted deductive reasoning in his *Discourse on Method* (1637). In addition to inventing a calculator after Pascal, Leibniz was a mathematician who appears to have discovered calculus (as did Isaac Newton, independent of Leibniz). Zwingli (D) was a Protestant reformer of the sixteenth century, and Leonardo da Vinci (E) was a Renaissance painter.

2. **(A)**   The repressiveness of Louis XIV's reign in France spurred some *philosophes* to advocate reform. The power of William III of Orange in England was checked by Parliament (E), and Joseph II (B), Frederick the Great (C), and Catherine the Great (D) were "enlightened despots" who put some reforms into effect with varying success.

3. **(B)**   Vesalius was an anatomist of the early Scientific Revolution. Paracelsus (A) is remembered for his observation that illness often comes from chemical imbalances in the body. Like Vesalius, Harvey (E) studied cadavers, but he is best remembered for his studies of the heart and blood circulation. Brahe (C) and Kepler (D) were astronomers.

4. **(D)**   Napoleon was not called the "first among equals," partly because he did not believe he had any equals. In Latin *primus inter pares* ("first among equals") refers to the pope. Napoleon was exiled to Elba (A) and later to St. Helena; he was declared King of Italy (B) as a result of conquests; his Continental System (C) was devised to choke England economically, as were his earlier Berlin Decrees (E), which prohibited his allies from importing British goods.

5. **(E)**   Several seventeenth-century monarchs claimed to rule by "divine right," that is, as a result of their selection by God. Even if a student does not immediately know the answer to this, the connection between the concepts of God and divinity provides a good clue. In a constitutional monarchy (A), the monarch's power is checked by another political body, usually a Parliament. Anarchists (B)

advocate the complete elimination of formal government. The terms *laissez-faire* (C) and mercantilism (D) refer to systems of economic thought.

6. **(E)** Cromwell acted essentially as a dictator. Following the English Civil War Cromwell tried to work with Parliament, but this did not prove to be workable. He dissolved Parliament and appointed eleven military governors to rule local regions of the country. He presided over these governors.

7. **(A)** Nobles in France's *ancien regime* (old regime) who gained their status by purchasing offices were called nobles of the robe. Those who had their status as a result of family heritage were called nobles of the sword (B). Some nobles of the sword were not really wealthy, but none could be called poor (C). Nobles of the robe and of the sword were French, not English (D and E).

8. **(A)** The United Nations was formed at the end of the Second World War and was designed to accomplish what the earlier League of Nations had failed to accomplish: to prevent another world war. The "Declaration of the Rights of Man and Citizen" (B) was the founding document of the French Revolution, and Burke's work (D) was a critique of that revolution. Bossuet's book (E) promoted the theory of "divine right." The U.S. Constitution is not explicitly interested in preventing future wars (C).

9. **(C)** Simone de Beauvoir was a post-Second World War feminist who wrote *The Second Sex.* Florence Nightingale (B) organized medical care for soldiers during the Crimean War. Catherine Booth (A), with her husband William, founded the Salvation Army in the mid-nineteenth century. Mary of Guise (D) was the mother of Mary Stuart, a sixteenth century queen of Scotland. Hannah Arendt (E) is a twentieth-century writer best known for her book *Eichmann in Jerusalem,* in which she recounts the trial in the early 1960s of a notorious Nazi criminal who had been living in Argentina.

10. **(B)** One of Freud's best-known books is *The Interpretation of Dreams.* Henry Mayhew (A) was a writer who described the lives of England's lower classes. Percy Bysshe Shelley (C) was a Romantic poet, John Stuart Mill (D) a political theorist who published *On Liberty,* and Rudyard Kipling (E) was a British writer in the late nineteenth and early twentieth century most remembered for his poem "The White Man's Burden."

11. **(E)** The Versailles Treaty limited post–First World War Germany in many ways. The Treaty of Ryswick (1697; D) concluded the War of the League of Augsburg between France on one side and Great Britain, the Netherlands, and Spain on the other. The Paris Peace Treaty of 1783 (C) ended the American

Revolution. The Treaty of Rome (B) established the European Economic Community in 1957, and the Treaty of Maastricht (A) led to the creation of the European Union in 1992.

12. **(B)** Fenelon was an admiring yet fierce critic of the king's warmongering. Bossuet (A) advocated "divine right," Chateaubriand (C) was a Romantic writer who opposed the anti-clericalism of the radical French Revolution, and Sartre (D) and Camus (E) were twentieth-century existentialist writers.

13. **(A)** In the 1840s the United States was busy settling its own West. It had no compelling interests in the Black Sea region. Supervision of Christian shrines (B), the Russian presence in Romania (C), the weakness of the Ottoman Empire (D), and British and French interests in the Mediterranean (E) were all causes of the Crimean War.

14. **(C)** Locke may have been in favor of all the choices given, but the phrase most associated with him is "life, liberty, and property." The phrase "life, liberty, and the pursuit of happiness" (B) appears in the U.S. Declaration of Independence; "liberty, equality, fraternity" (A) is a French slogan; and "peace, order, and good government" is Canadian (D). Public education (E) did not exist in the seventeenth century.

15. **(D)** Following the republican period associated with Cromwell's rule, the monarchy was restored in England. The Troubles (A) refer to violence between Irish nationalists and pro-British Irish in Ireland. The Renaissance (E) occurred in western Europe in the sixteenth century. The Age of Anxiety (C) is the term sometimes given to the twentieth century. The Reign of Terror (B) was experienced during the French Revolution.

16. **(B)** To answer this question correctly, students have to be careful. Answer (D) may be attractive, but it was Louis XVI, not Louis XIV who lost control of reforms. Through various wars, Louis XIV acquired imperial holdings in the Americas and in Asia. He did not increase the rights of the peasants (C); he actually revoked reforms that made life easier for Huguenots (French Protestants; E); and he was an absolute, not a constitutional, monarch (A).

17. **(D)** The Huguenots tended to be in the upper-middle class, and France's driving them away only hurt the country economically. Huguenots fled France and went to Prussia (C), the American colonies (E), England (A), and Holland (B).

18. **(E)** Montesquieu is best remembered for his writings on checks and balances and separation of political powers. Machiavelli (A) was a political

theorist of the Renaissance, Monteverdi (B) was a Baroque composer, Jules Michelet (C) was a nineteenth-century French historian, and Gregor Mendel (D) was a nineteenth-century theorist of heredity.

19. **(A)** Catherine the Great invited Diderot to Russia, partly to boost her own prestige, partly to benefit from Enlightenment learning. There were no public schools in Russia in the eighteenth century (D). Catherine was an "enlightened despot" and thus was generally in favor of some Enlightenment thought (C). No Russian philosophers of this period are considered prominent (E).

20. **(E)** Edinburgh, Scotland, was the center of the Scottish Enlightenment of the eighteenth century. Adam Smith and David Hume are associated with the movement.

21. **(A)** Of Europe's major powers, eighteenth-century England had the most liberal political system. The power of its monarch was checked by Parliament, and citizens had basic rights, such as trial by jury. The political system of the young United States was also admired by many *philosophes.*

22. **(E)** The "Declaration of the Rights of Man and Citizen" was a major early document of the French Revolution. The only other answer that might be tempting is (B), the American Revolution, which led to the Declaration of Independence.

23. **(D)** Between 1870 and 1914, European nations took imperial possession of all but a couple African nations. Indeed, most of the African nations we know today were created by Europeans. Nigeria, for example was given its name by an English journalist. Europeans did bring some industrialization to Africa (C), and there were some socialists (A) and liberals (E) among the colonizers, but (D) is by far the best answer.

24. **(C)** Napoleon sent forces into Portugal to prevent that country from trading with Britain. Going into and out of Portugal required movement through Spain. Spanish guerrillas cut Napoleon's communications and supply lines and launched hit-and-run raids on French troops.

25. **(A)** In his *Essay on the Principle of Population* (1798), Malthus argued that human population growth would outstrip growth in food production, thus leading to starvation and a reduced population. This was an early instance of an ongoing concern in the Western world—population growth and the ability of nature to meet the population's needs.

26. **(B)** Each of the five names listed is attached to a prominent psychologist, and Carl Jung was very interested in dreams, but *The Interpretation of Dreams* is one of Freud's best-known books. Carl Jung (C) looked to dreams for information about what he called "collective memory." He maintained that societies have memories just as individuals do.

27. **(C)** In that year there were revolutions and revolutionary movements in Austria, France, northern Italy, Prussia, and elsewhere. It was also the year of the publication of Karl Marx's *Communist Manifesto.* Germany defeated France in war in 1871 (D), and Britian's first major industrial reform came in 1833 (B). Napoleon was exiled for the second and last time in 1815 (E).

28. **(A)** Communists (B), liberals (E), monarchists (C), and Social Darwinists (D) all agitated for change in different places, but anarchists, though not widely influential, did assassinate a number of political leaders—among them, President McKinley in the United States.

29. **(E)** Austria-Hungary was Germany's one strong ally in the First World War. Austria and the Ottomans were allied with Germany (A). The Ottoman Empire was a weak power that went out of existence after the First World War. No parts of Italy were annexed by Austria in the early twentieth century (B), and one cause of the war was Austria's refusal to allow Serbs in its empire to join their land with Serbia's (C). The First World War preceded the rise of the Nazi Party by several years (D). In 1938 Austria was annexed by Germany. This was called the *Anschluss* ("joining").

30. **(B)** The goal of the Germany military in 1914 was to defeat France quickly and then to send its victorious troops to fight Russia in the east. The Schlieffen Plan, as this scheme was called, did not work, and the war in Western Europe was characterized by trench warfare.

31. **(A)** Owen's bleak, realistic poem describes some of the horrors of trench combat during the First World War. The poem is not nationalistic (B) because it does not promote or romanticize Britain's effort in the war. Nor could it have encouraged young men to volunteer to serve (C). Women's right to vote (D) and economic reform (E) are not mentioned in the poem.

32. **(C)** The Treaty of Brest-Litovsk ended conflict between Germany and Russia. The Paris Peace Treaty (A) ended the American Revolution, the Versailles Treaty (B) concerned agreements between the Allies and the Germans following the First World War, the Berlin Conference (D) involved

European powers dividing Africa into colonies, and the Munich Conference (E) preceded the Second World War.

33. **(D)**   The Social Darwinist Herbert Spencer is credited with coining this term. Some people might argue that *laissez-faire* economics has a "survival of the fittest" outlook (B), but the term does not originate with *laissez-faire*. Ideally, communism (A) and anarchism (E) lead to peace and community spirit. Mercantilism (C) refers to the economic systems of early modern France and Britain.

34. **(E)**   Hoping to promote instability in Russia, the Germans paid for Lenin's train ticket from exile outside Russia. The rest of the answers have no validity.

35. **(A)**   This book by Bossuet argued that the monarch was God's chosen person and, thus, his power was unquestionable. Locke's *Essay Concerning Human Understanding* (C) is concerned with psychology (though he did not use that term), and Thomas Hobbes's *Leviathan* (B) argues for a powerful ruler but, despite its frequent citations from the Bible, is a secular work, as is Gibbon's *The Decline and Fall of the Roman Empire* (E). Adam Smith's *The Wealth of Nations* (D) is a discussion of *laissez-faire* economic theory.

36. **(A)**   The Dutch established a republic in seventeenth-century Europe. Although England flirted with a republican form of government—that is, a government without a monarch—only briefly in the seventeenth century, the Dutch Republic prospered through the century. The French (B), Spaniards (C), Portuguese (D), and Prussians (E) all had monarchs.

37. **(D)**   Copernicus was the first person associated with the Scientific Revolution to question Ptolemy's astronomy. Galileo, Newton, Brahe, and Kepler were important astronomers/scientists of the Scientific Revolution, but Copernicus was the first to question the ancient astronomy of the Greeks.

38. **(C)**   Bacon called for the problem-solving method, which involved gathering information and deriving theories from the details of that information. In other words, the inductive method calls for movement from particular facts to general ideas. Descartes (A), on the other hand, said "I think, therefore I am" (*"Cogito ergo sum"*). He started with a general idea and derived particular facts from it, which is called the deductive method.

39. **(E)**   The Treaty of Westphalia is significant not only because it ended the Thirty Years' War but also because it signaled the secularization of European political life. The pope was not involved in the discussions leading to the treaty, though he wanted to be.

40. **(A)** Those are one of two best-known lines in Hobbes's *Leviathan*. The other well-known phrase refers to the lives of people in their natural state (that is, without government) as "nasty, brutish, and short." Like Hobbes, John Locke (B) was a seventeenth-century political theorist, but he was much less pessimistic than Hobbes, and unlike Hobbes, he called for representative government as opposed to a single strong ruler.

41. **(C)** The Edict of Nantes (1598) gave the Huguenots (French Protestants) limited freedoms, but Louis XIV revoked the edict in 1685. This led to a wave of Huguenot emigration which harmed France's economy, for many Huguenots were talented laborers, merchants, and nobles.

42. **(B)** Locke was an early advocate of individual political liberty. Richelieu (E) benefited from France's absolute monarchy, so he would not be interested in promoting the idea of personal rights. Neither would England's James I (C), who believed in his divine right to rule, nor Cromwell (A), who was essentially England's dictator following that country's civil war.

43. **(A)** Descartes' famous phrase in Latin means "I think, therefore I am." He started with a general idea—"I can think"—and derived particular facts from it ("I exist"), a process known as deductive reasoning. For information on inductive reasoning, see the answer to question 38.

44. **(C)** For most of the figures associated with the Scientific Revolution, there were two "books" one could read to learn about the world and God. One was the Bible, and the other was the natural world.

45. **(D)** If you know that the Edict of Nantes had to do with France, then you should be able to eliminate James I (A), Charles II (C), and William III (E), who were all English monarchs. Henry of Navarre (B), also known as Henry IV, published the Edict of Nantes. He himself had been a Protestant before converting to Catholicism before he took the throne, supposedly saying "Paris is worth a Mass."

46. **(A)** England's Glorious Revolution took place in 1688. With the exception of answer (D), all the possible answers took place in the seventeenth century. The year 1688 is a key date, however, because it marks the beginning of power sharing in England between the monarch and Parliament.

47. **(B)** Cavaliers fought for the king, Roundheads against the king. There were very few Lutherans (A) in England; Huguenots and *politiques* (C) were in France; England's American colonists (E) were essentially on their

own during England's civil war; and while the English and French (D) fought constantly, that was not a factor in the English Civil War.

48. **(E)** In many ways, the American Bill of Rights copies the English Bill of Rights, the first such document in the modern world. The "Declaration of Rights of Man and Citizen" also echoes some ideas in the English and American documents—not surprisingly, since French *philosophes* and reformers admired the system of rights that came out of the Glorious Revolution in England and the American Revolution.

49. **(D)** Louis XIV was the powerful Sun King who built an elaborate palace at Versailles and ruled by "divine right." Bossuet was Louis's tutor, and Cromwell was not a monarch.

50. **(A)** Pascal appears in histories of mathematics, philosophy, and theology. Marie Curie (E) was a late-nineteenth-century chemist. Galileo (B) engaged in philosophy and theology, but he is most remembered for his work with astronomy during the Scientific Revolution. Locke (C) was a political theorist, and Cromwell (D) was England's ruler in its years as a republic.

51. **(E)** Britain experienced political unrest and the possibility of revolution as a result of the Industrial Revolution and the Chartist movement, and the percentage of the British population that could vote expanded significantly in the nineteenth century. However, Britain's form of government did not fundamentally change in the nineteenth century. On the other hand, Belgium gained its independence from the Netherlands (D), and Spain (A), Greece (C), and Italy (B) all experienced revolutions.

52. **(A)** Most historians trace modern nationalism to the French Revolution. The "Declaration of the Rights of Man and Citizen" heavily emphasized the nation over the whims of individuals. Frenchmen were declared free, but only to the extent that their conduct did not disturb the nation.

53. **(C)** De Gouges wrote the "Declaration of the Rights of Woman and Female Citizen" because women were excluded from the vote by the National Assembly following the outbreak of the French Revolution. De Gouges was later executed for speaking out against the excesses of the revolution.

54. **(C)** Einstein's theory of relativity overthrew the assumptions people had about the universe as a result of Isaac Newton's theories. Freud (A) was the founder of psychoanalysis. Pasteur (B) discovered that illness is often caused by bacteria (thus, bacteria *in pasteur*ized milk has been killed).

Robert Koch (D) found the bacteria that caused cholera and isolated the tuberculosis bacillus. Marie Curie (E) was a chemist.

55. **(C)**   Joseph II, along with Frederick the Great of Prussia and Catherine the Great of Russia, was an "enlightened despot." William III of Orange (A) governed according to enlightened principles, but he is not included in the list of enlightened despots, mainly because, unlike Joseph II, he was not a despot, because his power was checked by Parliament. Louis XVI (D) instituted reforms only under pressure. Peter the Great of Russia (B) was an autocrat who brought French cultural practices to Russia but not western political reforms associated with the Enlightenment. George III (E) was the king the American colonies rebelled against in 1775–1776.

56. **(A)**   *Blitzkrieg* ("lightning war") was Hitler's mode of attack early in the Second World War. Sweden remained neutral during the war. Poland, Belgium, France and the Netherlands (B–E) were attacked in 1939–1940.

57. **(A)**   Many *philosophes* such as Voltaire were deists, believing that a supreme being created the world and now, like a watchmaker, let it run on its own according to natural laws. Arminianism (B) is a theological system that emphasizes human free will. Anabaptists (C) were opposed to the baptism of infants. Quakers (D) were Protestants who emphasized simple, heart-felt religion. Positivism (E) was a philosophy developed by August Comte that emphasized the capacity to find scientific solutions to human problems.

58. **(D)**   Rousseau (A), Descartes (B), Voltaire (C) and Condorcet (E) were all prominent figures in the Enlightenment, but the editorship of the first encyclopedia was Diderot's.

59. **(D)**   Beccaria's *Essay on Crimes and Punishments* is an early example of reform-minded people calling for rehabilitation of criminals instead of strict punishment.

60. **(B)**   The French Revolution was primarily a middle-class movement. King Louis XVI (C) was opposed to most of the Third Estate's program. Bishops (A) and high-ranking officers (D) were among the nobility and thus were not likely to favor reform. Most impoverished peasants (E) were illiterate and not as well informed as the literate middle classes.

61. **(C)**   Soon after the Russian Revolution (1917) it became clear that not many Russians would naturally embrace communism. Vladimir Lenin and other communist leaders became the "vanguard"—those who would lead the way to communist utopia.

62. **(E)**   The Committee of Public Safety was a danger—and was frequently deadly—to all who disagreed with its radical policies. The National Assembly (A) soon lost control of the French Revolution and in time seemed quite conservative. The National Convention (B) was more radical than the National Assembly; it declared France a republic, for example. But few were more radical than the agents of the Committee of Public Safety, directed by Robespierre. The committee's goal was to purge France of people who did not share its radical goals, such as the near-complete secularization of the country. Girondins (C) were conservatives within the National Convention, and the Directory (D) came out in reaction (in the revolutionary month of Thermidor) to the Reign of Terror.

63. **(A)**   Those who were opposed to the French Revolution and fled France were called émigrés. The émigrés were refugees (B), but they are remembered by their French name. The term *bourgeois* (C) was not an important term in the late eighteenth century, and the *sans-culottes* (D) and especially the Jacobins (E) were revolutionaries who favored radical reform.

64. **(D)**   Following Napoleon's entry into Moscow in 1812, winter descended on the French army, whose supply and communication lines were very strung out. As the French retreated, the Russians attacked. Hitler's forces would experience a similar fate during the Second World War.

65. **(B)**   The United States wished to trade with France and Britain, but neither France nor Britain wished the other to gain economically from trade with the United States. Consequently, both countries harassed American shipping. The United States fought an undeclared sea war with France in the 1790s and went to war with Britain in 1812.

66. **(C)**   Political revolutions broke out through much of Europe in 1848, the same year Karl Marx's *Communist Manifesto* was published. 1688 (A) is the year of England's Glorious Revolution, the French Revolution began in 1789 (B), the Bolshevik Revolution took place in 1917 (D), and in 1989 (E) the Soviet Union lost control of the East Bloc countries such as Poland, Hungary, and Czechoslovakia.

67. **(E)**   The Russians defeated Napoleon and Hitler, both of whom suffered from Russia's winter and the ability of the Russians to withdraw deep into their vast country. Russian troops also used slash-and-burn tactics and forced the enemy to string out long supply and communication lines.

68. **(D)** Despite its vast size and rich farmland, Russia was unable to feed its troops sufficiently. One reason was that many farmers were at the war front. Another reason was that Russia's transportation infrastructure was not elaborate, and it was difficult to get food to the troops. Finally, because of political instability, the country's economy was troubled.

69. **(B)** There were two revolutions in Russia in 1917. The provisional government came from the first revolution and comprised Socialists, liberals, and non-Bolshevik Communists. The Bolshevik movement, led by Lenin, launched another revolution in October and began to implement radical reform.

70. **(A)** The Treaty of Brest-Litovsk near the end of the First World War ended combat between Germany and Russia at the cost of the western portion of Russia's empire, including present-day Lithuania and Estonia. Norway gained its independence from Sweden in 1905 (C), Germany's unrestricted submarine warfare was the main cause of America's entry into the war (D), and the Treaty of Portsmouth ended the war between Japan and Russia (E).

71. **(C)** The New Economic Policy was a concession to small-scale private enterprise soon after the Russian Revolution. Farmers were allowed to sell some of their produce for a profit. It was designed to alleviate famine that developed during the First World War and was exacerbated by the revolution and ensuing civil war. Some Bolsheviks, such as Leon Trotsky, were opposed to this concession to capitalism.

72. **(E)** Rasputin was an unwashed mystic who appeared to have the power to help the Tsar's hemophiliac son. The only other Russian given as an option, Stalin (A), was no friend of the Tsar and had no influence on the Tsar's immediate household.

73. **(B)** Russia's communist revolution was led by Vladimir Lenin. Stalin (D) followed Lenin in power after a power struggle. Rasputin (C) and Nicholas (E) were not Bolsheviks, and Karl Marx (A) was a German Jew living in England, not a Russian.

74. **(D)** The cartoon depicts the Russo-German Non-Aggression Pact, also called the Molotov-Ribbentrop Pact, of 1939. This pact took much of the world aback, for the Soviets and the Nazis had openly hated and denounced one another for years. This was a pact of convenience and it led to Poland being occupied by both Germany and Russia. In less than two years Hitler would violate this pact and invade Russia in what he called Operation Barbarossa.

75. **(C)**   After the First World War, the Ottoman Empire went out of existence. From it emerged Syria, Jordan, Iraq, Turkey, and other Islamic nations. There was no such thing as an Empire of Scandinavia (B), and the British (A), Belgian (E), and American (D) empires continued to exist after the war.

76. **(B)**   Following the collapse of the Ottoman Empire, Britain and France were given "mandates" over Middle Eastern lands by the new League of Nations. Germany (A) lost all its colonies after the war, the United States (D) held colonies in East Asia but not the Middle East, Italy (C) did not govern in the Middle East, and the nation of Israel (E) did not exist until 1948.

77. **(A)**   Palestine, for example, became a British mandate. Dominions (E), such as Canada and Australia, had significant internal independence. Colonies (B) and dependencies (D) had significantly less independence. The term *associates* (C) was not formally applied to territories.

78. **(D)**   The French and British went to war briefly in the late 1950s to prevent Egypt from taking national control of the Suez Canal, for it was a vital transportation link between Europe and Asia. The Berlin to Baghdad Railway (A), like the Cape to Cairo Railway (B), was never completed. The Siberian Railroad (E) is in far eastern Russia, and the Panama Canal (C) is in Central America.

79. **(B)**   Sir Francis Drake, for example, attacked Spanish ships for plunder with the implicit approval of the English monarch. In the sixteenth century, neither free trade (as we think of it today), nor daily newspapers, nor the British East India Company, nor the concept of the separation of church and state existed.

80. **(C)**   Although the five-year plans of the interwar years caused great dislocations—for example, people were forced to move from the country into cities—they were quite successful in making Russia a serious industrial power. The New Economic Policy, which allowed farmers to sell some of their produce for a profit (B), was abolished by Stalin. The civil war (D) had been over for several years by the time the five-year plans were put into effect, and the monarchy had ended with the revolution of 1917 (A).

81. **(D)**   The Red Russians, or Bolsheviks, were able to rally Russians to the defense of Mother Russia. People may not like their governments, but they tend to like invaders less. The Soviets were able to capitalize on this fact.

82. **(C)**   Hitler had tried to stir up a coup to overthrow the state government of Bavaria. It was during his consequent time in prison the early 1920s that Hitler dictated his memoir and political testament, *Mein Kampf.* He had become the

leader of the Nazis before this, and he was named chancellor, formed an alliance with Mussolini, and militarized the Rhineland in the next decade.

83. **(A)** In German the word *Anschluss* means "joining." It refers to Germany's annexation of Austria in 1938. A central part of Hitler's political program was to unite all Germans in a single nation. There was little resistance in Austria to its annexation to Germany.

84. **(B)** The Molotov-Ribbentrop Pact was a nonaggression agreement between Nazi Germany and the Soviets. Hitler never intended to keep his promise not to attack Russia, but he did not want to worry about Russia while he was busy conquering and dominating most of western Europe. His decision to invade Russia in 1941 was fatal, for Russia's vast size and population, combined with its fierce winter and the determination of the Russians to repel an invader, played key roles in his defeat.

85. **(A)** President Wilson was the idealist who wanted to see the world made safe for democracy. He also proposed the idea of the League of Nations, which, ironically, the United States did not join. Clemenceau (B) and Lloyd George (C) were eager to punish Germany, Lenin (E) was too concerned with the Russian Revolution, and the kaiser (D) might have liked Wilson's idea but had no say in peacemaking.

86. **(E)** The United States did not join the League of Nations. All foreign treaties must be ratified by the U.S. Senate. Republicans in the Senate refused to approve the United States joining the league, largely because after the war many Americans wanted to pursue isolationist policies. Japan and Germany left the league in the early 1930s, indicating that they had no interest in abiding by its counsel.

87. **(A)** In exchange for the Catholic Church's recognition of his government, Mussolini recognized Catholicism as the official religion of Italy and gave the church jurisdiction over marriage matters. The Fascists did not close Italy's schools (B). All the other possible answers did take place but not as part of the Lateran Pact. The size of Germany's army was limited by the Treaty of Versailles (D); France guaranteed Poland's neutrality against Nazi threats in March of 1939 (E); and Germany, Italy and Japan formed the Axis in 1940 (C).

88. **(D)** Chamberlain said he believed he had achieved "peace in our time" and encouraged the people of Britain to go home and have a good night's rest. Hitler had already militarized the Rhineland (B) and occupied Austria

(C). Hitler's invasion of Poland (E) in 1939 led to Britain's declaration of war against Hitler.

89. **(B)** The Treaty of Westphalia was the document that in 1648 ended the Thirty Years' War. It is considered a major step on the road to separation of church and state because the pope was not a participant in the discussions, though he wanted to be.

90. **(C)** Among the prominent *philosophes* are Voltaire, Diderot, Montesquieu, and Condorcet. Anti-Nazi resisters were the *maquis*.

91. **(A)** Bossuet's *Politics Drawn from the Very Words of Scripture* is a classic statement of divine right theory.

92. **(B)** While seventeenth-century monarchs generally lived in luxury, no households compared to Louis XIV's Versailles, where all events were wrapped in elaborate ritual, and where the king was able to keep potential troublemakers contented by making them feel close to power.

93. **(D)** *Lyell's Principles of Geology* (1830) was an important work to Darwin. Spencer (A) later applied some of Darwin's ideas to societies and thus promoted the idea of social Darwinism. Nietzsche (B) was a late-nineteenth-century philosopher whose thought many Nazis later claimed to admire. Camus (C) was a post–Second World War existentialist philosopher and writer, and Daimler (E) was one of the early inventors of the automobile.

94. **(B)** Following France's rapid defeat at the hands of the Nazis in the summer of 1940, Germany occupied western and northern France, while a collaborationist government was established in southern France, at Vichy. Germany would later invade southern France as well, taking control of the whole country until its liberation by the Allies in 1944.

95. **(A)** The Glorious Revolution was bloodless. For fear that James II wished to return England to Catholicism, Parliament invited William III of Orange and his wife, Mary, to take England's throne. James II fled to France and his forces put up no resistance. The Glorious Revolution of 1688 came four decades after the English civil war. England began to take control of India in the eighteenth century (D), particularly as a result of the battle of Plassey (1757); and Napoleon was not a factor until the end of the eighteenth century (E).

96. **(C)** Postmodernists tend to be less interested in admiring the work of the powerful leaders than they are in pointing to leaders' foibles. Postmodernism is difficult to define but, in general, as an intellectual movement it rejects tradition and traditional ways of thinking about history, cultures, genders, and

truth. One effect of postmodernist thought is that history lessons often empha-size acts of hypocrisy and sheer power more than worthwhile achievements.

97. **(D)** This undeclared war involved French sailors seizing American ships and vice versa, though the French took many more American ships than the Americans took French ships. The French held colonies in the West Indies and the Americans conducted trade there.

98. **(B)** Mercantilists believed that the amount of wealth in the world is lim-ited, whereas capitalists believe that wealth can be created. For mercan-tilists, wealth was most represented by gold and silver. Thus mercantilists focused on selling exports which brought gold and silver into the home economy while discouraging imports, which sent wealth out of the country. Mercantilism spurred early colonialism as European nations competed for territories and their wealth.

99. **(C)** The photograph, taken in Austria, illustrates the resentment Germans and Austrians felt about the Versailles Treaty, which was signed after the First World War ended in 1918. Capitalizing on this resentment, Hitler came to power in 1933 and sparked the Second World War in 1939.

100. **(B)** The Archduke Franz Ferdinand was assassinated in Sarajevo in 1914. In the summer of that year, Serb nationalists who wished to leave the Austro-Hungarian Empire and join the nation of Serbia assassinated the archduke. This triggered a series of events that led to the First World War.

101. **(A)** Alsace-Lorraine was coveted by both Germany and France. Following France's defeat in the Franco-Prussian War (1870–1871), Alsace and Lor-raine were annexed by Germany. Following Germany's defeat in the First World War (1914–1918), Alsace and Lorraine were returned to France. Dur-ing Germany's control of France during the Second World War, through the years 1940–1944, the regions were once again controlled by Germans. Since the end of that war, Alsace and Lorraine have remained in French control.

102. **(C)** In the late nineteenth century inexpensive newspapers became widely available throughout the Western world. Public speeches (D) had always been available, but fewer people had regular access to them than to newspa-pers. Telephones (E) were not in wide use until the twentieth century, and radio (B) and television (A) were twentieth-century inventions.

103. **(E)** Suffragettes took their name from *suffrage,* a synonym for the vote. Many suffragettes wanted laws against alcohol consumption (A), wanted shops closed

on Sundays (B), worked within the dominant parties (C), and were pacifists (D). But their main goal, as their name suggests, was women's right to vote.

104. **(C)** In the late twentieth century, Western civilization experienced mass migration from former colonies. In the early twenty-first century, more Muslims from France's former African colonies attended mosques each week than French men and women attended Catholic churches. Britain hosted a large Pakistani population, and many Filipinos lived in the United States and served in its military, especially the navy.

105. **(C)** Though Germans fought Italians (D) and Russians (B) in the twentieth century, they also had alliances with them at other times. At no point in the late nineteenth and early twentieth centuries was an alliance formed between France and Germany, which shared lengthy borders.

106. **(C)** Italy was defeated by Ethiopia. This is one reason why Mussolini's forces invaded Ethiopia in 1935: to make up for the humiliation of losing a war to that African country in 1896 at the Battle of Adowa.

107. **(A)** France's navy, gunpowder, and soldiers were crucial to the Americans' victory. Without France, it is unlikely the Americans would have succeeded. The Dutch of the Netherlands (E) and the Spanish (B) also assisted the Americans against the common enemy (the British), but not nearly to the same extent. Mexico (D) did not exist as a nation (independent from Spain) until 1822. Some American loyalists who opposed the American Revolution went to present-day Canada (C) and thus helped to create there an English culture next to the French culture of Quebec.

108. **(B)** Christina of Sweden's eagerness to learn, along with the early hours she kept and Sweden's challenging climate, apparently contributed to the death of the philosopher Descartes.

109. **(A)** Newton was the first to write out a theory of gravity. Galileo (astronomy; B), Kepler (astronomy; C), Vesalius (anatomist; D), and Pascal (mathematician and theological writer; E) are all, like Newton, connected to the Scientific Revolution. But to Newton goes the credit for announcing a theory of gravity in his *Mathematical Principles of Natural Philosophy,* often referred to simply by part of its Latin title, *Principia.*

110. **(B)** Gibbon's multivolume and still much-read work, *The Decline and Fall of the Roman Empire,* is a classic of the Enlightenment, which emphasized human reason and secular explanations for events.

111. **(E)** Of the possibilities given, cotton is the commodity most associated with the first Industrial Revolution. Oil (B) would be correct if the question were about the Industrial Revolution. The first Industrial Revolution revolved in large measure around textile mills, which produced inexpensive clothing and cloth (textiles). This led to a demand for more cotton which, in return, led to a further entrenchment of slavery in the United States. Sugar (C) and tea (D) had been commodities important to the British economy since the seventeenth century. And a series of large gold (A) strikes began in the mid-nineteenth century in California, Australia, Canada, Alaska, and South Africa.

112. **(B)** After being locked out of deliberations at Versailles in 1789, the Third Estate met on an indoor tennis court and declared itself the National Assembly. Before long, King Louis XVI acknowledged that act but only with great reluctance.

113. **(B)** All the topics listed were taught at various places, but the general course of study was fairly uniform throughout the West. Latin continued to be emphasized in public education well into the twentieth century and was again growing in popularity in American high schools in the early twenty-first century.

114. **(D)** NATO was a strictly military organization interested in defense against the Soviets, so it left humanitarian work to other organizations. Many nations in NATO were involved in the fight against the communist North Koreans (E), but the Korean War was a U.S.-led United Nations conflict. In response, the Soviets formed their own military alliance system, the Warsaw Pact. The central premise of NATO was that if one member nation was attacked, all would consider themselves to have been attacked. This premise went into effect for the first time in September 2001, when radical Muslim terrorists flew commercial planes into buildings in New York City and Washington, D.C.

115. **(C)** A relativist maintains that there is no such thing as fixed right and wrong and that what is considered right and wrong depends on culture and viewpoint. With so many competing worldviews and philosophies at work in Western civilization by the late twentieth century, some had come to believe that the truth about life and its meaning and purpose could not be known for certain. The art form cubism (D), which emphasizes the fragmentation of modern life, can be seen as promoting relativistic thought, as can existentialism (B), which promoted the idea that each person needs to create his or her own meaning in life. Deism (A) argues that God is not involved in people's day-to-day affairs, and absolutism (E) refers to the theoretically complete power some monarchs—such as France's Louis XIV—held in the seventeenth century.

116. **(D)** Student demonstrations in France in 1968 almost toppled the government of Charles de Gaulle. By 1968 the civil war in Algeria had ended (A), and France had pulled its troops out of Vietnam in the mid-1950s (B). As in the United States, students in France demonstrated against police brutality and on behalf of reforms they wished to see put into effect in universities.

117. **(C)** Following the fall of the Soviet Union in 1991, nationalists in Chechnya began to fight for independence from Russia, while Basques, who had agitated from a homeland independent from Spain and France, continued to use terrorism into the early twenty-first century. In 1995 a majority of Quebec's French speakers voted in a referendum to begin a process that would lead to independence from Canada, but a French minority combined with other minorities very narrowly defeated the nationalists' project.

118. **(A)** The late-twentieth-century phenomenon of people traveling, attending church, or even going shopping in casual clothing was unique. Into the 1950s it was unusual for a man to be seen in public in anything other than a coat and tie. The teen cultures of the 1920s and 1950s, which emphasized distinct dress for youth, promoted an increasingly casual approach to dress.

119. **(D)** The twentieth century hosted the most repressive regimes in history. Louis XIV's France (C) never experienced the sort of intense control exercised by the Nazis and Soviets, the latter of which made traditional religion illegal (B). Twentieth-century dictators used radio and television (E) to further their own interests.

120. **(E)** Cromwell, like the Puritans who settled present-day New England in the seventeenth century, wished to purify churches of all that seemed Catholic, hence the name Puritan. Cromwell led the antimonarchical forces in England's civil war and later presided over the country during its republican period.

PRACTICE TEST 2

CLEP Western Civilization II

Also available at the REA Study Center (*www.rea.com/studycenter*)

This practice test is also offered online at the REA Study Center. Since all CLEP exams are computer-based, we recommend that you take the online version of the test to simulate test-day conditions and to receive these added benefits:

- **Timed testing conditions** – helps you gauge how much time you can spend on each question
- **Automatic scoring** – find out how you did on the test, instantly
- **On-screen detailed explanations of answers** – gives you the correct answer and explains why the other answer choices are wrong
- **Diagnostic score reports** – pinpoint where you're strongest and where you need to focus your study

PRACTICE TEST 2

CLEP Western Civilization II

(Answer sheets appear in the back of the book.)

TIME: 90 Minutes
120 Questions

DIRECTIONS: Each of the questions or incomplete statements below is followed by five possible answers or completions. Select the best choice in each case and fill in the corresponding oval on the answer sheet.

1.

```
REFLECTIONS
ON THE
REVOLUTION IN FRANCE,
AND ON THE
PROCEEDINGS IN CERTAIN SOCIETIES
IN LONDON
RELATIVE TO THAT EVENT.
IN A
L E T T E R
INTENDED TO HAVE BEEN SENT TO A GENTLEMAN
IN PARIS.
BY THE RIGHT HONOURABLE
E D M U N D    B U R K E.

THE SECOND EDITION.

L O N D O N:
PRINTED FOR J. DODSLEY, IN PALL-MALL.
M.DCC.XC.
```

In the book illustrated above, Edmund Burke primarily

(A) denounced the French revolution
(B) praised the French revolution
(C) dispassionately compared it to the American Revolution
(D) dispassionately compared it to the Russian Revolution
(E) correctly predicted that it would lead to democracy by 1812

2. France's defeat in the Franco-Prussian War of 1870 led to

   (A) France losing its African and Asian colonies
   (B) France losing its American colonies
   (C) the sale of Louisiana to the United States
   (D) the loss of Alsace-Lorraine
   (E) German military occupation of Paris through the year 1899

3. "Every foot of ground contested; every hundred yards another trench; and everywhere bodies—rows of them!" This wartime letter comes from which conflict?

   (A) Franco-Prussian War
   (B) Seven Years' War
   (C) First World War
   (D) Korean War
   (E) Operation Desert Storm

4. The demand for rubber from the Belgian Congo was partly driven by a demand for

   (A) synthetic clothing
   (B) aircraft parts
   (C) bicycle tires
   (D) toys
   (E) Tupperware

5. Who of the following believed that people use "defense mechanisms" to defend their egos?

   (A) Thomas Carlyle
   (B) Herbert Spencer
   (C) Joseph Goebbels
   (D) Giuseppe Mazzini
   (E) Sigmund Freud

6.

This cartoon is a caricature of which of the following?

(A) Charles Darwin
(B) Herbert Spencer
(C) Thomas More
(D) F. Scott Fitzgerald
(E) William Gladstone

7. The ideas of which of the following were most accepted by Adolf Hitler?

(A) Andrew Carnegie
(B) Florence Nightingale
(C) Friedrich Nietzsche
(D) Karl Marx
(E) John Calvin

8. The appearance of the German warship *Panther* off the coast of Morocco

(A) signaled the beginning of that country becoming a German colony
(B) prevented British and French troops from clashing at Fashoda
(C) suggested that Kaiser Wilhelm II intended to support the Boers in their war against the British
(D) sparked talk of war between Germany and France
(E) sparked talk of war between Germany and Belgium

9. Late nineteenth-century Belgium's largest colony was in

   (A) central Africa
   (B) central Asia
   (C) Malaysia
   (D) the West Indies
   (E) the South Pacific

10. Which of the following places important European leaders in the correct chronological order?

    (A) Bismarck, Lenin, George III, Christina of Sweden, Gorbachev
    (B) Lenin, Bismarck, George III, Christina of Sweden, Gorbachev
    (C) Gorbachev, Bismarck, Lenin, George III, Christina of Sweden
    (D) Christina of Sweden, George III, Bismarck, Lenin, Gorbachev
    (E) George III, Christina of Sweden, Gorbachev, Lenin, Bismarck

11. The Boers were

    (A) South African settlers of Dutch ancestry
    (B) Argentines of Welsh ancestry
    (C) Gaelic-speaking Scots
    (D) Dutch settlers in Indonesia
    (E) British colonists in Hong Kong

12. In 1914 Germany invaded France

    (A) from the west, via the sea
    (B) from the south, via Italy
    (C) from the northeast, via Belgium
    (D) directly from the east
    (E) from all directions simultaneously

13. Germany's unrestricted submarine warfare in the First World War was designed to

    (A) prevent Mexico from joining the war on the side of the United States
    (B) provoke Mexico into joining the war against the United States
    (C) assist ships bringing goods to England
    (D) eliminate ships bringing goods to England
    (E) Germany had no submarines in the First World War

14. The Brest-Litovsk Treaty

    (A) brought Germany out of the First World War
    (B) brought Britain out of the First World War
    (C) brought Russia out of the First World War
    (D) ended the First World War
    (E) threatened to bring Mexico into the First World War

15. In Soviet terminology, wage earners were the

    (A) bourgeoisie
    (B) capitalists
    (C) robber barons
    (D) proletariats
    (E) hoi-polloi

16. Civil war in which country gave Hitler a chance to test his weaponry?

    (A) Greece
    (B) Germany
    (C) Czechoslovakia
    (D) Spain
    (E) Ethiopia

17. In 1939 what two countries agreed to a nonaggression pact?

    (A) Britain and Germany
    (B) Germany and the Soviet Union
    (C) Soviet Union and Japan
    (D) Germany and Italy
    (E) Britain and Austria

18. Neville Chamberlain is most remembered for

    (A) reporting on Joseph Stalin's methods
    (B) leading the Abraham Lincoln Brigade
    (C) gaining U.S. assistance to Britain during the Second World War
    (D) trying to appease Hitler
    (E) taking Britain out of the League of Nations

19. The beginning of the end of the Nazi regime in northwestern Europe was

    (A) the Battle of the Bulge
    (B) Stalingrad
    (C) the "phony war"
    (D) Hitler's invasion of Norway
    (E) D-Day

20.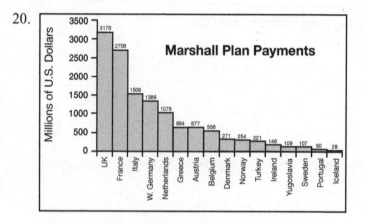

    This graph illustrates an American economic program that went into effect

    (A) after the First World War
    (A) during the Great Depression
    (C) during the Second World War
    (D) after the Second World War
    (E) at the height of European imperialism

21. The Soviet-dominated counterpart to NATO was

    (A) collectivization
    (B) East Berlin
    (C) the Warsaw Pact
    (D) the European Economic Union
    (E) North Korea

22. The United States was to Vietnam as the Soviet Union was to

    (A) Pakistan
    (B) Afghanistan
    (C) Iran
    (D) Turkmenistan
    (E) Azerbaijan

23. *Sputnik* was

    (A) the first satellite successfully launched into space
    (B) the first dog to survive in space
    (C) a space creature on the Cold War-era television program *Outer Limits*
    (D) the Soviet leader after Khrushchev
    (E) a *Star Trek* code word for the Soviets

24. Soviet missiles in which of the following countries nearly led to war with the United States?

    (A) Mexico
    (B) Turkey
    (C) Cuba
    (D) East Germany
    (E) Philippines

25. The first book printed in African languages was almost always

    (A) Shakespeare
    (B) the Bible
    (C) *Gulliver's Travels*
    (D) a collection of Rudyard Kipling's poetry
    (E) a school grammar textbook

26. Which late-nineteenth-century European power drew resources from Africa substantial enough to make a positive difference to it economically?

    (A) Britain
    (B) France
    (C) Portugal
    (D) Spain
    (E) Belgium

27. By 1900 the British had a strong presence in Hong Kong and the French had a strong presence in

    (A) Indochina
    (B) Japan
    (C) Korea
    (D) Indonesia
    (E) Singapore

28. Napoleon met his final defeat at

    (A) Leipzig
    (B) Sarajevo
    (C) Moscow
    (D) Brussels
    (E) Waterloo

29. Generally speaking, the new large-circulation newspapers of early-twentieth-century Western civilization were

    (A) written for the educated elite
    (B) usually bilingual
    (C) sensationalistic
    (D) owned by Socialists
    (E) owned by monarchists

30. In 1901, nationalism was the greatest internal threat to which of the following?

    (A) Austria-Hungary
    (B) Russia
    (C) Britain
    (D) Spain
    (E) Germany

31. For Woodrow Wilson, the primary purpose of the League of Nations was to

    (A) keep Germany weak militarily
    (B) contain the Soviet Union
    (C) maintain Europe's borders as they existed in 1918
    (D) promote democracy
    (E) prepare for war

32. Which of the following nations emerged from the First World War a new significant international power?

    (A) Germany
    (B) France
    (C) Italy
    (D) Russia
    (E) United States

33. The Weimar Republic refers to the government in

(A) Britain before the First World War
(B) Germany at the end of the First World War
(C) Russia between the February and October revolutions
(D) Belgium's empire in the Congo
(E) Hitler's government

34. In 1932 Germany's Nazi Party

(A) lost an election to the Communists
(B) took complete control of Germany
(C) was outlawed by the socialist government
(D) outperformed all other parties in elections
(E) was created

35.

The event depicted in this photograph

(A) gave Hitler an excuse to gain complete control of Germany
(B) enraged Hitler and led him to form the Nazi Party
(C) led to the militarization of the Rhineland
(D) was blamed on gypsies, who were placed in camps
(E) led to Hitler's temporary removal from power

36. The assertion that the United States would support free peoples who were resisting communist revolution and political subjugation was central to the

    (A) Truman Doctrine
    (B) Treaty of Versailles
    (C) Marshall Plan
    (D) Domino Theory
    (E) Yalta Conference

37. In 1948 the Organization for European Economic Cooperation was established to implement the

    (A) Truman Doctrine
    (B) Treaty of Versailles
    (C) Marshall Plan
    (D) Domino Theory
    (E) Yalta Conference

38. From June 1948 through May 1949, goods were airlifted into

    (A) West Germany to feed occupying forces
    (B) Algeria to assist anti-French fighters
    (C) the Soviet Union to prevent starvation
    (D) West Berlin to prevent it from becoming communist
    (E) Belgium to help it clear away war debris

39. To keep India's loyalty during the Second World War, Britain

    (A) offered postwar independence
    (B) sent a large occupying army to India
    (C) forcibly sent thousands of Indians to Australia and New Zealand
    (D) offered to turn India's government over to France
    (E) withdrew all British troops from India

40. "[The French government's] objective is the same as ours—to obtain the collaboration of all nations, not excluding the totalitarian States, in building up a lasting peace for Europe." The statement was made by Neville Chamberlain

(A) following the assassination of Franz Ferdinand in Sarajevo.
(B) before the fall of the Berlin Wall.
(C) after the Munich Conference.
(D) at the Congress of Vienna.
(E) in response to the reading of Woodrow Wilson's Fourteen Points.

41. The first European nation to be defeated by an Asian nation in modern times was

(A) Russia
(B) Spain
(C) Italy
(D) Belgium
(E) Portugal

42. In 1919 the pope declared

(A) his disapproval of the vote for women
(B) his approval of the vote for women
(C) his approval of birth control
(D) his disapproval of birth control
(E) that Latin would no longer be the language of Catholic church services

43. The "youth culture" that is now taken for granted became a widespread reality

(A) during the Great Depression
(B) during the student demonstrations of the 1960s
(C) on the eve of the First World War
(D) following the Second World War
(E) with the advent of radio in the early twentieth century

44. Apartheid was the name given to a political system existent until 1993 in what country?

(A) Netherlands
(B) South Africa
(C) France
(D) Germany
(E) Soviet Union

45. The key to stability in eastern Europe from 1950 to 1989 was

(A) economic prosperity
(B) a widespread belief in the virtues of communism
(C) the Soviet military
(D) occasional elections
(E) freedom of religion

46. In 1978 a pope was selected from which of the following countries?

(A) Albania
(B) Greece
(C) United States
(D) Poland
(E) Russia

47. Which of the following Soviet leaders is associated with promoting greater political openness?

(A) Trotsky
(B) Brezhnev
(C) Khrushchev
(D) Putin
(E) Gorbachev

48. The first East Bloc country to open its borders to the West was which of the following?

(A) Poland
(B) Lithuania
(C) Latvia
(D) Hungary
(E) Romania

49. In 1990 the Polish dissident and reformer Lech Walesa

    (A) was elected president of Poland
    (B) was imprisoned
    (C) was exiled to the United States
    (D) was assassinated by Soviet agents
    (E) concluded that reforms had gone too far

50. The first president of Russia within the Commonwealth of Independent States was

    (A) Putin
    (B) Gorbachev
    (C) Zhirinovsky
    (D) Yeltsin
    (E) Lenin

51. At the end of the 1980s Soviet troops did not stop anticommunist movements in Eastern Europe partly because

    (A) the Soviet Union no longer existed
    (B) the East Bloc nations had built up formidable armies
    (C) the U.S. threatened military response if Soviet troops moved in
    (D) part of the Soviet military was tied up in a central Asian war
    (E) Pope John Paul II personally led the anticommunist rallies

52. After the collapse of the Soviet Union and East Bloc, NATO became involved in war in

    (A) Romania
    (B) Iran
    (C) Yugoslavia
    (D) South Africa
    (E) Falkland Islands

53. By 1945 a million people of French ancestry lived in which North African country?

    (A) Algeria
    (B) Tunisia
    (C) Morocco
    (D) Egypt
    (E) Libya

54. U.S. funds were funneled to anti-Soviet fighters in Afghanistan via

   (A) India
   (B) Pakistan
   (C) Iran
   (D) Saudi Arabia
   (E) Turkmenistan

55.

Courtesy of Steve Raper

The person on the left is Mikhail Gorbachev. The cartoon was drawn in which of the following periods?

   (A) 1905–1917
   (B) 1935–1940
   (C) 1956–1964
   (D) 1970–1979
   (E) 1989–1992

56. In 1935 Italy invaded

   (A) Bulgaria
   (B) Morocco
   (C) Austria
   (D) Spain
   (E) Ethiopia

57. Catholicism was declared the official religion of Italy as part of the

    (A) Lateran Pact
    (B) Balfour Declaration
    (C) Molotov-Ribbentrop Pact
    (D) Berlin Congress
    (E) Congress of Vienna

58. An agreement in Dayton, Ohio, in 1995 brought an end to war in

    (A) Haiti
    (B) Sudan
    (C) Yugoslavia
    (D) Falklands
    (E) Israel

59. Who among the following is most associated with the rejection of Woodrow Wilson's plans for peace after the First World War?

    (A) Georges Clemenceau
    (B) Victoriano Orlando
    (C) Kaiser Wilhehm II
    (D) Leon Trotsky
    (E) Benito Mussolini

60. Which of the following countries left the League of Nations in 1933?

    (A) Britain
    (B) Portugal
    (C) France
    (D) South Africa
    (E) Germany

61. Against the Treaty of Versailles, in 1935 Hitler sent troops into

    (A) Poland
    (B) the Rhineland
    (C) Ethiopia
    (D) Denmark
    (E) Sudetenland

62. Adolf Hitler wrote this book

(A) while in prison
(B) during the First World War
(C) after he gained power in 1933
(D) in response to France's declaration of war against Germany
(E) before he committed suicide in May 1945

63. What led to the industrialization of Russia in the 1930s?

(A) The New Economic Policy
(B) The show trials
(C) The five-year plans
(D) Allied intervention during the Soviet Union's civil war
(E) The collectivization of agriculture

64. Which Soviet leader is most associated with purges of the military leadership?

(A) Lenin
(B) Trotsky
(C) Brezhnev
(D) Stalin
(E) Gorbachev

65. Which of the following dictators was the first to gain power?

(A) Stalin
(B) Mussolini
(C) Franco
(D) Hitler
(E) Lenin

66.

The sketch above of a spinning jenny, which was used to make cloth from cotton, is MOST related to which of the following?

(A) the beginning of English settlement in the New World
(B) the first Industrial Revolution
(C) the second Industrial Revolution
(D) the Great Depression
(E) *perestroika* and *glasnost*

67. All the following are true of the Glorious Revolution EXCEPT

(A) it led to a fundamental change in England's government
(B) it led to the publication of a bill of rights
(C) it placed a Protestant king and queen on England's throne
(D) it was bloodless
(E) it ended the possibility of Catholic rule in England

68. The eighteenth-century European country that provided the greatest, if still small, opportunity for economic upward mobility was

(A) Prussia
(B) Russia
(C) Spain
(D) England
(E) Portugal

69. In his *Enquiry Concerning Human Understanding*, the British philosopher David Hume argued or suggested all of the following EXCEPT

    (A) all religious "truths" are open to question
    (B) all beliefs people have are derived from the perceptions of their senses
    (C) God plants certain truths in people's minds
    (D) Descartes' belief about the idea of perfection being God-given is false
    (E) the nature of the world made skepticism the best philosophical point of view

70. Which philosopher is most associated with the concept of the "noble savage"?

    (A) David Hume
    (B) Jean-Jacques Rousseau
    (C) John Locke
    (D) Thomas Jefferson
    (E) Sigmund Freud

71. The late-eighteenth-century writer who argued for greater access to education for women was

    (A) John Stuart Mill
    (B) Florence Nightingale
    (C) Simone de Beauvoir
    (D) Rachel Carson
    (E) Mary Wollstonecraft

72. The convening of the Assembly of Notables preceded all of the following EXCEPT

    (A) the Thermidorian Reaction
    (B) the Glorious Revolution
    (C) Napoleon's Concordat with the pope
    (D) the Reign of Terror
    (E) the Great Fear

73. Between 1789 and 1794 throughout France, books were

    (A) collected by the government and sold to pay down the national debt
    (B) burned by the thousands
    (C) confiscated from monasteries and nobles' houses and placed in a national library
    (D) distributed to peasants
    (E) banned

74. The majority of African slaves brought by Europeans to the New World went to

    (A) the Middle East
    (B) Brazil and the Caribbean
    (C) Virginia
    (D) New England
    (E) India

75. The report of the Sadler Committee led to

    (A) the Factory Act of 1833
    (B) the American Revolution
    (C) the Boer War
    (D) urbanization in England
    (E) the Munich Crisis

76. The greatest symbol of the Holocaust is the death camp at

    (A) Berlin
    (B) Auschwitz
    (C) Brussels
    (D) Bastogne
    (E) Stutthof

77. As a result of the Bretton Woods Agreement

    (A) NATO was formed
    (B) the decision was made to drop the atomic bomb on Japanese cities
    (C) the U.S. dollar was declared the world's reserve currency
    (D) the Berlin Wall was built
    (E) France agreed to leave Vietnam

78.

This painting by Picasso, "Guernica" (1937), is an example of what artistic school?

(A) Baroque
(B) Impressionism
(C) Realism
(D) Cubism
(E) Existentialism

79. The European Economic Community, also called the Common Market, was formed in 1957

(A) as a military counterpart to the Warsaw Pact
(B) to limit the power of France
(C) to reintegrate East and West Berlin
(D) to promote cooperation among western European countries
(E) to facilitate the independence of India and Algeria from European colonial powers

80. Green parties have been allied with all the following movements EXCEPT

(A) feminist writers
(B) animal rights advocates
(C) antiwar protestors
(D) unregulated free trade advocates
(E) Social Democrats

81. *Kristallnacht* refers to

(A) the Allies' bombardment of the German city of Dresden
(B) the effort to eliminate Europe's Jews
(C) widespread vandalism directed against Jewish property in prewar Germany
(D) Germany's secret code broken by the British during the Second World War
(E) Hitler's call for "living space"

82. The European New Left of the generation after the Second World War

(A) advocated a form of socialism free of Soviet-style dictatorship
(B) abandoned socialism as an unworkable economic theory
(C) called for the United States to eliminate the communist government in Vietnam
(D) enjoyed its greatest success in Spain
(E) opposed decolonization

83. The Scramble for Africa took place in which of the following eras?

(A) 1914–1945
(B) 1870–1914
(C) 1775–1800
(D) 1815–1870
(E) 1945–1965

84. The philosophical outlook that emphasizes the "greatest good for the greatest number of people" is

(A) nihilism
(B) postmodernism
(C) utilitarianism
(D) social Darwinism
(E) Zionism

85. The Second Vatican Council did all the following EXCEPT

    (A) require Latin to remain the language of the Mass
    (B) continue to require that priests remain celibate
    (C) acknowledge that sexual relations within marriage were not only for procreation
    (D) recognize that parents might have good reasons to limit the number of children they have
    (E) maintain that only men can be Catholic priests

86. When the term *Third World* was coined in 1955 it referred to

    (A) Africa
    (B) the Southern Hemisphere
    (C) communist nations
    (D) nations not aligned either with the United States or the Soviet Union
    (E) countries hosting U.S. or Soviet military bases

87. In 1948 Zionism led to

    (A) the establishment of Israel as a nation
    (B) civil war in Algeria
    (C) the election of Harry Truman as U.S. president
    (D) the evacuation of France from Vietnam
    (E) the launching of the space race

88. The "Declaration of the Rights of Man and Citizen" calls for all the following EXCEPT

    (A) all persons to be considered innocent of a crime until proven guilty
    (B) complete freedom of speech
    (C) recognition of the right of each person to his or her own property
    (D) taxation based upon ability to pay
    (E) the elimination of tax exemptions for nobles

89. The English Bill of Rights called for all the following EXCEPT

    (A) freedom of speech in Parliament
    (B) political equality for Jews
    (C) abolition of cruel and unusual punishments for crimes
    (D) Parliament's consent for laws to be suspended
    (E) the right of the people to petition the king

90. "[Each man has] his own advantage…in view. But the study of his own advantage naturally…leads him to prefer that employment which is most advantageous to the society." This view of economics was written by

   (A) Adam Smith
   (B) Karl Marx
   (C) Friedrich Engels
   (D) Jean-Baptiste Colbert
   (E) F. A. Hayek

91. "The frequent [parties], the private promenades at Versailles, the journeys, were means on which the King seized in order to distinguish or mortify the courtiers, and thus render them more assiduous in pleasing him." This quote recalls the lifestyle of

   (A) Charles I
   (B) Napoleon III
   (C) James I
   (D) Joseph II
   (E) Louis XIV

92. "A well conducted government must have an underlying concept so well integrated that it could be likened to a system of philosophy. All actions taken must be well reasoned… The sovereign is the first servant of the state." This statement best fits which of the following political systems?

   (A) Enlightened despotism
   (B) Absolutism
   (C) Marxism
   (A) Divine right
   (E) Social democracy

93. "What is the Third Estate? All, but an all that is shackled and oppressed." These words helped to trigger which of the following?

   (A) American Revolution
   (B) Glorious Revolution
   (C) Russian Revolution
   (D) French Revolution
   (E) Industrial Revolution

94. "What is the will of a Nation? It is the result of individual wills..." This claim, made in France in 1789, echoes the view of which prominent philosopher?

    (A) Descartes
    (B) Locke
    (C) Rousseau
    (D) Pascal
    (E) Hobbes

95. "The principle of all sovereignty resides essentially in the nation." This view expresses a central idea of

    (A) "Declaration of the Rights of Man and Citizen"
    (B) Declaration of Independence
    (C) *Communist Manifesto*
    (D) *Emile*
    (E) *The Descent of Man*

96. "[T]he raising or keeping a standing army within the kingdom in time of peace, unless it be with consent of Parliament, is against the law." This quote comes from the

    (A) Versailles Treaty
    (B) Edict of Nantes
    (C) Vatican II
    (D) Bretton Woods Agreement
    (E) English Bill of Rights

97. "[F]rom this day forward no Egyptian shall be excluded from admission to eminent positions nor from acquiring high ranks...." This statement was made by

    (A) Lloyd George
    (B) Winston Churchill
    (C) Gandhi
    (D) Mussolini
    (E) Napoleon

98. "Workers arriving 2 minutes late shall lose half an hour's wages." In what period were rules like this one in Berlin FIRST posted?

(A) 1770–1800
(B) 1810–1850
(C) 1900–1920
(D) 1870–1890
(E) 1740–1770

99. "The slave is sold once and for all, the proletarian has to sell himself by the day and by the hour." This claim was made by which of the following?

(A) Mussolini
(B) Emmeline Pankhurst
(C) Olympia de Gouges
(D) Friedrich Engels
(E) George Orwell

100. Who is best remembered for claiming that, though people have "exalted powers," they still bear in their bodies "the indelible stamp of [their] lowly origin"?

(A) Charles Darwin
(B) Andrew Carnegie
(C) Albert Einstein
(D) Marie Curie
(E) John Watson

101. "Gentlemen, I must speak from a higher and more truthful plane. It must be stated openly that…superior races have rights over inferior races." This view, expressed by the French politician Jules Ferry, most helped to spur

(A) the social gospel movement
(B) the Crimean War
(C) the Scramble for Africa
(D) anarchism
(E) the Russian Civil War

102. "Yes, an unfortunate, a 'dirty Jew' has been sacrificed. Yes, what an accumulation of madness, stupidity, unbridled imagination, low police tactics, inquisitorial and tyrannical methods this handful of officers have got away with!" These lines were written by Emile Zola during

   (A) the Dreyfus Affair
   (B) the Holocaust
   (C) *Kristallnacht*
   (D) the Nuremberg Trials
   (E) the Munich Conference

103. Rudyard Kipling's famous poem "The White Man's Burden" was written at

   (A) the completion of the Spanish-American War
   (B) the beginning of the Boxer Rebellion
   (C) the end of the Boer War
   (D) the opening of Japan-to-Western trade
   (E) the end of the Russo-Japanese War

104. "Whither is God?... I will tell you. We have killed him...." These lines were written by which of the following?

   (A) Einstein
   (B) Pascal
   (C) Marx
   (D) George Bernard Shaw
   (E) Nietzsche

105. The so-called Lost Generation emerged following which conflict?

   (A) Franco-Prussian War
   (B) Seven Years' War
   (C) First World War
   (D) Korean War
   (E) Operation Desert Storm

106. "Against individualism, the Fascist conception is for the State; and it is for the individual in so far as he coincides with the State...." Who among the following is most likely to have said this?

(A) Adolf Hitler
(B) Joseph Stalin
(C) Vladmir Lenin
(D) Benito Mussolini
(E) Georges Clemenceau

107. "A spirit of innovation is generally the result of a selfish temper, and confined views. People will not look forward to posterity, who never look backward to their ancestors." These lines came from which of the following texts?

(A) Charter of the United Nations
(B) National Assembly's "Declaration of the Rights of Man and Citizen"
(C) U.S. Constitution
(D) Edmund Burke's *Reflections on the Revolution in France*
(E) Bishop Bossuet's *Politics Drawn from the Very Words of Holy Scripture*

108. Which of the following caused many eighteenth-century Europeans to question the belief in a loving divine providence?

(A) A tidal wave that killed thousands in Ireland
(B) A fire that destroyed much of Amsterdam, the Netherlands
(C) An earthquake that shattered Lisbon, Portugal
(D) A crime wave that overtook St. Petersburg, Russia
(E) An outbreak of bubonic plague in London

109. Jean-Jacques Rousseau's novel *Emile* argues that

(A) education should allow children to pursue their own interests
(B) education should be closely monitored by the government
(C) education should be strictly controlled by monks and nuns
(D) education was necessary only for an elite minority
(E) new technology would make traditional education unnecessary

110. Following the Second World War, prominent Nazis were tried for crimes in what city?

(A) San Francisco
(B) Nuremberg
(C) Stalingrad
(D) Potsdam
(E) Tehran

111. The Frenchman Beaumarchais

(A) funneled assistance to the Americans during their war with Britain
(B) funneled assistance to the British during their war with the Americans
(C) governed Quebec through the end of the Seven Years' War
(D) led France's persecution of the Huguenots
(E) led France's Huguenots in their struggles against the French government

112. The Treaty of Versailles required all the following EXCEPT

(A) that Germany's army be limited to 100,000 men
(B) that Berlin be occupied by forces from the victorious Allies
(C) the abolition of Germany's air force
(D) a prohibition against Germany building tanks
(E) payment of reparations by the war's victors

113. Which writer urged Westerners to "send forth the best ye breed...to serve your captives' need"?

(A) Alfred Lord Tennyson
(B) H. G. Wells
(C) Bertrand Russell
(D) G. K. Chesterton
(E) Rudyard Kipling

114. "We demand the unification of all Germans in the Greater Germany on the basis of the right to self-determination of peoples." The language of this plank from the Nazi Party's political platform echoes the earlier words of whom?

(A) Woodrow Wilson
(B) Karl Marx
(C) Edmund Burke
(D) Harry Truman
(E) Charles Dickens

115. Which of the following wars was NOT fought in the eighteenth century?

(A) War of Jenkins's Ear
(B) War of Austrian Succession
(C) Seven Years' War
(D) American Revolution
(E) Crimean War

116. Descartes argued that people were able to understand the idea of perfection because

(A) they could see and learn about perfect things in the world
(B) human beings are basically good and capable of achieving perfection
(C) people have a subconscious desire for perfection
(D) a perfect being more powerful than people gives them the idea
(E) actually, Descartes argued that people really could not contemplate the idea of perfection

117. Descartes fell ill and died while teaching philosophy to whom?

(A) Christina of Sweden
(B) Catherine the Great
(C) Queen Victoria
(D) Marie Antoinette
(E) Beatrice Webb

118. Jean-Jacques Rousseau's influential book is titled

   (A) *Democracy in America*
   (B) *The Social Contract*
   (C) *London Labour and the London Poor*
   (D) *Faust*
   (E) *Philosophy of History*

119. Cardinal Richelieu is remembered for

   (A) renouncing Louis XVIII and fleeing to England
   (B) joining forces with the Third Estate
   (C) organizing France's public affairs
   (D) discovering Quebec
   (E) surrendering to the English during the Seven Years' War

120. "The mightiest counterpart to the Aryan is represented by the Jew. . . . Not through him does any progress of mankind occur, but in spite of him." This statement was written by

   (A) Adolf Hitler
   (B) Joseph Stalin
   (C) Vladimir Lenin
   (D) Benito Mussolini
   (E) Georges Clemenceau

PRACTICE TEST 2

Answer Key

1.	(A)	31.	(D)	61.	(B)	91.	(E)
2.	(D)	32.	(E)	62.	(A)	92.	(A)
3.	(C)	33.	(B)	63.	(C)	93.	(D)
4.	(C)	34.	(D)	64.	(D)	94.	(C)
5.	(E)	35.	(A)	65.	(E)	95.	(A)
6.	(A)	36.	(A)	66.	(B)	96.	(E)
7.	(C)	37.	(C)	67.	(A)	97.	(E)
8.	(D)	38.	(D)	68.	(D)	98.	(B)
9.	(A)	39.	(A)	69.	(C)	99.	(D)
10.	(D)	40.	(C)	70.	(B)	100.	(A)
11.	(A)	41.	(A)	71.	(E)	101.	(C)
12.	(C)	42.	(B)	72.	(B)	102.	(A)
13.	(D)	43.	(D)	73.	(C)	103.	(A)
14.	(C)	44.	(B)	74.	(B)	104.	(E)
15.	(D)	45.	(C)	75.	(A)	105.	(C)
16.	(D)	46.	(D)	76.	(B)	106.	(D)
17.	(B)	47.	(E)	77.	(C)	107.	(D)
18.	(D)	48.	(D)	78.	(D)	108.	(C)
19.	(E)	49.	(A)	79.	(D)	109.	(A)
20.	(D)	50.	(D)	80.	(D)	110.	(B)
21.	(C)	51.	(D)	81.	(C)	111.	(A)
22.	(B)	52.	(C)	82.	(A)	112.	(B)
23.	(A)	53.	(A)	83.	(B)	113.	(E)
24.	(C)	54.	(B)	84.	(C)	114.	(A)
25.	(B)	55.	(E)	85.	(A)	115.	(E)
26.	(E)	56.	(E)	86.	(D)	116.	(D)
27.	(A)	57.	(A)	87.	(A)	117.	(A)
28.	(E)	58.	(C)	88.	(B)	118.	(B)
29.	(C)	59.	(A)	89.	(B)	119.	(C)
30.	(A)	60.	(E)	90.	(A)	120.	(A)

PRACTICE TEST 2

Detailed Explanations of Answers

1. **(A)**   Edmund Burke's *Reflections on the Revolution in France* marks what many historians see as the beginning of modern conservatism. Burke argued that radical change that had no roots in the history and traditions of a people could not work. In the case of the French Revolution, he was correct, for the revolution eventually slid into Napoleon Bonaparte's dictatorship.

2. **(D)**   France's defeat in the Franco-Prussian War led to the loss of Alsace-Lorraine. France lost all but a few small American colonies (B) as a result of the Seven Years' War (1756–1763), and it lost its large African and Asian colonies (A) during the decolonization period following the Second World War. France sold Louisiana (C) to the United States in 1803. Germany did lay siege to and occupy Paris as a result of the war, but this had ended long before 1899 (E).

3. **(C)**   The key word in this quote is *trench*. Trench warfare was the chief characteristic of the western front during the First World War. Trenches were used in the Korean War (D) and Operation Desert Storm (E), but they did not characterize those conflicts the way they did in the First World War.

4. **(C)**   Initially, bicycles had uncomfortable wooden wheels. Rubber tires helped to make riding more comfortable, but the rubber had to be gotten from somewhere outside western Europe. It was available in Latin America, Asia, and Africa. The Belgians capitalized on the rubber available in the Congo and made the lives of many Congolese a living hell in the process. Sometimes, Congolese who did not collect enough rubber to satisfy the Belgians had their hands cut off.

5. **(E)**   Defense mechanisms such as repression, projection, and transference came into public consciousness with the work of Freud. Carlyle (A) was a nineteenth-century British historian and social writer. Spencer (B) was a promoter of social Darwinism. Goebbels (C) was Hitler's propaganda minister and Mazzini (D) was a leading Italian nationalist.

6. **(A)**   Darwin's theory suggests that humans and apes derive from a common ancestor. The idea of natural selection is most famously spelled out in Darwin's *On the Origin of Species*. Thomas More (C) was a sixteenth-century

English assistant to the king and a writer. F. Scott Fitzgerald (D) was a post-First World War novelist associated with the "lost generation." Gladstone (E) was a British prime minister who, among other things, supported the idea of Irish Home Rule—that is, limited political freedom.

7. **(C)** Many Nazis claimed to have been influenced by the writings of Friedrich Nietzsche. Some historians argue that the Nazis misunderstood and misapplied Nietzsche's writings, but it is clear that many considered Nietzsche an intellectual mentor. Nietzsche's writing seem to suggest that the strong should rule the weak and that the powerful individual is the highest expression of humanity. The Nazis would have little interest in the philanthropy of Carnegie (A) and Nightingale (B); they were fiercely anti-Marxist (D); and because they were anti-Christian, they had no use for the Reformation theologian John Calvin (E).

8. **(D)** The *Panther* affair sparked war talk between France and Germany. This was one of several incidents that helped to set the stage for the First World War. The Germans' support of the Boers in their war against the British (1900–1902; C) was another. Germany did take African colonies in the southeast and southwest but not in the north (A).

9. **(A)** Unlike Britain and France, Belgian colonial holdings were limited. Its only significant colony was Congo in central Africa.

10. **(D)** Christina of Sweden ruled in the seventeenth century. George III was on the British throne during the American Revolution in the late eighteenth century. Bismarck created modern Germany in the 1860s and early 1870s. Lenin came on the scene in 1917, and Gorbachev presided over the unraveling of the Soviet Union in the early 1990s.

11. **(A)** The Boers were Dutch settlers in South Africa. Britain assumed it would be easy to beat the Boers in war (the Boers wanted independence from British rule). But the Boers employed hit-and-run tactics, and they proved themselves tough fighters. During the Boer War (1900–1902), the British employed scorched-earth tactics (i.e., burning farmland to starve the enemy) and established concentration camps, which, though nothing like the camps set up for Jews during the Second World War, were certainly unpleasant and conducive to the spreading of disease and misery.

12. **(C)** Early in the First World War, Germany invaded France from the northeast, via Belgium. This was part of the Schlieffen Plan to capture Paris quickly and then turn the German army's attention to defeating Russia.

Germany's invasion of Belgium gave Britain a formal reason to declare war on Germany.

13. **(D)** Germany's unrestricted submarine warfare was designed to eliminate ships bringing goods to England. Before the beginning of the war in 1914, the United States traded much more with Britain than it did with Germany. The United States hoped to remain neutral and to carry on its trade. As one of its war measures, Germany was compelled to end this trade, which helped the British. The Germans also knew that the Americans were secretly providing the British with ammunition and other war materiel. The most famous passenger ship en route to Britain to be sunk was the *Lusitania*. Nearly 1,200 people aboard died. Germany did want to lure Mexico into the war (B), stating in the Zimmermann Telegram that the American Southwest would go back into Mexican hands in the event of an American defeat.

14. **(C)** The Brest-Litovsk Treaty ended conflict between Germany and Russia. While this treaty brought peace between Germany and Russia, Germany still had enemies to face in western Europe, and the United States, which had only recently (in 1917) declared war.

15. **(D)** The Soviets called wage-earners the proletariat. This term, which comes from ancient Rome, was used by Karl Marx and Friedrich Engels to refer to wage earners. *Hoi-polloi* (E) is a Greek term referring to the people. The bourgeoisie (A), capitalists (B) and so-called robber barons (C) were owners of wealth who, in the Marxian view, exploited the proletariat.

16. **(D)** From 1936 through 1939, civil war raged in Spain. The republican (i.e., antimonarchical) forces were assisted by the Soviets and committed atrocities against Catholic priests and nuns. The antirepublicans, who also committed atrocities, were assisted by Italy's Mussolini and Germany's Hitler. The antirepublicans won the civil war and their leader, Francisco Franco, remained in power into the 1970s. Though Franco had some things in common with Hitler and, more so, with Mussolini, Spain remained neutral during the Second World War.

17. **(B)** The Nazi-Soviet Pact, also called the Molotov-Ribbentrop Pact, surprised the world—not to mention committed Nazis (who had always been ferociously anti-Soviet) and Communists (for whom fascism and nazism were the ultimate evils). Hitler had no intention of keeping his promise, and he invaded the Soviet Union in 1940. Also, a secret part of this pact

provided for both countries occupying Poland, which happened in the fall of 1939.

18. **(D)** Neville Chamberlain is most remembered for a short speech he gave after meeting with Hitler at Munich in 1938. To great acclaim, he said he believed he had achieved "peace in our time." Meanwhile, Hitler prepared for war. *Appeasement* was not a bad word until after it became clear that Hitler would always take advantage of the governments that tried to be reasonable with him. Hitler only understood force, whereas Chamberlain believed he could come to agreements through conversations with the Fuehrer.

19. **(E)** The D-Day invasion, or the invasion of Normandy, marked the beginning of the end of Hitler's hold on northwestern Europe. It is true that Hitler's substantial losses in the east, such as at Stalingrad (B), made his task more difficult in the west. But it is difficult to see how France and Belgium could have been liberated without a land invasion, which took place on June 6,1944. The "phony war" period (C) took place during the winter of 1939–1940; Hitler invaded Norway (D) in 1940; and the Battle of the Bulge (A) followed the D-Day invasion, marking Hitler's last major offensive operation in the west.

20. **(D)** The Marshall Plan is the popular term for the European Economic Recovery Program. The plan was designed to prevent freezing and starvation after the Second World War, and also to prevent communist influence from growing in western Europe. This program laid the foundation for Western Europe's postwar prosperity. By all accounts, it was a great success.

21. **(C)** The Warsaw Pact was the Soviet Union's counterpart to the North Atlantic Treaty Organization. East Berlin (B) was a Warsaw Pact member, and North Korea (E) received economic and military assistance from the Soviets. *Collectivization* (A) is a term used to describe the Soviets' taking of private farms and making them the property of the nation. The term *European Economic Union* (D) is an incorrect mixing of two terms associated with economic agreements reached after the Second World War: the European Economic Community and its successor the European Union.

22. **(B)** The Soviet Union bogged down in Afghanistan just as the United States bogged down in Vietnam. In both Vietnam and Afghanistan rural, seemingly backward people defeated superpowers in long wars that were characterized by guerrilla warfare. Where the U.S. war in Vietnam led to a

loss of international prestige, the Soviet war in Afghanistan contributed to the collapse of the Soviet Union.

23. **(A)** *Sputnik* was the first successful satellite. After the Soviets launched it into space, many Americans came to believe that their country was falling behind in the race for world—and galactic—domination. Consequently, John F. Kennedy ran for president in 1959 calling for significant growth in the American space program. Ten years later American astronauts planted an American flag on the moon.

24. **(C)** In 1963 the U.S. and Soviet Union came close to war as a result of Soviet missiles in Cuba. The Soviets' agreement to take the missiles out of Cuba was based partly on a secret promise from the United States later to remove U.S. missiles from Turkey.

25. **(B)** Since early modern times the first book to be translated into languages new to Europeans was the Bible. Much that scholars know about native languages that have changed significantly over time comes from translations of the Bible. Often hymns and prayer books were translated at the same time as or soon after translations of the Bible or portions of the Bible were made available.

26. **(E)** Belgium extracted great wealth from its colony, the Congo. Historians disagree about the extent to which the European powers benefited from imperialism, though the general view is that imperialism cost the colonizers more than they gained. Belgium is an exception, for it drew substantial wealth from the Congo in the form of rubber, ivory, and other commodities.

27. **(A)** Indochina, present-day Vietnam, was a French colony. The French experienced defeat at the hands of the Indochinese, or Vietnamese, in 1954 at Dienbienphu in northern Vietnam. Fearing that communism would spread through Southeast Asia, the United States picked up in Vietnam where France left off and, eventually, also experienced defeat. In the early twentieth century, the Japanese had influence in Korea (C), the Dutch in Indonesia (D), and the British in Singapore (E), where Britain suffered the greatest defeat, in terms of men captured, of its history during the Second World War.

28. **(E)** Napoleon suffered his final defeat at Waterloo. This battle followed Napoleon's return to France following his first banishment to the island of Elba. Following his defeat at Waterloo he was exiled to St. Helena, a small

island in the Atlantic. Napoleon suffered earlier defeats at Leipzig (A) and Moscow (C).

29. **(C)** Beginning in the late nineteenth century, newspapers became increasingly sensationalistic. What we now call the "tabloid press" got its start at this time. Nationalistic, jingoistic newspapers often beat the war drum, sometimes (as in the case of the Spanish-American War of 1898) stirring up significant sentiment in favor of war.

30. **(A)** Austria-Hungary faced great internal difficulties as a result of nationalist movements within its borders. Each of the countries listed hosted ethnic and linguistic minorities with nationalistic feelings—for example, the Welsh and Gaelic speakers of Britain (C). But nationalism was the greatest threat to Austria-Hungary. Serbian nationalism hurled that country into a war with Russia, which quickly developed into the First World War. After that war Austria-Hungary ceased to exist; it was killed partly by internal nationalism.

31. **(D)** Wilson hoped to "make the world safe for democracy" and peace. He advised against treating the defeated Germans harshly (A), and he favored adjusting borders to allow some ethnic groups to have their own nations (C). For example, Poland, which ceased to exist in the 1790s, emerged again on the map after the First World War. Wilson wished to see the Soviet Union fail and, barring that, he favored limiting its influence (B), but that was not his chief design for the League of Nations.

32. **(E)** The United States emerged from the First World War an international military power. It fought in the war less than a year, yet it emerged from the war strong and influential. One reason was that no part of the war had been fought on its soil. Another was its massive industrial power and wealth. Russia (D), Germany (A), France (B), and Italy (C) all faced significant internal difficulties following the war.

33. **(B)** The Weimar Republic was formed in Germany at the end of the First World War. Before Germany sued for peace, the Kaiser abdicated under threat of a revolt similar to the Soviet Union. The socialists and liberals who applied this pressure established a republic in Weimar and sued for peace. Hitler and the Nazis, along with many others in Germany, viewed the Weimar Republic as traitorous—as having stabbed Germany in the back.

34. **(D)** The Nazis outperformed all other parties in Germany's 1932 elections. The Nazis never gained 50 percent of the vote, but parties in European countries rarely do. For the Nazis to gain the vote of more than four in ten Germans only a decade after the party's formation suggests that Hitler's program had wide appeal.

35. **(A)** The German Reichstag was burned by a Dutch Communist. This gave Hitler an opportunity to claim that the Communists were staging a revolution. It was not true, but Communists were active in Germany—especially in Berlin—and many feared them.

36. **(A)** The Truman Doctrine was the first in a series of American policies to contain communism. As a result of this doctrine, the United States assisted Greece and Turkey in fights against communist forces. The Marshall Plan (C) involved providing millions of dollars to Europeans to rebuild after the Second World War and, as a result, ensuring that communism did not become deeply and widely rooted in western Europe. The Domino Theory (D) maintained that the fall of one country to communism would lead to another falling, and so on. This was the theory that drove the United States to fight communism in Vietnam.

37. **(C)** The Organization for European Economic Cooperation (OEEC) was formed to implement the Marshall Plan. The United States provided the funds and the OEEC organized the spending of it. (See the explanation of question 20 for further information on the Marshall Plan.)

38. **(D)** In 1948 the Soviets blockaded West Berlin in an effort to bring it under Soviet control. The Allies, led by the United States, flew goods into West Berlin day and night for a year. The Soviets backed down and reopened the routes between West Berlin and West Germany, and West Berlin remained free of communist government through the Cold War.

39. **(A)** Britain promised India its independence, which it gained in 1947, two years after the Second World War ended. An organized nationalist movement had been growing in India since the late nineteenth century. Its best-known leader was Mohandas Gandhi. Fearing a Japanese invasion of India, Britain did maintain some troops there, though Britons never outnumbered Indians (B).

40. **(C)** Answering this question correctly involves knowing when Chamberlain gave his most enduring speech. In 1938 at Munich, Hitler promised Chamberlain that he had no further desires to gain more territory than he

had already (having annexed Austria and parts of Czechoslovakia). Chamberlain believed—or wanted to believe—Hitler. The following year Hitler ordered his forces to invade Poland.

41. **(A)**   In 1905 Russia lost the Russo-Japanese War. For such a large country to be defeated by one so small was humiliating. More humiliating was the fact that Japan had only begun to modernize fifty years before.

42. **(B)**   In 1919 the pope endorsed the idea of women's suffrage—i.e., the vote for women. In the late nineteenth and early twentieth centuries women gained the vote in most of western Europe, in the United States and Canada, and in Australia and New Zealand. The Catholic Church still formally disapproves of non-natural methods of birth control, and Latin ceased to be the language of Mass following Vatican II in the 1960s.

43. **(D)**   The first wave of the baby boom generation brought rock music, blue jeans, and distinctive ways of talking into mainstream western culture. The 1920s had seen the advent of a youth culture, but it was dealt a blow by the Depression and the Second World War. The baby boomers enjoyed unprecedented wealth. Since the 1950s, youth culture has defined much of popular culture.

44. **(B)**   Under the apartheid regime black Africans who made up the large majority in South Africa had little political and economic power. South African society was strictly segregated Many countries limited trade with South Africa as a result of its policies and these, along with the general wave of change taking place in central and eastern Europe, led to the demise of the apartheid government.

45. **(C)**   The key to stability in the East Bloc was the Soviet military. Uprisings in 1956 (Hungary and Poland) and Czechoslovakia (1968) were put down by the Soviet military. In the late 1980s the Soviet military was occupied with a failing war in Afghanistan. Without the threat of the military to keep things together, the communist East Bloc would not have survived as long as it did.

46. **(D)**   Pope John Paul II, elected in 1978, was Polish. Unlike in other Soviet-dominated countries, the Catholic churches of Poland were not closed. They served as centers for discussion, and the Solidarity movement, which demanded reforms in communist Poland, had a strong Catholic identity. Pope John Paul II visited Poland and sparked hopes among the people there for greater freedom. Before John Paul II, popes had long been selected

from among Italians. Mother Teresa, who worked among the impoverished of Calcutta, was from Albania (A).

47. **(E)** The terms most associated with Gorbachev are *glasnost* ("openness") and *perestroika* ("restructuring"). Gorbachev ended the war in Afghanistan and legalized dissent. He believed that communism would benefit from criticism and challenges. Khrushchev (C) and Brezhnev (B) were earlier Soviet dictators, although they were not as harsh as Stalin. Trotsky (A) was a prominent early Bolshevik revolutionary, later assassinated by Stalin's agents. Putin (D) was elected president of the post-Soviet Russia in 2000.

48. **(D)** Hungary was the first East Bloc country to open its doors to the West. Once there was a breach in the so-called Iron Curtain separating communist eastern Europe from democratic western Europe, the flood of people who wanted out of the communist countries could not be stopped. Unlike in most East Bloc countries, Romania's dictator Nicolae Ceausescu tried to resist the winds of change (E). He and his wife were captured by reformers and shot.

49. **(A)** Walesa had led the Solidarity workers' movement in Poland. He is considered a key figure in sparking the end of the communist system in eastern Europe. His movement led to elections, which in turn led to the communists losing power. Unlike in earlier times, the Soviets did not step in to prevent or roll back the reforms of the late-1980s.

50. **(D)** Boris Yeltsin was post–Soviet Russia's first president. Putin (A) followed Yelstin in office as the second president of post–Soviet Russia. Among the challenges Putin faced were a separatist movement in Chechnya, which was aided by radical Muslims from central Asia, large-scale corruption, and a fragile economy.

51. **(D)** The Soviet military was bogged down in a losing war in Afghanistan. This was endured from 1979 to 1989. The East Bloc nations had their own militaries (B), but they were overseen by the Soviet military, and the Soviets based troops throughout the East Bloc. The United States boycotted the 1980 Olympics in Moscow as a result of the Soviet invasion of Afghanistan, but it did not threaten military action in the event the Soviets moved to stop reform movements in Poland, Hungary, and elsewhere (C). Pope John Paul II was an outspoken opponent of communism, and his visit to Poland in 1979 met with great enthusiasm, but the pope did not personally lead anticommunist rallies (E).

52. **(C)** After the collapse of the Soviet system, civil war broke out in Yugoslavia. The same region of eastern Europe that seethed before the First World War boiled again after the death of Marshal Tito and after the influence of the Soviet Union was gone (though the U.S.S.R. had not dominated Yugoslavia the way it had the East Bloc countries). Within Yugoslavia were major ethnic groups of different religions who had mistrusted one another for centuries—Serbs, Bosnians, Albanians, Croats, Montenegrins, Macedonians. War began in the summer of 1990 when Slovenia and Croatia declared their independence from Yugoslavia. In the course of the war, the Serbs followed a policy of "ethnic cleansing"—that is, the killing and forced removal of Muslims from Serbia. The Serb leader Slobodan Milosevic was later tried for war crimes.

53. **(A)** These were the *pieds-noirs* (literally, the "black feet"). The best known among them was the philosopher and playwright Albert Camus. Many of the Muslims who later emigrated to France came from France's former colony, Algeria.

54. **(B)** In the same way that the Chinese and Soviets assisted the Vietnamese in their war against the U.S., the U.S. assisted the anti-Soviet fighters in Afghanistan. There are no known cases of direct U.S. military involvement in the Soviet-Afghan War, but millions of dollars and weapons were funneled to the Afghan fighters through Pakistan's intelligence service.

55. **(E)** Mikhail Gorbachev unintentionally presided over the demise of the Soviet Union. By allowing greater political freedoms, he opened a door that could not be shut. The Soviet Union ceased to exist in late December 1991.

56. **(E)** Mussolini's forces invaded Ethiopia largely to compensate for Italy's loss in war against that country in the 1890s. Also, the League of Nations' failure to prevent Mussolini from conquering Ethiopia showed Mussolini and, more important, Hitler that they could buck the league's will.

57. **(A)** The Lateran Pact was the pope's agreement with Mussolini. In exchange, Mussolini gained the political recognition of the Catholic Church. Also as a result of this agreement the pope gained control over Vatican City. Mussolini was an atheist, but the majority of Italians were Catholics.

58. **(C)** The Dayton Accords followed NATO bombing strikes against Serbian targets. As a result of the agreement, Bosnia gained its independence,

and NATO troops remained in the Balkans for years thereafter to keep the peace. Haiti (A) experienced persistent chaos, and American and French troops went there in 2004 to reinstitute order. In the early 2000s the United Nations tried to bring peace to Sudan (B), a former British holding that had experienced decades of war. The war between Britain and Argentina over the Falkland Islands (D), or the Malvinas, as the Argentines called them, ended in 1982, and up to early 2005 Israel had fought no large-scale wars since the 1970s (E), probably because it alone in the Middle East at that time possessed nuclear weapons.

59. **(A)** Georges Clemenceau was the French premier in 1906–1909 and 1917–1920, and he, like many French people generally, wanted revenge. Following the First World War, the French could say that the Germans had fired the first shot, that the Germans had been belligerent for years before the war, and that the Germans had invaded and devastated much French territory. Following the war, the French were not eager to act on Wilson's call for "peace without victory," instead advocating significantly altering Germany's borders, seizing its colonies, and forcing it to repay the costs of the war (reparations).

60. **(E)** Germany left the League of Nations in 1933. When he was campaigning for the Nazi party, Hitler promised that he would pull Germany out of the League of Nations if he were placed in high office. He did so soon after gaining power. He did not like multilateral agreements, and he especially despised the league, which he believed intended to keep Germany hemmed in.

61. **(B)** Hitler sent troops into the Rhineland in 1935. According to the Versailles Treaty, that region on France's eastern border was not to have military personnel based in it. France, however, did have military personnel on its eastern border with Germany guarding the Maginot Line, France's system of defense. For Hitler, that was intolerable.

62. **(A)** Hitler dictated *Mein Kampf* to Rudolph Hess, who later became a key figure in the Nazi regime. Both were in prison for attempting to orchestrate a coup in the German state of Bavaria. *Mein Kampf* became a best seller following Hitler's rise to power, and it was easily available to all who wished to read it.

63. **(C)** Stalin's series of five-year plans began in 1928, and they focused on building the Soviet Union's heavy industry. The plans did not lead to the production levels Stalin hoped for, but they did make the U.S.S.R. much

more industrialized than it had been before. Thus they helped to prepare the Soviets for the devastating war Hitler would bring to them in the 1940s, though the Soviets would rely on U.S. assistance throughout the war.

64. **(D)**   In terms of body count, Stalin is one of the greatest killers of all time. About one-third of the members of the Soviet Communist Party were purged (i.e., executed, imprisoned, or exiled) in the early 1930s. Among those purged were many leading military officers. That purge of the military leadership led Hitler to believe that the Soviets, lacking significant experienced leadership, would be easy to beat in war.

65. **(E)**   Answering this question correctly depends on the student's ability to place events in chronological order. Lenin came to power in 1917, and he was followed by Stalin (A). Mussolini (B) came to power in 1922, Hitler (D) in 1933, and Spain's Franco (C) in 1939.

66. **(B)**   The word *cotton* in the question provides the essential clue. A demand for cotton cloth was a major force behind the first Industrial Revolution.

67. **(A)**   The transition to the rule of William III was orderly, and Parliament maintained its power and ability to check the power of the monarch. There was no radical change of governmental practice. The English Bill of Rights stated on paper what already existed as a result of previous political conflict and effort.

68. **(D)**   Though eighteenth-century England by early twenty-first century standards would not seem full of liberty, relative to Europe's other powers, it did provide greater opportunities to prosper. Some Huguenots (French Protestants) who fled to England contributed to England's wealth. It was this relative liberty that the French *philosophes* of the eighteenth century admired.

69. **(C)**   Hume denied that God plants essential ideas into the minds of people. This question can be answered using the process of elimination. All the choices besides (C) suggest modern ways of seeing the world. Before and after Hume, many theologians and philosophers (including Descartes) have argued that humans can only contemplate the idea of eternity and perfection— things they have not seen or experienced—because a perfect, eternal being has given them the capacity to do so.

70. **(B)**   Rousseau argued that man was by nature good—a "noble savage"— but was corrupted by society. For him, human societies stunted people's originality and true natures. Thus, in his novel *Emile,* he advocates a

system of education that allows students to follow their own natural interests. Rousseau is also associated with the concept of the *general will*, or the common interests of the people. If a minority is opposed to the general will, Rousseau maintains, it should be forced to abide by the general will for its own good.

71. **(E)** Mary Wollstonecraft argued in the eighteenth century for greater access to education for women. Of all the possibilities given, only Mary Wollstonecraft was an eighteenth-century writer. Simone de Beauvoir (C) was a twentieth-century feminist, and in the nineteenth century John Stuart Mill (A) advocated giving the vote to women. Rachel Carson (D) and her book *Silent Spring* is associated with the early environmentalist movement. Florence Nightingale (B) was a popular nurse during the Crimean War.

72. **(B)** The convention of the Assembly of Notables preceded the French Revolution. The Thermidorian Reaction (A), Napoleon's Concordat (C), the Reign of Terror (D) and the Great Fear (E) are all linked to the revolution, which began in 1789. The Assembly of Notables failed to agree to reforms that would put France's fiscal house in order; thus Louis XVI was compelled to convene the Estates General. The Glorious Revolution took place in England in 1688 (B).

73. **(C)** Though France's radical revolutionaries were hardly tolerant of people with different views, they did value books, reason, and learning. At the time public libraries were not yet a norm in Western civilization; Benjamin Franklin in the United States advocated opening them. Many book collections were held in monasteries, and when the church came under attack in revolutionary France, much church property, including its books, was confiscated.

74. **(B)** Slaves went to North America (C & D) in the hundreds of thousands, but they went to Latin America (especially Brazil), the Caribbean, and the West Indies by the millions. The most lucrative crop the slaves produced was sugar. In North America most slaves went to the South. Few went to New England, and very few went to Canada.

75. **(A)** The report of the Sadler Committee led to the Factory Act of 1833. In 1832 the parliamentarian Michael Sadler launched an investigation of conditions in England's textile factories. The stories the Sadler Committee heard of children working long hours with little rest and under the threat of violence led to the beginning in England of industrial reforms that would

continue through the nineteenth and twentieth centuries. The Sadler report was a response to industrialization, not a cause of it.

76. **(B)** The camp at Auschwitz, about 40 miles from Cracow, Poland, was the largest built by the Nazis. Well over one million Jews, Poles, gypsies (or Roma) and Soviet prisoners were killed there. Among its roles was putting prisoners to forced labor prior to exterminating them. The camp at Stutthof (E), near present-day Gdansk, Poland, was the first concentration camp built outside Germany. It was a relatively small camp and, though many died there, it was not an extermination camp. There were no death camps at Berlin (A), Brussels (C), or Bastogne (a site of a major campaign related to the Battle of the Bulge; D).

77. **(C)** The Bretton Woods Agreement (1944) made the U.S. dollar the world's reserve currency. This reveals the power the U.S. possessed as the Second World War began to wind down. Through the war the British Empire and, to a lesser extent, the Soviets had depended on American goods and material to keep their war machines running. American military power was also decisive in defeating the Nazis and, in the Pacific, the Japanese. Following the war, partly as a result of the U.S. mainland having been untouched by conflict and largely as a result of the jobs created by the war, the U.S. was the world's economic powerhouse—a position it held into the twenty-first century.

78. **(D)** Cubism emphasizes the fragmentation of human experience. *Baroque* (A) refers to seventeenth-century painting, architecture, and music. As the term *impressionism* (B) suggests, this school of art emphasized reproduction of people's impression of scenes. Edges and borders are not clearly defined. Among impressionism's best-known practitioners was Claude Monet. Realism (C), in literature and painting, attempts to depict reality from a detached, dispassionate point of view. Existentialism (E) was an intellectual movement expressed in literature and philosophical writing. It emphasized the need for people to create meaning for themselves, and its two best-known figures are Albert Camus and Jean-Paul Sartre.

79. **(D)** The European Economic Community was formed to promote cooperation among western European nations. In the late twentieth century, war between western European nations seemed unthinkable. This was partly because of the experience of two devastating world wars. But it was also because as the century wore on, the western European nations (and increasingly eastern European nations) were bound together by elaborate economic and political agreements.

80. **(D)**   Green parties, which emphasize environmental protection, are on the political left and do not advocate unregulated trade. Unlike free-market advocates, they believe that the environment and the rights of the poor are best preserved through government regulation and action. In political campaigns the Green parties regularly make common cause with feminists (A), animal rights groups (B), Social Democrats (i.e., socialist-leaning liberals; E), and pacifists (C).

81. **(C)**   In November 1938 the Nazi party called for Jewish stores and synagogues to be destroyed. This led to a night of terror called *Kristallnacht*, the "night of broken glass." Many buildings owned by Jews were looted, vandalized, and burned. At the time Hitler did not yet envision eliminating all Jews (B); the Nazis' intent at that point was for Jews to leave Germany. Many did, though others stayed, believing that the worst had passed. Hitler's effort to eliminate Europe's Jews is referred to as the Holocaust, or the *Shoah*. Germany's secret code—broken by the British—was produced by the Enigma machine (D).

82. **(A)**   Though some on the politically far left in the years following the Second World War would make excuses for the Soviet Union or argue that anti-Soviet news was capitalist propaganda, others believed, rightly, that the Soviets used the language of socialism and democracy as a cover for tyranny. The New Left called for genuine social democratic politics that relied on elections, political debates, and free speech. The New Left's influence is seen in the welfare states that prevail in western Europe, where taxes are high and government-sponsored health care is available to all.

83. **(B)**   Europeans had been busy collecting colonies since the 1500s, but Africa became a colonial focus in the late nineteenth and early twentieth centuries (1870–1914). The division of Africa into colonies and spheres of influence was the focus on the Berlin Conference of 1885. Today, European languages—especially English and French—are common in Africa. This is one legacy of colonialism.

84. **(C)**   Utilitarianism, which calls for the "greatest good for the greatest number," is most associated with Jeremy Bentham (1748–1832). Nihilism (A) claims that nothing can be known for certain and that all truth claims are baseless—a somewhat self-refuting school of thought since its own claims are taken by its adherents as true. Postmodernism (B) is a movement that is hard to define, and it expresses itself differently in politics, art, and literature. Essentially, it shares with nihilism a distrust of claims to

truth and, in particular, it rejects big-picture theories and ideas that claim to be true for all people, such as Christianity, Islam, and communism. A postmodernist might say, "What's true for you is true for you, and what's true for me is true for me."

85. **(A)** As a result of the Second Vatican Council (Vatican II), Latin was abandoned as the common global language of the Mass. While the Catholic Church recognized that a family could have good reasons to limit the number of children in it, the church remained opposed to artificial, non-natural birth control (C & D).

86. **(D)** When the term *Third World* was first coined, it referred to nations not aligned with either the United States or the Soviet Union. Now more often referred to as the developing world, the countries of the so-called Third World became synonymous with poverty, overpopulation, unhealthy living conditions, and political corruption. In that sense (not the original one), much of the Third World is in the Southern Hemisphere. Through the Cold War the United States and Soviet Union had military personnel based throughout the world, and their navies and air forces tracked one another in the air and at sea.

87. **(A)** Zionism, or Jewish nationalism, gave birth to the state of Israel in 1948. Minutes after Israel declared itself a nation, the United States recognized it as such. The United States was the first nation to do so, and the two countries have been close, if not always easy, allies since that time.

88. **(B)** The "Declaration of the Rights of Man and Citizen" allows for free speech only to the extent that that speech does not limit another person's freedoms and that public order is not disturbed. For the revolutionaries, the nation was more important than the individual's whims. Thus, most historians see the French Revolution as the first real nationalist movement.

89. **(B)** The English Bill of Rights did not grant political equality to Jews. Jews would not be granted political equality in England until the nineteenth century, and after that they faced discrimination, which was the norm in Europe, though anti-Semitism in England was much less severe than it was in Germany, Austria, and eastern Europe. A nineteenth-century British prime minister, Benjamin Disraeli, was a Jew by birth, but he was a convert to Christianity.

90. **(A)** In *The Wealth of Nations* (1776) Adam Smith maintains that as people pursue their own economic interests they do well for their society. For

example, if I want to succeed, then I will ask prices that are affordable and will attract customers. Low prices are good for others because that leaves them with money to invest in other projects. F A. Hayek (E) was a twentieth-century theorist who also advocated making room for substantial individual freedom in the economy. Jean-Baptiste Colbert (D) directed France's finances during the reign of Louis XIV and did not promote ideas similar to Smith's. Marx (B) and Engels (C) are the most prominent nineteenth-century theorists of communism, which does not allow for individuals creating wealth for their own benefit.

91. **(E)** The word *Versailles* in the quote signals that Louis XIV is the best of the available choices. Louis XIV built his elaborate living space outside France to awe foreigners and the French people, and to keep potentially troublesome nobles close at hand.

92. **(A)** The quote comes from Frederick II of Prussia, an "enlightened despot." This answer can be arrived at through the process of elimination. There is nothing in the quote about the monarch being God's elected person to rule, and thus "divine right" (D) can be eliminated. A quote exemplifying Marxism (C) would include language about class struggle, the proletariat, the bourgeoisie, and/or revolution. No absolutist ruler (B) would refer to himself as a servant of the state. In Louis XIV's view, he was the state. And we would expect an illustrative statement from a Social Democrat (E) to include language about equality, social justice, rights, reform, welfare programs, and so on.

93. **(D)** The pamphlet *"What Is the Third Estate?"* was written by Abbe Sieyes before the Estates General convened at Versailles in the early summer of 1789. Similarly, Thomas Paine's small book *Common Sense* helped to spur support for the American Revolution.

94. **(C)** Rousseau argued that a nation should be governed according to the "general will." Just what the general will is has been debated. Some who have promoted dictatorship and others who have called for democracy have referred to Rousseau's concept of the general will. Perhaps this ambiguity means that the concept itself is not very helpful.

95. **(A)** The French Revolution emphasized the nation as the source of sovereignty, rather than in a monarch or ruling class. During the French Revolution social distinctions were deemphasized, and in the eyes of the law they completely eliminated. In their place came the label *citoyen* (citizen).

96. **(E)** Like the revolutionaries later in Britain's American colonies, many seventeenth-century Britons feared that a standing army could be used by a monarch to eliminate liberties. Thus the English Bill of Rights limits the monarch's power to maintain a standing army in peace time.

97. **(E)** Napoleon made this statement while he was a military officer with the army of revolutionary France in Egypt. Wherever French armies went during the revolution and Napoleon's rule, they spread revolutionary ideas such as the one expressed in this quote.

98. **(B)** The Industrial Revolution began in England in the late 1700s but had spread to the European continent by the 1830s. This quote comes from 1844. By the late nineteenth century regulations and laws throughout Western civilization had made factories less harsh than they had been decades before, though they were still difficult places to work. By the late twentieth century, most factory work had been shipped to nations outside the West, where products produced with cheap labor were affordable to Europeans and Americans.

99. **(D)** Communists like Friedrich Engels called factory workers "wage slaves." Engels, with Karl Marx was the most important nineteenth century promoter of communism. Together they wrote the *Communist Manifesto* (1848). Mussolini (A) had been a Socialist as a young man but is most associated with fascism. Pankhurst (B) was a prominent late nineteenth-century British suffragette. Olympia de Gouges (C) argued for women's rights during the French Revolution. George Orwell (E) was a Socialist who is best known for his criticisms of dictatorship in his novels *Animal Farm* and *1984*.

100. **(A)** Students can answer this question correctly if they are familiar with the general thesis of Darwinism—namely, that more complicated organisms develop from simpler forms over long periods through natural processes. Andrew Carnegie (B) was a steel magnate and philanthropist; Einstein (C) was the most eminent physicist of the twentieth century; Marie Curie (D) was an important chemist; and John Watson (E) was a psychologist who focused on the ways behaviors are shaped through punishments and rewards. He is considered the father of American behavioral psychology.

101. **(C)** If students do not know the correct answer immediately, they can arrive at it through the process of elimination. The quote exemplifies an aspect of social Darwinism, which was one motivation behind the Scramble for Africa—that is, the belief that some races had a right or an obligation to

rule over and either civilize or exploit other races. Some British and French believed the Russians were inferior (and some Russians believed the British and French were inferior), but this manner of speaking belongs more to the late nineteenth century than to the 1840s, when the Crimean War (B) was fought. The social gospel movement (A) emphasized assisting the urban poor and downtrodden, and while some members of this movement would have agreed with the quotation, it does not exemplify the central thought of the social gospel.

102. **(A)**   Zola's famous article, in which he repeated the assertion "*j'accuse*" ("I accuse"), rallied many French people against the injustice dealt to Captain Dreyfus. The Dreyfus Affair, in which the Jewish officer was falsely charged and imprisoned for spying, is a prominent example of European anti-Semitism. Answering this question with certainty requires knowing about Zola's involvement in the Dreyfus case.

103. **(A)**   Kipling wrote his famous poem after the United States joined the club of global empires. Americans were in China during the Boxer Rebellion (B), an uprising of Chinese nationalists against foreigners. The United States was a key player in forcing nineteenth-century Japan to trade with the outside world (D), and U.S. President Theodore Roosevelt played a key role in bringing Russia and Japan to the peace table (E).

104. **(E)**   Nietzsche certainly was not Europe's first outspoken atheist—or, perhaps better to say, *anti*-theist—but he did popularize the phrase "God is dead." By this he meant that civilized society had progressed to the point where God was no longer necessary. Now, he said, the world looked to the strong man to arrange the world's affairs. Many Nazis, who later claimed Nietzsche as an inspiration, were also fervent atheists.

105. **(C)**   The slaughter of the First World War, which seemed to solve no substantial problems, caused many to doubt the goodness or existence of God, the reliability of traditions and the trustworthiness of governments. Artists of the Lost Generation exuded cynicism and world weariness.

106. **(D)**   Though the term *fascist* came to be applied to the Italian, German, and Japanese governments of the 1930s, the term itself was Italian, and Italian fascism was different in important respects from nazism. For example, Mussolini was not murderously anti-Jewish as leading Nazis were. Stalin (B) and Lenin (C) were Communists and completely opposed to fascism. Neither was Clemenceau (E), French premier at the end of the First World War, a fascist.

107. **(D)**   Burke's argument against the French Revolution was that it could not succeed because it was led by people who had no experience in leadership and because the reforms called for and instituted did not stem from natural societal evolution but from a radical break with custom and tradition. The "Declaration of the Rights of Man and Citizen" (B) has nothing reverential to say about the political traditions of France. In contrast, much that is in the U.S. Constitution (C) had existed in British common law for a long time.

108. **(C)**   The earthquake in Lisbon took place on All Saints Day while church services were being conducted. Fire and flood caused more damage, and tens of thousands died. Voltaire used this as an occasion to attack the idea that everything was controlled by a loving, all-powerful God. Some came to believe that the only explanation was simply that such things happen in the natural world. This event and its aftermath caused some in Europe to begin to doubt traditional theological answers to questions about the causes and reasons for pain and evil.

109. **(A)**   Rousseau maintained that educational systems should allow children to pursue their own interests. As he wrote: "Instead of keeping him [the student] cooped up in a stuffy room, take him out into a meadow every day. There let him run, let him frisk about. If he falls a hundred times, so much the better. He will learn all the sooner how to pick himself up. The well-being of liberty will make up for many wounds. My pupil will often have bruises; in return he will always be [happy]. Your pupils may have fewer bruises, but they are always constrained, always enchained, always sad."

110. **(B)**   Following the Second World War, Nazis were tried for war crimes in Nuremberg. This was the same city from which the Nuremberg Laws take their name. Passed in 1935, they stripped Jews in Germany of their civil rights. San Francisco (A) is where the United Nations first convened. The UN later moved to New York. Stalingrad (C) in the Soviet Union was where the Germans suffered one of many heavy defeats. Potsdam (Germany; D) and Tehran (Iran; E) were meeting places for the Allied leadership during the war. Divisions between the Americans and Soviets became clear at the Potsdam Conference (1945), as U.S. President Truman correctly accused the Soviet leader, Stalin, of wanting to make satellite states of the eastern European countries that Soviet forces liberated from the Nazis. Also at Potsdam, Truman revealed to the Soviets and British that the United States possessed a new weapon vastly more powerful than any seen before. Four

days after the end of this conference, on August 6, 1945, the United States dropped an atomic bomb on Hiroshima.

111. **(A)** Beaumarchais funneled war goods to the American revolutionaries. Posing as the fictional firm Rodrique, Hortalez, and Company, Beaumarchais sent large quantities of gunpowder, cannon, clothing, camping equipment, and firearms to the Americans during their revolution. This French help to the Americans was essential for the revolution to succeed. The French had an interest in seeing their long-time enemy, Britain, humbled.

112. **(B)** Berlin would be occupied following the Second World War, but it was not occupied after the First World War. After he came to power in 1933, Hitler ignored every other requirement listed as options—and many more.

113. **(E)** Answering this question correctly requires that students know that Kipling's writing is associated with Western imperialism of the late nineteenth and early twentieth centuries. The "captives" specifically referred to are the Filipinos that came under U.S. control after Spain lost the Philippines to the Americans after the Spanish-American War, but it can be considered to apply to the colonized generally. Tennyson (A) was a prominent nineteenth-century British poet. Among his best known poems is the "Lady of Shalott." H. G Wells (B) was a British writer of the late nineteenth and early twentieth centuries, most remembered for his science fiction in the novels *The Time Machine, War of the Worlds*, and *Invisible Man*. Bertrand Russell (C) was a British philosopher and essayist who argued for the dismantling of traditional views on sexuality and the family. G K. Chesterton (D) was a Catholic writer who made a stiff and witty defense of traditional Catholicism. His work is still much read.

114. **(A)** Woodrow Wilson promoted the idea of the self-determination of ethnic groups as a way of avoiding future wars, because the First World War was sparked by ethnic nationalism in Austria-Hungary. Many German nationalists would be angered that this principle did not apply to them: Germans lived in Czechoslovakia, Poland, Austria (which the League of Nations prohibited from joining Germany), and elsewhere. The Nazis wanted to see all Germans living within a single German nation.

115. **(E)** Answering this question correctly simply involves having a sense of when the Crimean War was fought: 1853–1856. This war pitted France and Britain against Russia.

116. **(D)** Descartes maintained that people are able to understand the idea of perfection because a perfect being has planted the idea in their minds. This is the essence of several arguments put forward to make an intellectual case for the existence of God. Since the 1600s Christian intellectuals have felt compelled to devise rational arguments to defend belief in God. Among the better-known early intellectuals was Pascal.

117. **(A)** Apparently the cold northern weather and early hours were too much for Descartes. Russia's Catherine the Great also hosted the Enlightenment encyclopedist Diderot, whose library she purchased.

118. **(B)** In *The Social Contract* Rousseau theorizes about the "general will." He claims that individuals should give up some of their personal freedoms for the good of the community.

119. **(C)** Richelieu and Colbert are remembered for organizing France's public affairs in the *ancien regime*. Among Richelieu's reforms was the establishment of professional tax-collectors, called *intendents*, who were responsible to no one but the king. This angered many nobles, who avoided paying taxes, for now they could not get away as easily with not paying. France's finances were a continual problem before the Revolution. Expensive wars were waged with insufficient funds.

120. **(A)** Nazism's anti-Semitic program was predicated on the belief that Germany's problems were the fault of the Jews. Hitler blamed Germany's loss in the First World War on a Jewish conspiracy, and he laid the decadence of German culture in the 1920s at the feet of the Jews. For Hitler, Jews were somehow both very powerful and subhuman.

PRACTICE TEST 1

Answer Sheet

1. Ⓐ Ⓑ Ⓒ Ⓓ Ⓔ	27. Ⓐ Ⓑ Ⓒ Ⓓ Ⓔ	53. Ⓐ Ⓑ Ⓒ Ⓓ Ⓔ
2. Ⓐ Ⓑ Ⓒ Ⓓ Ⓔ	28. Ⓐ Ⓑ Ⓒ Ⓓ Ⓔ	54. Ⓐ Ⓑ Ⓒ Ⓓ Ⓔ
3. Ⓐ Ⓑ Ⓒ Ⓓ Ⓔ	29. Ⓐ Ⓑ Ⓒ Ⓓ Ⓔ	55. Ⓐ Ⓑ Ⓒ Ⓓ Ⓔ
4. Ⓐ Ⓑ Ⓒ Ⓓ Ⓔ	30. Ⓐ Ⓑ Ⓒ Ⓓ Ⓔ	56. Ⓐ Ⓑ Ⓒ Ⓓ Ⓔ
5. Ⓐ Ⓑ Ⓒ Ⓓ Ⓔ	31. Ⓐ Ⓑ Ⓒ Ⓓ Ⓔ	57. Ⓐ Ⓑ Ⓒ Ⓓ Ⓔ
6. Ⓐ Ⓑ Ⓒ Ⓓ Ⓔ	32. Ⓐ Ⓑ Ⓒ Ⓓ Ⓔ	58. Ⓐ Ⓑ Ⓒ Ⓓ Ⓔ
7. Ⓐ Ⓑ Ⓒ Ⓓ Ⓔ	33. Ⓐ Ⓑ Ⓒ Ⓓ Ⓔ	59. Ⓐ Ⓑ Ⓒ Ⓓ Ⓔ
8. Ⓐ Ⓑ Ⓒ Ⓓ Ⓔ	34. Ⓐ Ⓑ Ⓒ Ⓓ Ⓔ	60. Ⓐ Ⓑ Ⓒ Ⓓ Ⓔ
9. Ⓐ Ⓑ Ⓒ Ⓓ Ⓔ	35. Ⓐ Ⓑ Ⓒ Ⓓ Ⓔ	61. Ⓐ Ⓑ Ⓒ Ⓓ Ⓔ
10. Ⓐ Ⓑ Ⓒ Ⓓ Ⓔ	36. Ⓐ Ⓑ Ⓒ Ⓓ Ⓔ	62. Ⓐ Ⓑ Ⓒ Ⓓ Ⓔ
11. Ⓐ Ⓑ Ⓒ Ⓓ Ⓔ	37. Ⓐ Ⓑ Ⓒ Ⓓ Ⓔ	63. Ⓐ Ⓑ Ⓒ Ⓓ Ⓔ
12. Ⓐ Ⓑ Ⓒ Ⓓ Ⓔ	38. Ⓐ Ⓑ Ⓒ Ⓓ Ⓔ	64. Ⓐ Ⓑ Ⓒ Ⓓ Ⓔ
13. Ⓐ Ⓑ Ⓒ Ⓓ Ⓔ	39. Ⓐ Ⓑ Ⓒ Ⓓ Ⓔ	65. Ⓐ Ⓑ Ⓒ Ⓓ Ⓔ
14. Ⓐ Ⓑ Ⓒ Ⓓ Ⓔ	40. Ⓐ Ⓑ Ⓒ Ⓓ Ⓔ	66. Ⓐ Ⓑ Ⓒ Ⓓ Ⓔ
15. Ⓐ Ⓑ Ⓒ Ⓓ Ⓔ	41. Ⓐ Ⓑ Ⓒ Ⓓ Ⓔ	67. Ⓐ Ⓑ Ⓒ Ⓓ Ⓔ
16. Ⓐ Ⓑ Ⓒ Ⓓ Ⓔ	42. Ⓐ Ⓑ Ⓒ Ⓓ Ⓔ	68. Ⓐ Ⓑ Ⓒ Ⓓ Ⓔ
17. Ⓐ Ⓑ Ⓒ Ⓓ Ⓔ	43. Ⓐ Ⓑ Ⓒ Ⓓ Ⓔ	69. Ⓐ Ⓑ Ⓒ Ⓓ Ⓔ
18. Ⓐ Ⓑ Ⓒ Ⓓ Ⓔ	44. Ⓐ Ⓑ Ⓒ Ⓓ Ⓔ	70. Ⓐ Ⓑ Ⓒ Ⓓ Ⓔ
19. Ⓐ Ⓑ Ⓒ Ⓓ Ⓔ	45. Ⓐ Ⓑ Ⓒ Ⓓ Ⓔ	71. Ⓐ Ⓑ Ⓒ Ⓓ Ⓔ
20. Ⓐ Ⓑ Ⓒ Ⓓ Ⓔ	46. Ⓐ Ⓑ Ⓒ Ⓓ Ⓔ	72. Ⓐ Ⓑ Ⓒ Ⓓ Ⓔ
21. Ⓐ Ⓑ Ⓒ Ⓓ Ⓔ	47. Ⓐ Ⓑ Ⓒ Ⓓ Ⓔ	73. Ⓐ Ⓑ Ⓒ Ⓓ Ⓔ
22. Ⓐ Ⓑ Ⓒ Ⓓ Ⓔ	48. Ⓐ Ⓑ Ⓒ Ⓓ Ⓔ	74. Ⓐ Ⓑ Ⓒ Ⓓ Ⓔ
23. Ⓐ Ⓑ Ⓒ Ⓓ Ⓔ	49. Ⓐ Ⓑ Ⓒ Ⓓ Ⓔ	75. Ⓐ Ⓑ Ⓒ Ⓓ Ⓔ
24. Ⓐ Ⓑ Ⓒ Ⓓ Ⓔ	50. Ⓐ Ⓑ Ⓒ Ⓓ Ⓔ	76. Ⓐ Ⓑ Ⓒ Ⓓ Ⓔ
25. Ⓐ Ⓑ Ⓒ Ⓓ Ⓔ	51. Ⓐ Ⓑ Ⓒ Ⓓ Ⓔ	77. Ⓐ Ⓑ Ⓒ Ⓓ Ⓔ
26. Ⓐ Ⓑ Ⓒ Ⓓ Ⓔ	52. Ⓐ Ⓑ Ⓒ Ⓓ Ⓔ	78. Ⓐ Ⓑ Ⓒ Ⓓ Ⓔ

(Continued)

PRACTICE TEST 1

Answer Sheet

79. Ⓐ Ⓑ Ⓒ Ⓓ Ⓔ
80. Ⓐ Ⓑ Ⓒ Ⓓ Ⓔ
81. Ⓐ Ⓑ Ⓒ Ⓓ Ⓔ
82. Ⓐ Ⓑ Ⓒ Ⓓ Ⓔ
83. Ⓐ Ⓑ Ⓒ Ⓓ Ⓔ
84. Ⓐ Ⓑ Ⓒ Ⓓ Ⓔ
85. Ⓐ Ⓑ Ⓒ Ⓓ Ⓔ
86. Ⓐ Ⓑ Ⓒ Ⓓ Ⓔ
87. Ⓐ Ⓑ Ⓒ Ⓓ Ⓔ
88. Ⓐ Ⓑ Ⓒ Ⓓ Ⓔ
89. Ⓐ Ⓑ Ⓒ Ⓓ Ⓔ
90. Ⓐ Ⓑ Ⓒ Ⓓ Ⓔ
91. Ⓐ Ⓑ Ⓒ Ⓓ Ⓔ
92. Ⓐ Ⓑ Ⓒ Ⓓ Ⓔ

93. Ⓐ Ⓑ Ⓒ Ⓓ Ⓔ
94. Ⓐ Ⓑ Ⓒ Ⓓ Ⓔ
95. Ⓐ Ⓑ Ⓒ Ⓓ Ⓔ
96. Ⓐ Ⓑ Ⓒ Ⓓ Ⓔ
97. Ⓐ Ⓑ Ⓒ Ⓓ Ⓔ
98. Ⓐ Ⓑ Ⓒ Ⓓ Ⓔ
99. Ⓐ Ⓑ Ⓒ Ⓓ Ⓔ
100. Ⓐ Ⓑ Ⓒ Ⓓ Ⓔ
101. Ⓐ Ⓑ Ⓒ Ⓓ Ⓔ
102. Ⓐ Ⓑ Ⓒ Ⓓ Ⓔ
103. Ⓐ Ⓑ Ⓒ Ⓓ Ⓔ
104. Ⓐ Ⓑ Ⓒ Ⓓ Ⓔ
105. Ⓐ Ⓑ Ⓒ Ⓓ Ⓔ
106. Ⓐ Ⓑ Ⓒ Ⓓ Ⓔ

107. Ⓐ Ⓑ Ⓒ Ⓓ Ⓔ
108. Ⓐ Ⓑ Ⓒ Ⓓ Ⓔ
109. Ⓐ Ⓑ Ⓒ Ⓓ Ⓔ
110. Ⓐ Ⓑ Ⓒ Ⓓ Ⓔ
111. Ⓐ Ⓑ Ⓒ Ⓓ Ⓔ
112. Ⓐ Ⓑ Ⓒ Ⓓ Ⓔ
113. Ⓐ Ⓑ Ⓒ Ⓓ Ⓔ
114. Ⓐ Ⓑ Ⓒ Ⓓ Ⓔ
115. Ⓐ Ⓑ Ⓒ Ⓓ Ⓔ
116. Ⓐ Ⓑ Ⓒ Ⓓ Ⓔ
117. Ⓐ Ⓑ Ⓒ Ⓓ Ⓔ
118. Ⓐ Ⓑ Ⓒ Ⓓ Ⓔ
119. Ⓐ Ⓑ Ⓒ Ⓓ Ⓔ
120. Ⓐ Ⓑ Ⓒ Ⓓ Ⓔ

PRACTICE TEST 2

Answer Sheet

1. Ⓐ Ⓑ Ⓒ Ⓓ Ⓔ	27. Ⓐ Ⓑ Ⓒ Ⓓ Ⓔ	53. Ⓐ Ⓑ Ⓒ Ⓓ Ⓔ
2. Ⓐ Ⓑ Ⓒ Ⓓ Ⓔ	28. Ⓐ Ⓑ Ⓒ Ⓓ Ⓔ	54. Ⓐ Ⓑ Ⓒ Ⓓ Ⓔ
3. Ⓐ Ⓑ Ⓒ Ⓓ Ⓔ	29. Ⓐ Ⓑ Ⓒ Ⓓ Ⓔ	55. Ⓐ Ⓑ Ⓒ Ⓓ Ⓔ
4. Ⓐ Ⓑ Ⓒ Ⓓ Ⓔ	30. Ⓐ Ⓑ Ⓒ Ⓓ Ⓔ	56. Ⓐ Ⓑ Ⓒ Ⓓ Ⓔ
5. Ⓐ Ⓑ Ⓒ Ⓓ Ⓔ	31. Ⓐ Ⓑ Ⓒ Ⓓ Ⓔ	57. Ⓐ Ⓑ Ⓒ Ⓓ Ⓔ
6. Ⓐ Ⓑ Ⓒ Ⓓ Ⓔ	32. Ⓐ Ⓑ Ⓒ Ⓓ Ⓔ	58. Ⓐ Ⓑ Ⓒ Ⓓ Ⓔ
7. Ⓐ Ⓑ Ⓒ Ⓓ Ⓔ	33. Ⓐ Ⓑ Ⓒ Ⓓ Ⓔ	59. Ⓐ Ⓑ Ⓒ Ⓓ Ⓔ
8. Ⓐ Ⓑ Ⓒ Ⓓ Ⓔ	34. Ⓐ Ⓑ Ⓒ Ⓓ Ⓔ	60. Ⓐ Ⓑ Ⓒ Ⓓ Ⓔ
9. Ⓐ Ⓑ Ⓒ Ⓓ Ⓔ	35. Ⓐ Ⓑ Ⓒ Ⓓ Ⓔ	61. Ⓐ Ⓑ Ⓒ Ⓓ Ⓔ
10. Ⓐ Ⓑ Ⓒ Ⓓ Ⓔ	36. Ⓐ Ⓑ Ⓒ Ⓓ Ⓔ	62. Ⓐ Ⓑ Ⓒ Ⓓ Ⓔ
11. Ⓐ Ⓑ Ⓒ Ⓓ Ⓔ	37. Ⓐ Ⓑ Ⓒ Ⓓ Ⓔ	63. Ⓐ Ⓑ Ⓒ Ⓓ Ⓔ
12. Ⓐ Ⓑ Ⓒ Ⓓ Ⓔ	38. Ⓐ Ⓑ Ⓒ Ⓓ Ⓔ	64. Ⓐ Ⓑ Ⓒ Ⓓ Ⓔ
13. Ⓐ Ⓑ Ⓒ Ⓓ Ⓔ	39. Ⓐ Ⓑ Ⓒ Ⓓ Ⓔ	65. Ⓐ Ⓑ Ⓒ Ⓓ Ⓔ
14. Ⓐ Ⓑ Ⓒ Ⓓ Ⓔ	40. Ⓐ Ⓑ Ⓒ Ⓓ Ⓔ	66. Ⓐ Ⓑ Ⓒ Ⓓ Ⓔ
15. Ⓐ Ⓑ Ⓒ Ⓓ Ⓔ	41. Ⓐ Ⓑ Ⓒ Ⓓ Ⓔ	67. Ⓐ Ⓑ Ⓒ Ⓓ Ⓔ
16. Ⓐ Ⓑ Ⓒ Ⓓ Ⓔ	42. Ⓐ Ⓑ Ⓒ Ⓓ Ⓔ	68. Ⓐ Ⓑ Ⓒ Ⓓ Ⓔ
17. Ⓐ Ⓑ Ⓒ Ⓓ Ⓔ	43. Ⓐ Ⓑ Ⓒ Ⓓ Ⓔ	69. Ⓐ Ⓑ Ⓒ Ⓓ Ⓔ
18. Ⓐ Ⓑ Ⓒ Ⓓ Ⓔ	44. Ⓐ Ⓑ Ⓒ Ⓓ Ⓔ	70. Ⓐ Ⓑ Ⓒ Ⓓ Ⓔ
19. Ⓐ Ⓑ Ⓒ Ⓓ Ⓔ	45. Ⓐ Ⓑ Ⓒ Ⓓ Ⓔ	71. Ⓐ Ⓑ Ⓒ Ⓓ Ⓔ
20. Ⓐ Ⓑ Ⓒ Ⓓ Ⓔ	46. Ⓐ Ⓑ Ⓒ Ⓓ Ⓔ	72. Ⓐ Ⓑ Ⓒ Ⓓ Ⓔ
21. Ⓐ Ⓑ Ⓒ Ⓓ Ⓔ	47. Ⓐ Ⓑ Ⓒ Ⓓ Ⓔ	73. Ⓐ Ⓑ Ⓒ Ⓓ Ⓔ
22. Ⓐ Ⓑ Ⓒ Ⓓ Ⓔ	48. Ⓐ Ⓑ Ⓒ Ⓓ Ⓔ	74. Ⓐ Ⓑ Ⓒ Ⓓ Ⓔ
23. Ⓐ Ⓑ Ⓒ Ⓓ Ⓔ	49. Ⓐ Ⓑ Ⓒ Ⓓ Ⓔ	75. Ⓐ Ⓑ Ⓒ Ⓓ Ⓔ
24. Ⓐ Ⓑ Ⓒ Ⓓ Ⓔ	50. Ⓐ Ⓑ Ⓒ Ⓓ Ⓔ	76. Ⓐ Ⓑ Ⓒ Ⓓ Ⓔ
25. Ⓐ Ⓑ Ⓒ Ⓓ Ⓔ	51. Ⓐ Ⓑ Ⓒ Ⓓ Ⓔ	77. Ⓐ Ⓑ Ⓒ Ⓓ Ⓔ
26. Ⓐ Ⓑ Ⓒ Ⓓ Ⓔ	52. Ⓐ Ⓑ Ⓒ Ⓓ Ⓔ	78. Ⓐ Ⓑ Ⓒ Ⓓ Ⓔ

(Continued)

PRACTICE TEST 2

Answer Sheet

79. Ⓐ Ⓑ Ⓒ Ⓓ Ⓔ	93. Ⓐ Ⓑ Ⓒ Ⓓ Ⓔ	107. Ⓐ Ⓑ Ⓒ Ⓓ Ⓔ
80. Ⓐ Ⓑ Ⓒ Ⓓ Ⓔ	94. Ⓐ Ⓑ Ⓒ Ⓓ Ⓔ	108. Ⓐ Ⓑ Ⓒ Ⓓ Ⓔ
81. Ⓐ Ⓑ Ⓒ Ⓓ Ⓔ	95. Ⓐ Ⓑ Ⓒ Ⓓ Ⓔ	109. Ⓐ Ⓑ Ⓒ Ⓓ Ⓔ
82. Ⓐ Ⓑ Ⓒ Ⓓ Ⓔ	96. Ⓐ Ⓑ Ⓒ Ⓓ Ⓔ	110. Ⓐ Ⓑ Ⓒ Ⓓ Ⓔ
83. Ⓐ Ⓑ Ⓒ Ⓓ Ⓔ	97. Ⓐ Ⓑ Ⓒ Ⓓ Ⓔ	111. Ⓐ Ⓑ Ⓒ Ⓓ Ⓔ
84. Ⓐ Ⓑ Ⓒ Ⓓ Ⓔ	98. Ⓐ Ⓑ Ⓒ Ⓓ Ⓔ	112. Ⓐ Ⓑ Ⓒ Ⓓ Ⓔ
85. Ⓐ Ⓑ Ⓒ Ⓓ Ⓔ	99. Ⓐ Ⓑ Ⓒ Ⓓ Ⓔ	113. Ⓐ Ⓑ Ⓒ Ⓓ Ⓔ
86. Ⓐ Ⓑ Ⓒ Ⓓ Ⓔ	100. Ⓐ Ⓑ Ⓒ Ⓓ Ⓔ	114. Ⓐ Ⓑ Ⓒ Ⓓ Ⓔ
87. Ⓐ Ⓑ Ⓒ Ⓓ Ⓔ	101. Ⓐ Ⓑ Ⓒ Ⓓ Ⓔ	115. Ⓐ Ⓑ Ⓒ Ⓓ Ⓔ
88. Ⓐ Ⓑ Ⓒ Ⓓ Ⓔ	102. Ⓐ Ⓑ Ⓒ Ⓓ Ⓔ	116. Ⓐ Ⓑ Ⓒ Ⓓ Ⓔ
89. Ⓐ Ⓑ Ⓒ Ⓓ Ⓔ	103. Ⓐ Ⓑ Ⓒ Ⓓ Ⓔ	117. Ⓐ Ⓑ Ⓒ Ⓓ Ⓔ
90. Ⓐ Ⓑ Ⓒ Ⓓ Ⓔ	104. Ⓐ Ⓑ Ⓒ Ⓓ Ⓔ	118. Ⓐ Ⓑ Ⓒ Ⓓ Ⓔ
91. Ⓐ Ⓑ Ⓒ Ⓓ Ⓔ	105. Ⓐ Ⓑ Ⓒ Ⓓ Ⓔ	119. Ⓐ Ⓑ Ⓒ Ⓓ Ⓔ
92. Ⓐ Ⓑ Ⓒ Ⓓ Ⓔ	106. Ⓐ Ⓑ Ⓒ Ⓓ Ⓔ	120. Ⓐ Ⓑ Ⓒ Ⓓ Ⓔ

Glossary

absolutism—A political trend after the Thirty Years' War that emphasized the complete authority of a nation's ruler.

agricultural revolution—Eighteenth-century revolution brought on by a need to feed a growing population and enabled by improved growing methods.

Al Qaeda—Terrorist network created by Osama bin Laden; undertook major attacks against the United States.

Alien and Sedition Acts—U.S. security laws passed in anticipation of war in 1798; restricted alien naturalization and banned the press from writing malicious statements against the government.

Allies—Military alliance during both World War I and World War II; generally made up of Great Britain, France, and their supporters, including the United States; during World War I, included Italy; during World War II, included the Soviet Union.

anarchists—Those who advocate the overthrow of all government.

ancien regime—French term describing the old order of absolute monarchs.

Anschluss—Forced joining of Germany and Austria in 1938.

anti-Semitism—Anti-Jewish sentiment and persecution.

apartheid—South African government policy of strict racial segregation; ended in 1993.

Assembly of Notables—An assembly of France's elite convened to help reform the country's finances in 1787.

Atlantic Charter—Document signed by U.S. President Franklin D. Roosevelt and British Prime Minister Winston Churchill in 1941; encouraging self-government and global cooperation; set the stage for the formation of the United Nations.

atomic bomb—Powerful nuclear weapon; most famously used by the United States against Japan to hasten the end of World War II.

Auschwitz—Largest death camp built by the Germans during World War II; site of the murder of more than one million Jews.

Axis Powers—Alliance of Germany, Italy, and Japan during World War II.

Bacon, Sir Francis—English theorist (1561–1626) who popularized the inductive method of scientific reasoning.

Bare Bones Parliament—English Parliament after it was purged of Puritan members under Cromwell.

Battle of Britain—Air campaign between Great Britain and Germany fought during 1940; prevented Germany from taking Britain.

Bentham, Jeremy—English economist and philosopher (1748–1832) who advocated utilitarianism.

273

Berlin Conference—Conference held in 1885 to divide Africa among the leading European powers for purposes of colonization; contributed to the Scramble for Africa.

Berlin Wall—Physical wall dividing communist East Berlin and democratic West Berlin; constructed in 1961; fell in 1989; symbol of the division between the West and the Eastern Bloc.

Bishop Bossuet—Tutor to Louis XIV and philosopher; advocated for absolutism from a strictly religious point of view.

Bismarck, Otto von—Late nineteenth-century German statesman; primary force behind the unification of Germany.

Blitz—German bombing of British cities during World War II.

blitzkrieg—German style of rapid, land- and air-based warfare during World War II; literally, "lightning war."

Boston Tea Party—When American settlers, protesting the tax on tea imports and monopoly of the East India Company, dressed as Mohawk Indians and dumped 342 chests full of tea into Boston Harbor.

bourgeoisie—The middle-class; group opposed by Marx and other communists.

Brahe, Tycho—Danish astronomer (1546–1601) who studied the positions of planets and stars; work supported Kepler's studies of elliptical orbits.

Brest-Litovsk Treaty—Treaty signed by Russia and Germany in 1918; granted independence to several former Russian states, including Finland, Poland, Estonia, and Lithuania.

Brezhnev Doctrine—Cold War–era Soviet doctrine stating that the Soviet Union reserved the right to interfere in the domestic policies of communist nations.

British East India Company—Joint-stock company established to conduct trade in Asia; based on the Dutch model.

bureaucracy—Complex form of governmental organization; relies on a division of labor and a strict chain of command.

capitalism—Economic system in which the majority of the production of goods is privately owned and income is distributed through the operation of markets; also known as the free-market system.

Carnegie, Andrew—American industrialist and multimillionaire (1835–1919); supported the concept of the gospel of wealth.

Catherine the Great—Eighteenth-century Russian empress who advocated liberal humanitarian political theories for government reform.

Cavaliers—Supporters of Charles I during the English Civil War.

Central Directory—Organized Prussian government bureaucracy organized by the Fredericks; staffed by nobles and professional civil servants.

Central Powers—World War I alliance of Germany and its comrade nations, including Austria and the Ottoman Empire.

Charles I—17th century English king, son of James I, who believed, as his father did, that he ruled by a divine right; distrusted and repressed Parliament.

Charles II—Seventeenth-century English king who was restored to the throne after being exiled during the era of the Puritan Commonwealth.

Chartist movement—British working-class movement for parliamentary reform.

Chechnya—Russian region; site of civil war between Russian forces and Muslim separatists after the fall of the Soviet Union.

checks and balances—Governmental system establishing policies or structures so that no one governing unit has too much power.

Chernobyl—Site of a major nuclear disaster that took place in 1986 in Ukraine.

Churchill, Winston—British prime minister during World War II; led strong national opposition to Hitler's Germany.

Civil Code—Napoleonic Code of 1804; sought to encourage advancement in government and the military through merit rather than by status.

Civil Constitution of the Clergy—French document of 1790 requiring clergy to take an oath of loyalty to the nation.

Colbert, Jean-Baptiste—Chief Minister to Louis XIV; centralized the French economy by employing mercantilism.

Cold War—Lengthy period of conflict, mostly between the United States and the Soviet Union, over global dominance; contributed to the outbreak of several regional conflicts, including the Korean War and the Vietnam War.

Committee of Public Safety—French Revolutionary body that led the nation against powers seeking to end the Revolution; led by Danton and, later, Robespierre; created the first European national army.

Commonwealth of Independent States—National unit that replaced the Soviet Union upon its fall in 1991.

Communist Manifesto—Work written by Karl Marx in 1848; argued for a workers' revolution to end capitalism and institute a utopian, egalitarian society with no economic divisions.

Congress of Vienna—European conference that reorganized the continent following the defeat of Napoleon; created new buffer states; sought to ensure lasting peace.

conservatism—Political belief that tradition helps determine whether an idea is worthwhile.

containment—Cold War-era U.S. policy of preventing the spread of communism.

Convention of Westminster—Alliance in 1756 between England and Prussia against France.

Copernicus, Nicolaus—Polish astronomer (1473–1543) who concluded that Earth revolved around the Sun, also known as the heliocentric theory.

Crimean War—War fought between an alliance of Britain, France, and the Ottoman Empire against Russia; aimed to gain control of oversight of certain Christian shrines in the Middle East; granted French and British ships the right to trade in the Black Sea.

Cromwell, Oliver—Leader of the New Model Army for Parliament during the English Civil War; became leader of England alongside Parliament following the conflict.

Cuban Missile Crisis—Incident in 1962 during which the United States and the Soviet Union almost came to physical war; occurred over the presence of Soviet missiles on the island of Cuba.

Curie, Marie—Polish-born French physicist (1867–1934); with her husband Pierre, discovered radium; shared a Nobel Prize for her work.

Darwin, Charles—British naturalist (1809–1882) who formed the theory of evolution through natural selection.

Dayton Accord—Agreement signed in 1995 that granted Bosnia independence and stationed NATO troops in the Balkans for several years.

D-Day—Major allied invasion of German-occupied France during World War II; gave the Allies a foothold from which to regain control of France.

de Chateaubriand, Réné—French writer and diplomat (1768–1848) who wrote of the influence of religious feeling on history, government, the arts, nature, and the conscience.

de Condorcet, Marie Jean—French philosopher (1743–1794) who believed that through reason, study, and tolerance humans could achieve perfection.

de Gaulle, Charles—French general and leader of the Free French movement; later served as president of France.

de Gouges, Olympia—French playwright (1748–1793) who wrote the *Declaration of the Rights of Woman and Female Citizen* calling for political equality of men and women.

Decembrist Revolt—A badly planned revolt against the Russian government following the death of Tsar Alexander I.

Declaration of Pillnitz—Declaration by Leopold II and Friedrich Wilhelm II that they would invade France if the royal family was harmed.

Declaration of the Rights of Man and Citizen—French document of 1789 declaring that all citizens were politically equal and enjoyed inherent right to "liberty, property, security, and resistance to oppression."

deductive method—Logical system based on making smaller conclusions based on general principles.

deists—Those who believed that God had created the world but then stood back from it to let it function on its own.

Descartes, Réné—French philosopher (1596–1650) who believed that true knowledge about the world could be attained only through the use of human reason; author of the influential *Discourse on Method*.

Diderot, Denis—French philosopher (1713–1778); edited the first multivolume collection of learning, *Encyclopedia, or Dictionary of the Sciences, Arts, and Trades*.

Directory—Five-man group that oversaw the French legislature under the 1795 constitution written by the National Convention.

divine right—The authority to govern given to kings directly from God.

Drake, Sir Francis—English admiral who circumnavigated the globe; began career as a privateer.

Dutch East India Company—Joint-stock company established to conduct trade in Asia.

Easter Rising—Irish civil conflict in 1916; pitted Irish republicans against British forces for the right to a free Ireland.

Eastern Question—The diplomatic problem caused by the disintegrating Ottoman Empire, which endangered trade routes important to France and England.

Edict of Nantes—French decree of 1598 granting the Huguenots freedom of worship.

Edict of Toleration—Austrian law affirming freedom of religious practice for all Christians.

Einstein, Albert—German-American physicist (1879–1955) who developed several influential scientific theories, including the theory of relativity.

Emerson, Ralph Waldo—American transcendentalist writer (1803–1882) greatly influenced by romanticism.

émigrés—French nobles and military officers who fled France when the revolution broke out.

Emperor Napoleon III—Nineteenth-century emperor of France who had been elected to rule France in 1850 as president and later took the title of emperor; nephew of Napoleon Bonaparte.

enclosure movement—Privatization of previously shared agricultural land in England; increased farming productivity but damaged small farmers.

English Bill of Rights—English government document; denied the power of a monarch to pass laws without Parliament's consent; protected people from excessive bail and cruel and unusual punishments; and allowed residents the right to address grievances with the government.

English Civil War—Power struggle sparked by Charles I's attempt to arrest five members of Parliament for treason; pitted forces supporting Parliament against those supporting the king; resulted in a brief rule by Cromwell and Parliament before the restoration of the monarchy.

Essay on Crimes and Punishments—Book written by Cesare Baccaria in 1764; advocated for the humane treatment of criminals.

Estates General—French legislative body.

ethnic cleansing—Organized genocide undertaken against the Muslims in Serbia by Serbs.

European Economic Community—Economic alliance eliminating tariffs on goods from other member states; formed in 1957; forerunner of the European Union.

European Union (EU)—Alliance of several European nations established in 1993; focused mostly on shared economic goals with some limited political privileges for citizens of all member states.

existentialism—Philosophic movement of the twentieth century that stresses the individual's responsibility to make life meaningful for him- or herself despite life's apparent absurdity.

Factory Act of 1833—Act passed in England prohibiting children under the age of 13 to work more than 9 hours and young people between ages 13–18 from working more than 69 hours a week.

Falklands War—Conflict between Britain and Argentina over a group of small islands near South America in 1982.

Fascist Party—Italian political party headed by the dictator Benito Mussolini.

Fenelon, Francois—French writer and Catholic bishop (1651–1715); called for limited monarchy and equality for all people in the eyes of the law.

Ferdinand VII—Nineteenth-century king of Spain who ignored Spain's constitution and disbanded its parliament after Napoleon's defeat; an ensuing military revolt led Ferdinand to agree to follow the constitution.

Ferdinand, Franz—Austrian archduke assassinated by a Serbian nationalist in 1914; death triggered the outbreak of World War I.

First Estate—The first of the three classes of French society consisting of clergy, who paid no taxes.

Franco, Francisco—Spanish military officer (1892–1975); led antisocialist forces during the Spanish Civil War; dictator of Spain from the mid-1930s until his death.

Franco-Prussian War—Conflict between France and Prussia in 1870; led to the capture of Napoleon III and a crushing defeat of France.

Franklin, Benjamin—American scientist, philosopher, and statesman (1706–1790); believed that perfection is beyond the grasp of humans.

Frederick II (Frederick the Great)—Eighteenth-century king of Prussia; considered an "enlightened despot"; invaded Saxony, beginning the Seven Years' War in Europe; led Prussian forces to victory.

Frederick William—Sixteenth-century Prussian Great Elector during and after the Thirty Years' War.

Free French—Group of French opponents of the Vichy government who sought to oppose Nazi Germany during World War II.

free trade—Trade policy that does not discriminate against imports or interfere with exports by applying tariffs or subsidies.

French and Indian War—Conflict between the French and English over control of North America; American arm of the Seven Years' War.

Freud, Sigmund—Austrian psychologist (1856–1939) who believed that humans are only conscious of a small portion of their mental lives; innovated the field of psychoanalysis.

Galileo Galilei—An Italian natural philosopher, astronomer, and mathematician (1564–1642); contributed to the spread of the heliocentric theory.

Garibaldi, Giuseppe—Nineteenth-century Italian revolutionary; helped unify the Kingdom of Italy.

geocentrism—The belief that Earth is the center of the universe.

Girondins—Within the French Revolution–era National Convention, representatives of the French countryside who favored a federal system and were opposed to eliminating the monarchy.

Gladstone, William—Nineteenth-century British prime minister who expanded the vote of the majority of the British male population.

glasnost—Soviet policy of increased openness in government operations undertaken by Gorbachev; literally, "openness."

Glorious Revolution—England's bloodless revolution that resulted in the deposing of James II, the accession of William III, and the taking of ruling power by Parliament.

Gorbachev, Mikhail—Soviet reformist president during the 1980s; supported economic and political liberalization policies.

gospel of wealth—Social theory promoted by Andrew Carnegie; suggested that the wealthy had a duty to help the poor help themselves.

Grand National Consolidated Trades Union—A broad English trade union that petitioned for an 8-hour workday; founded by British social reformer Robert Owen.

Great Depression—Period of worldwide economic decline and high unemployment during the 1930s.

Great Purges—Series of Soviet political murders during the late 1930s; undertaken by Stalin; sought to remove all possible political dissidents.

Greek Revolution—Revolution of 1821 led by Greek liberals and nationalists who sought independence from the Ottoman Empire.

Grotius, Hugo—Dutch statesman and philosopher who advocated for free trade among nations.

Hegel, Friedrich—German philosopher (1770–1831) who believed that history takes shape as long-held beliefs clash with newly emerging ideas and then, from the clash, a new set of beliefs is formed.

heliocentrism—The belief that the sun is the center of the universe.

Hitler, Adolf—German political leader; head of the Nazi Party and later the German state; led Germany into World War II; extremely anti-Semitic.

Hobbes, Thomas—English philosopher and writer of *Leviathan*; advocated for absolutism.

Holocaust—Systematic murder of European Jews by Hitler's Germany; also known as the Final Solution.

Holy Alliance—An alliance of Austria, Prussia, and Russia; formed after radical movements occurred in Spain and Italy made the three nations uneasy.

Home Rule—Freedom granted to Ireland by Britain 1914 to manage many of its own political affairs.

Huguenots—French Calvinists who were systemically persecuted under Henry II during the sixteenth century.

Hussein, Saddam—Iraqi dictator who opposed the United States in Operation Desert Storm in 1990–91 and again in 2003.

inductive method—Logical system based on pulling information together to arrive at a general theory.

Industrial Revolution—Eighteenth-century revolution in which technological advancements were made, machines were used to mass-produce goods, new efficient fuels were used, and new, stronger ores were created.

Irish Republican Army—Irish nationalist army formed in the early twentieth century; sometimes used violent tactics to support Irish independence through much of the century.

Iron Curtain—Term created by Winston Churchill after World War II to identify the division between democratic Western nations and communist Eastern Bloc nations.

Jacobin Club—The most famous political group known for egalitarianism and extreme violence that led to the French Revolution.

James I—Seventeenth-century English king who asserted that he ruled by divine right and that the Parliament's role was to advise him.

James II—Seventeenth-century Catholic English king who was dethroned in the Glorious Revolution.

Jefferson, Thomas—American statesman (1743–1826); author of The Declaration of Independence.

joint-stock investment bank—Banks that undertook financing large projects by getting many investors to support them financially.

Joseph II—Eighteenth-century Austrian emperor who strove to govern through sound political and moral philosophy.

Junkers—Prussian nobility.

Kennedy, John F.—U.S. president during the early 1960s; oversaw U.S. actions during the Cuban Missile Crisis and Bay of Pigs incidents.

Kepler, Johannes—German mathematician and astronomer (1571–1630) who argued for the heliocentric theory; argued for the existence of elliptical, rather than round, orbits.

Khrushchev, Nikita—Soviet leader during the Cuban Missile Crisis and Bay of Pigs incidents, among others.

"king cotton"—Term describing the economic dominance of cotton in the American South.

King George III—King of England during the American Revolution.

King William IV—Nineteenth-century English king; passed measures that allowed representation of the middle class in Parliament.

Korean War—Cold War conflict (1950–1953) between communist forces supporting North Korea and democratic forces supporting South Korea; resulted in the creation of a highly militarized border between the two Koreas.

labor unions—Associations of trades made to protect workers from unfair practices.

laissez-faire—Economic idea calling for minimal government interference in the economy.

League of Nations—International organization founded after World War I; attempted to maintain world peace; lacked sufficient power and influence to succeed.

Leibniz, Gottfried—German mathematician (1646–1716) who independently developed integral calculus, and developed another calculating machine thirty years after Pascal.

Lend Lease Act—U.S. law allowing the United States to send war supplies to Britain during World War II.

Lenin, Vladimir—Russian communist radical (1870–1924) who helped lead the overthrow of the tsar and institute the Soviet Union; instituted the New Economic Policy; led the Soviet Union until his death in 1924.

Levellers—English radical republicans who wanted a vote for every man who owned property; formed part of the Parliament after the English Civil War.

liberalism—Political belief that enhancing and protecting an individual's freedom is the main goal of politics.

Locke, John—An English philosopher who promoted the idea that a ruler could only rule so long as he or she kept the people's trust.

Lost Generation—Generation of young people who came of age after World War I; included many notable writers, such as Ernest Hemingway and F. Scott Fitzgerald.

Louis XIV—King of France who strived for complete power over France; took away decision-making power from nobles, censored books, and tortured opponents; also promoted science.

Louis XVI—Eighteenth-century king of France who ruled until the French Revolution; was eventually guillotined on counterrevolution charges with his wife Marie Antoinette.

Louis XVIII—Nineteenth-century king of France; conservative ruler; allowed the people who wished the old regime to return to terrorize Protestants and liberals.

Louisiana Territory—French territory in North America that Napoleon sold the United States in order to help pay for his military campaigns.

Luddites—Workers opposed to industrialization; attacked factories where machines had taken over their jobs.

Madison, James—American statesman (1743–1836) who was most responsible for the American Constitution.

Marie Antoinette—Eighteenth-century French queen who was overthrown during the French Revolution and executed by guillotine.

Marshall Plan—Economic assistance granted to European countries by the United States following World War II.

Mazzini, Giuseppe—Italian nationalist (1805–1872) who headed the Young Italy movement; supported the unification of Italy.

mercantilism—Economic and political system that held that the state must generate wealth in precious metals and raw materials, often provided by colonial holdings.

Mill, John Stuart—Liberal philosopher (1806–1873) who wrote *On Liberty* in 1859; argued that people should be allowed to pursue their interests, and advocated for the value of keeping an open mind.

Montesquieu, Charles—French political philosopher (1689–1755); wrote The Spirit of the Laws, and tried to explain the "natural laws" governing politics.

Mountain—Within the French Revolutionary–era National Convention, representatives of Paris who favored eliminating the monarchy.

Mussolini, Benito—Italian Fascist dictator; led Italy during World War II.

Napoleon Bonaparte—Emperor of France and military conqueror (1769–1821); reformed the organization of the military and education; conquered widely in Europe; was ultimately defeated and exiled.

Nasser, Gamal Abdal—Egyptian leader who nationalized the Suez Canal in 1956.

National Assembly—Legislative assembly comprising the Third Estate; created in 1789.

National Convention—Elected officials charged with the task of writing a new French constitution after they ended the monarchy in September of 1792.

nationalism—Idea that one's nation is superior to all other nations; contributed to the growth of imperialism and the outbreak of World War I and World War II.

NATO (North Atlantic Treaty Organization)—Military alliance of the United States and several Western European countries to oppose the spread of communism.

natural selection—Scientific idea argued by Charles Darwin; held that advantageous traits became more dominant over time.

Nazi Party—German political party headed by Adolf Hitler; rose to power in Germany during the 1930s; opposed democracy and communism; supported massive anti-Semitic policies.

neutrality acts—Series of U.S. laws passed during the 1930s and early 1940s aimed at keeping the United States out of foreign wars.

New Model Army—Forces recruited by Parliament during the English Civil War; operated under the leadership of Oliver Cromwell.

Newton, Isaac—British scientist (1642–1727) who explained the elliptical orbit of the planets by arguing that gravity's consistent attraction causes Earth to move in a consistent, predictable order; support led to greater acceptance of the heliocentric theory.

Nicholas II—Last tsar of Russia; overthrown and later executed by Red Russian communist forces.

Nietzsche, Friedrich—German philosopher (1844–1900); opposed Christianity, criticized the emphasis on reason, and supported raw, irrational, emotional responses.

Nightingale, Florence—English nurse (1820–1910) during the Crimean War who advanced the role of women as nurses, created more sanitary conditions for patients, and was the first woman to receive the Order of Merit.

noble savage—Enlightenment-era concept that idealized those lacking the trappings of modern civilization.

Northern War—War in which Russia successfully challenged Sweden's supremacy in the Baltic region using tactics learned from the defenders.

Nuremberg War Crimes Trials—Series of trials against Nazi leaders after World War II; tried crimes relating to the execution of the war and the Holocaust.

On the Origin of Species—Work written by Charles Darwin (1809–1882); argued for the theories of evolution and natural selection.

Operation Desert Storm—Brief war between the United States and Iraq in 1991; sparked by the Iraqi invasion of Kuwait.

Osama bin Laden—Wealthy Muslim radical; financed the Taliban in Afghanistan; orchestrated a series of major terrorist attacks against the United States through the Al Qaeda terrorist network.

Ottoman Empire—Turkish empire that covered the majority of Eastern Europe; reigned for about 600 years until it fell apart in 1922.

Pankhurst, Emmeline—British women's rights activist who campaigned for women's right to vote; led the Women's Social and Political Union.

Paracelsus—Swiss physician (1493–1541) who believed that illness happened because of a chemical imbalance in the body.

Paris Commune—The revolutionary government of Paris; consisted of members from the city's 48 wards.

Parliament—The original legislative body of the United Kingdom.

Pascal, Blaise—French mathematician (1623–1662) who invented a calculating machine and devised an influential theory of chance and probability.

Pasteur, Louis—French scientist (1822–1895) who investigated the source of infectious diseases and created the process of pasteurization of milk.

penny press—Inexpensive mass media newspapers that formed a mass culture during the nineteenth century.

People's Charter—A bill drafted in England in 1838 for working-class parliamentary reform.

perestroika—Soviet policy of economic and political liberalization undertaken by Gorbachev; generally considered to have contributed to the fall of communism; literally, "restructuring."

Petition of Right—Document passed by Parliament in 1628; stated that English subjects had basic rights that could not be repressed by the king.

philosophes—Enlightenment-era thinkers, scientists, and writers who believed in the power of human reason.

Picasso, Pablo—Spanish Cubist painter (1881–1973); one of the most influential modern artists.

Pitt, William (the Elder)—British Secretary of State during the Seven Years' War; gave Prussia financial assistance to attempt to weaken France.

Plassey—Site of a major British victory against France in India; set the stage for the British East India's influence in India.

Prague Spring—Period of attempted revolt and reform in communist Czechoslovakia in 1968; quashed by Soviet forces.

privateers—Government-sanctioned pirates active in the West Indies during the seventeenth and eighteenth centuries.

Proclamation of 1763—English act barring American settlers from moving west of the Appalachian Mountains.

Protestant Reformation—Series of religious reforms to simplify worship, achieve salvation through a personal connection with God, and end excesses of the Catholic Church that arose during the early sixteenth century; led to the creation of Protestant denominations that separated from the Catholic Church.

Protocol of Troppau—An 1820 measure created by the Holy Alliance that allowed them to intervene in the affairs of other countries that were unable to maintain conservative order on their own.

Ptolemy—Greek philosopher who believed that Earth was the center of the universe.

Pugachev, Emelyn—Eighteenth-century leader of a rebellion against Russia's wealthy landowners that resulted in greater repression of peasants.

Quadruple Alliance—Alliance of Russia, Prussia, Austria, and Britain; formed to challenge Napoleon.

Realpolitik—Theory of politics based on what is possible rather than what is ideal.

Red Russians—Russian Bolsheviks who sought to institute communism.

Red Shirts—Italian revolutionaries under the command of Giuseppe Garibaldi; conquered Sicily and formed a new government at Naples; ultimately helped unify Italy.

Reign of Terror—A period during the French Revolution in which supposed supporters of the crown were tortured and executed by the revolutionary government.

Rembrandt—Dutch painter (1606–1669); innovator of realism; emphasized the use of light and shade.

Revolutions of 1848—Series of revolutions across Europe that sought to replace monarchies with republican governments; generally failed.

Risorgimento—Ninteenth-century Italian unification movement.

Robespierre, Maximilien—Eighteenth-century Jacobin leader of the French Revolution; leader in the revolutionary government during the Reign of Terror; overthrown and executed in 1794.

Romantic movement—An eighteenth-century intellectual and artistic movement that focused more on emotions than on reason.

Roundheads—Armed forces of Parliament during the English Civil War; named for the shaped of their Puritan hats.

Rousseau, Jean-Jacques—Swiss-born French philosopher (1712–1778) who wrote Social Contract; believed that government was a necessary evil.

Rump Parliament—English Parliament after the Presbyterians were purged from it during the English Civil War; governed the brief English republic.

Russo-Japanese War—Conflict between Russia and Japan over land in eastern Asia; ended in Japanese victory in 1905; contributed to Russian discontent with its government.

Sadler Committee—British reform committee led by Michael Thomas Sadler; led to the regulating of factory conditions and children's working hours.

Salvation Army—A religious organization founded in 1865 in London's East End; created to feed and house those in need; exemplary of the social gospel movement.

Schlieffen Plan—German strategy during World War I; relied on attacking France through Belgium, quickly capturing Paris, and then focusing on Russia; led a massive stalemate along the Western Front.

scientific method—Scientific system of finding facts based on observation and verifiable facts; also known as the empirical method.

Scottish Enlightenment—A period in the eighteenth century during which Scotland was considered a thought leader; connected philosophers include David Hume and Adam Smith.

Scramble for Africa—European efforts to establish imperial colonies in Africa during the mid- to late nineteenth century.

Second Estate—The second of the three classes of French society consisting of nobles of the sword (passed through the generations) and nobles of the robe (who bought their status), who paid few taxes.

Second Vatican Council—Ecumenical council that significantly altered and liberalized some Catholic forms and beliefs; held during the early 1960s.

separation of powers—Governmental system dividing the ruling powers among multiple governing units.

Seven Years' War—Conflict spanning 1756–1763; involved all the great powers in Europe; sparked, in part, by the French and English conflict over control of North America and India.

Silent Spring—Environmental work written by Rachel Carson in 1962; sparked a global environmental movement.

Social Darwinism—Social theory popularized by Herbert Spencer during the nineteenth century; suggested that the fittest leaders naturally rose to the top of society, and the weakest to the bottom; supported the growth of imperialism.

Social Democratic Party (SDP)—German political party; became the most influential socialist organization in Europe.

social gospel—Reform movement based on religious ideals of those who wanted to build a perfect world on Earth.

Society of United Irishmen—An organized underground movement formed in 1791 to fight for Ireland's independence from England.

Soviet-Afghan War—Conflict between the Soviet Union and Afghanistan mostly spanning the 1980s, during which the Soviets sought to occupy Afghan territory.

Spanish Civil War—Spanish conflict in the 1930s that pitted the forces of Franco against government loyalists; resulted in the establishment of a fascist Spain under Franco.

Spanish-American War—Conflict between the United States and Spain in 1898; fought largely in the islands of Cuba and the Philippines; resulted in U.S. acquisition of Guam, the Philippines, Puerto Rico, and other imperial holdings.

spinning jenny—Early industrial invention that greatly increased textile production.

Sputnik—Soviet satellite that became the first to be successfully launched in 1957, inaugurating the space age and the Cold War space race between the U.S.S.R. and U.S.

Stalin, Joseph—Led the Soviet Union after the death of Lenin; oversaw a brutal regime responsible for the deaths of millions.

Sudentenland—German-speaking region of western Czechoslovakia; granted to Hitler's Germany as part of the policy of appeasement in the late 1930s.

Taliban—Muslim fundamentalist government of Afghanistan that took power after the Soviet defeat in the Soviet-Afghan War.

tariff—Tax on goods that cross national borders.

Tennis Court Oath—Oath signed by members of the Third Estate affirming their desire to remain united until the creation of a written constitution; set off the French Revolution.

Thatcher, Margaret—Late twentieth-century British prime minister; known for conservative economic policies that cut government programs and expenses.

The Wealth of Nations—Book written by Adam Smith promoting the laissez-faire approach to the economy.

theory of relativity—Theory put forth by Einstein; suggested that the world was subject to four dimensions—height, width, depth, and time.

Thermidorian Reaction—The reaction against the radical Jacobin revolutionaries that resulted in their purge from political groups and the Jacobin Club in Paris being dismantled.

Third Estate—The third of the three classes of French society; contained everyone not in the first two classes; paid the most taxes.

Third International—Socialist organization founded by Russian communists in 1919; set conditions for socialists throughout Europe; called for the rapid institution of communism; also known as the Comintern.

Thirty Years' War—Conflict lasting from 1618 to 1648; initially fought over religious disputes, but came to involve much of Europe over time; greatly destructive to Germany.

Tories—Supporters of Charles II during the Glorious Revolution.

transcendentalism—Nineteenth-century movement in which writers and philosophers believed in the innate goodness of man, and that insight was more important than logic when searching for truths.

Treaty of Paris—1763 treaty ending the Seven Years' War and the French and Indian War.

Treaty of Rome—Treaty signed in 1957 that created the European Economic Community.

Treaty of Versailles—Treaty ending World War I; sought to humiliate and punish Germany for World War I; placed heavy reparations on Germany; contributed greatly to the tensions that later caused World War II.

Treaty of Westphalia—Treaty signed in 1648; ended the Thirty Years' War; expanded religious recognition to Calvinists; granted increased power to France.

Triple Alliance—Alliance of Germany, Austria, and Italy formed in 1882; also known as the Triple Entente.

Trotsky, Leon—Russian communist radical (1877–1940) who helped lead the overthrow of the tsar and institute the Soviet Union; instituted government control of farms and used farm products to fund industrial growth.

Truman Doctrine—Cold War-era U.S. policy of supporting nations that opposed communism.

Tsar Peter III—Eighteenth-century emperor of Russia; reversed the country's stand to make it pro-Prussia; supported Prussia during the Seven Years' War.

Tsar Peter the Great (Peter I)—Seventeenth-century Russian tsar whose rule was largely influenced by Western Europe.

Tull, Jethro—British agronomist (1674–1741) who found that using a metal plow to plant seeds, instead of casting them on the ground, produced a greater crop yield.

ultraroyalists—French group of the early nineteenth century that sought to return France to an earlier political system dominated by the *ancien regime*.

United Nations—International organization founded after World War II; designed to manage international affairs and deter conflicts; replaced the failed League of Nations.

Utilitarianism—Theory that people should work to create happiness for the greatest number of people; focused on ends rather than means; developed during the late eighteenth and early nineteenth centuries.

V-E Day—Day on which German surrendered unconditionally in World War II: May 7, 1945.

Vesalius, Andreas—Belgian physician (1514–1564) who dissected animals and human cadavers to learn more about anatomy; wrote *On the Structure of the Human Body*.

Vichy Regime—French puppet government controlled by the Nazis during World War II.

Victor Emmanuel III—Italian king (1900–1946); invited Mussolini to become the prime minister in the early 1920s.

Volksgeist—Romantic notion of the spirit of a group of people; proposed by German writer Johann Gottfried Herder; literally, "people's spirit."

Voltaire, Francois—French writer (1694–1778) who believed in religious freedom, and urged the use of ideas brought on by the Enlightenment to create a better society.

War of Austrian Succession—Power struggle between Prussia and Austria from 1740 to 1748; came to involve France and Britain.

War of Jenkins's Ear—Eighteenth-century naval war between Spain and England; spurred by the treatment of British sailors in the West Indies; eventually became part of the War of Austrian Succession.

Warsaw Pact—Soviet-controlled military alliance of Eastern European states formed in 1955 to oppose NATO.

Washington, George—American colonial officer; fired the first shots on the French and Indian War at French forces in the Ohio Valley.

Waterloo—Site where Napoleon's forces were defeated for the last time in Belgium; defeat unseated Napoleon and led to his exile.

Watt, James —English inventor (1736–1819) of the first steam-powered machine.

Whigs—Members of Parliament who fought against James II taking the English throne during the Glorious Revolution.

White Russians—Russian anti-Bolsheviks; included liberals, monarchists, and others.

William Harvey—Sixteenth-century English physician who was the first to understand the circulation of blood through the human body.

William III of Orange—Seventeenth-century Protestant king of England who took the throne from James II after he was invited to do so by Parliament as part of the Glorious Revolution; co-ruled with wife Mary.

Wollstonecraft, Mary—English writer (1759–1797) who advocated for equal education for women; author of *The Vindication of the Rights of Women*.

Zimmermann Telegram—German message to the Mexican government promising Mexico lands occupied by the United States should Mexico enter World War I on the side of Germany; direct cause of U.S. entry into World War I.

Zionism—Jewish nationalism; movement that contributed to the foundation of the state of Israel.

Zollverein—German customs union established in 1834; encouraged community and a shared culture among German-speaking peoples.

Index

Notes

Notes

REA's Test Preps

The Best in Test Preparation

- REA "Test Preps" are **far more** comprehensive than any other test preparation series
- Each book contains full-length practice tests based on the most recent exams
- **Every** type of question likely to be given on the exams is included
- Answers are accompanied by **full** and **detailed** explanations

REA publishes hundreds of test prep books. Some of our titles include:

Advanced Placement Exams (APs)
Art History
Biology
Calculus AB & BC
Chemistry
Economics
English Language & Composition
English Literature & Composition
European History
French Language
Government & Politics
Latin Vergil
Physics B & C
Psychology
Spanish Language
Statistics
United States History
World History

College-Level Examination Program (CLEP)
American Government
College Algebra
General Examinations
History of the United States I
History of the United States II
Introduction to Educational Psychology
Human Growth and Development
Introductory Psychology
Introductory Sociology
Principles of Management
Principles of Marketing
Spanish
Western Civilization I
Western Civilization II

SAT Subject Tests
Biology E/M
Chemistry
French
German
Literature
Mathematics Level 1, 2
Physics
Spanish
United States History

Graduate Record Exams (GREs)
Biology
Chemistry
Computer Science
General
Literature in English
Mathematics
Physics
Psychology

ACT - ACT Assessment

ASVAB - Armed Services Vocational Aptitude Battery

CBEST - California Basic Educational Skills Test

CDL - Commercial Driver License Exam

COOP, HSPT & TACHS - Catholic High School Admission Tests

FE (EIT) - Fundamentals of Engineering Exams

FTCE - Florida Teacher Certification Examinations

GED

GMAT - Graduate Management Admission Test

LSAT - Law School Admission Test

MAT - Miller Analogies Test

MCAT - Medical College Admission Test

MTEL - Massachusetts Tests for Educator Licensure

NJ HSPA - New Jersey High School Proficiency Assessment

NYSTCE - New York State Teacher Certification Examinations

PRAXIS PLT - Principles of Learning & Teaching Tests

PRAXIS PPST - Pre-Professional Skills Tests

PSAT/NMSQT

SAT

TExES - Texas Examinations of Educator Standards

THEA - Texas Higher Education Assessment

TOEFL - Test of English as a Foreign Language

USMLE Steps 1,2,3 - U.S. Medical Licensing Exams

For information about any of REA's books, visit www.rea.com

Research & Education Association
61 Ethel Road W., Piscataway, NJ 08854
Phone: (732) 819-8880

Notes

Notes

Notes